P9-DCM-463

THE
ULTIMATE
BOOK OF
BOXING
LISTS

★ THE ULTIMATE BOOK OF ★

BOXING LISTS

BERT
SUGAR AND ### TEDDY
ATLAS

© 2010 by Bert Randolph Sugar and Teddy Atlas

All rights reserved under the Pan-American and International Copyright Conventions

This book may not be reproduced in whole or in part, in any form or by any means, electronic or mechanical, including photocopying, recording, or by any information storage and retrieval system now known or hereafter invented, without written permission from the publisher.

Digit on the right indicates the number of this printing

Library of Congress Control Number: 2010922441
ISBN 978-0-7624-4013-9

Cover and Interior Design: Joshua McDonnell
Editor: Greg Jones

PHOTO CREDITS:
Front cover: Muhammad Ali: AP Photo; Sugar Ray Leonard: AP Photo/Dennis Cook
p. 19: Courtesy Everett Collection, p. 51: Ken Sax/Courtesy Everett Collection
p. 76: CSU Archives/Courtesy Everett Collection, p. 86: AP Photo
p. 155: Mirrorpix/Courtesy Everett Collection, p. 118: Courtesy Everett Collection
p. 204: CORBIS TK (photo of Graziano), p. 218: AP Photo,
p. 236: AP Photo/Anthony Camerano

Running Press Book Publishers
Hachette Book Group
1290 Avenue of the Americas
New York, NY, 10104

Visit us on the web!
www.runningpress.com

CONTENTS

FOREWORD

Within the small world of the pro boxing media, you would be hard pressed to find two more disparate characters than Bert Sugar and Teddy Atlas. I've spent quite a bit of time with each, working, researching, and dining. Each has his own positives. When you eat out with Teddy, there's actually food. But there's no one breaking out spontaneously into vaudeville songs, either. You take the good with the bad.

Bert, of course, has the best recall in broadcasting. His encyclopedic knowledge of boxing, baseball, and college football is legendary, and I've never seen anyone better. He's been at most every major fight over the last half century, and can give you a round-by-round of most any major fight. Working with Bert requires three things: Naming the winner first in any fight conversation (Ali-Frazier I is actually Frazier-Ali); a high tolerance for cigar smoke; and a quick answer to the question, "Where the hell can I find a good scotch around here?"

Teddy's view of life is quite different. I remember picking him up for breakfast at a local hotel one Saturday morning after we both worked *Friday Night Fights* at ESPN the night before. I parked in view of the main entrance, and while I cleaned up my car a bit, I continuously kept checking ahead to the doors to make sure I didn't miss him when he walked out. Behind me was a steep landscaped hill that led to the local highway, so I wasn't looking in that direction. Before I knew it, Teddy had silently walked up from behind, his mere presence startling me. I said, "I kept checking over there so you couldn't sneak up on me." Teddy said, smiling, "But when they come for you, they'll come from over there."

Despite their differences, they have one overriding similarity in their approach to boxing: Making sense of the chaos.

For Bert, the chaos is the decades of fights, the unending parade of champions, spreading out to more and more weight classes and the insidious explosion of so-called sanctioning bodies. Bert's lists put things in historical perspective and make a century of fights into a narrative. Separated by decades and different cultures, Benny Leonard and Roberto Duran would seem to have very little in common. But we want to know how they, their careers, and their performances compared. Bert has been crystallizing his thoughts on just these things for years. We want to know how Benny Leonard rates with Roberto Duran; how Bernard Hopkins' incredible durability at middleweight stacks up against the punishing reign of Marvelous Marvin Hagler; and where Roy Jones, with the great peak but steep decline, lands among the all-time greats.

For Teddy, the chaos to be deciphered is in the ring itself. An uneducated eye sees a violent clash of strength and speed. Teddy sees the patterns, the angles, and how each fighter's repertoire interlocks into his opponents'. Styles do indeed make fights, and how those styles mesh determines the flow of the battle. He senses the ebb and flow of energy, the clash of wills, the struggle with inner stamina, and frequently sees the outcome rounds before it happens. Teddy's technical expertise combined with his ability to dig into a man's psyche is what sets him apart.

So I am happy to be able to introduce this collaboration of two men who have seen, and can see, what so few of us can. We are blessed to have both.

Brian Kenny, ESPN
August, 2010

INTRODUCTION BY BERT SUGAR

Controversy is to boxing what garlic is to a salad: it enlivens it. One of the longest-running controversies in boxing is "Who's the greatest?" And boxing fans, never fearful of communicating their opinions vocally, will debate it every which way, like religious contemplatives of old arguing over the number of angels on the head of a pin, arguments ever at the ready. Another classic subject that commands debate is the old "Who would win between 'So-and-so' versus 'What's-his-face' in their primes?"—yet another exercise in futility with each side talking of ships and sealing-wax and the other meaningless twaddle.

Having already had enough of these bar arguments, whether bellying up to the bar at my favorite watering hole or wearing down a carload of pencils to stubs reducing my thoughts to paper, whenever someone aims a scotch at my head asking for my opinion I reach for my coat and head for the door, crying out like the raven, "Nevermore!"

And so when Running Press editor Greg Jones asked if I would be interested in writing a book of boxing lists, sort of a grab bag of different subjects, I was more than underwhelmed. But the more I thought about it, the more intrigued with the idea I became. After all, or so my reasoning went, lists have always been with us, going all the way back to Moses handing down a list of Commandments from the Mount. And everybody, including Santa who had a list he was always "checking twice," seemed to have one. Even boxing fans have their lists, but they were almost always of the roster-like variety—you know, most KO's, most wins, most disa, most data, with an emphasis on the latta. Somehow subjective lists, the ones that stir controversy, were missing in action from boxing's list of lists. As I thought more and more about undertaking such a project, the more I could see it taking form as a collection of orderly miscellanea that when stitched together would provide a shorthand history of the sport. And, not incidentally, spark controversy of its own.

There I was in a full-crouch position, ready to start assembling a group of lists rivaling these found in the Yellow Pages, my bookkeeper's mind rattling at the number of possibilities and inclusions, not to mention their order, when a vagrant thought occurred to me. Rather than staging quarrels with myself, or looking for wisdom in the bottom of an empty scotch glass, I needed a vital collaborator who would bring a new perspective to the construction of these lists, someone who could provide a wide-angle lens more than a mere connect-the-dots picture, and spark new ideas. A different view from a different pew, if you will. And to me there was only one person who fit the bill: Teddy Atlas.

For even though Teddy is readily identifiable as the "voice" of ESPN boxing and has served as the announcer for the last three Olympic boxing telecasts, he is more, much more, than an announcer. With on-the-ground experience both as a boxer and as a trainer, Teddy brings an insider's view to his announcing, his analysis alone worth the price of admission. He can parse a fight the way a schoolmarm can a sentence, breaking down everything in simple terms even the most casual fan can appreciate. Add to that his deep reverence, even passion, for the sport, its traditions and its participants, having sat at the knee of the venerable Cus D'Amato and absorbing boxing's rich history going back almost to the time Father Adam first heard the rush of the apple salesmen. You can hear that amazing inner library on almost every broadcast, one he exhibits by dropping in little historic tidbits to match the situation he is describing. Or coming up with lists of his own that include names as overlooked as the second man to fly the Atlantic—for instance, including Young Griffo on his list of great defensive fighters. (Young Griffo?) Put all those qualities together and you have the reasons why Teddy Atlas was the perfect complement to the making of *The Ultimate Book of Boxing Lists*.

Thankfully, Teddy was open to the idea of helping to pull together such a work and now, proving that old adage about "two heads being better than one," or some-such, we played off each other, arguing and re-arguing the merits of the lists themselves, those to be included, and the order of their inclusion—which, at times, seemed to be monstrous quicksand, its particles changing rapidly. One time I suggested that Two-Ton Tony Gallento belonged in the "Most Awkward" category, but Teddy argued that he wasn't awkward so much as he was just there to be hit, saying, "You didn't have to look for him." And voila!, we had a new list, the "Takes Two-to-Give-One" fighters.

There were others to be included or excluded, some entrants not standing up to the vaguest sort of examination with other potential names emerging and re-emerging, depending upon the list. We constantly ran through a long laundry list of fighters from the present and recent past along with those from the long-ago whose names are preserved only in yellowing newspapers in equally yellowing albums, pressed between the pages of time, looking to see which fighters belong where, if anywhere. After examining both the bottle and its contents, so to speak, we were finally able to come up with approximately 100 lists—sure to provoke 100-plus arguments.

Along with several whose advice and help made this book possible—people like Thom Loverro, Mike Silver, Steve Farhood, Cornell Richardson, Peter Wood, and all our "celebrity" contributors—we have gone over the lists and names many times almost as if we were constantly touching the paint to see if it were dry. And yet, unlike red wine blushing at the certificate of purity on its label, we do not put any such certificate on these lists. For we realize that in the mind's eye of many they are open to discussion and that somewhere out there are those who will pick up any glove cast at them in the name of challenge to dispute our choices.

But that is the nature of the sport of boxing: controversy. So gentlemen and gentlewomen, at the bell, start your arguments!

INTRODUCTION BY TEDDY ATLAS

Did he run enough? Was it early enough in the morning? Did he eat the proper foods? Did he weaken himself making the proper weight? How strong-willed will the other guy be? Can he keep his thoughts steered away from the possible dangers that lie ahead and direct them in a positive stream?

Now the call comes, the gruff voice screams, "You're up!" It's time to go. He lets his feet drop to the floor from the table occupied by gauze and tape and scissors. His handlers pull the robe onto him and place the hood over his head. He shoots a couple of punches in the air as he heads down a long hallway that never seems to end. And then, into the lights and cheers, calls for primitive behavior and violent acts. His calf muscles twitch a nervous dance as he steadies his breathing with deep slower breaths. He bends and steps through the ropes while his eyes survey the ring like a hunter who knows the one he seeks also seeks him. The microphone drops from the sky, introductions are made, the cloth leaves his body and a last coat of cold Vaseline is applied to his face, and a last reminder of the battle plan is whispered into his ear.

The bell rings and he knows it tolls for him. He is a prizefighter. And he is at work in his workplace.

Professional boxers, practicing the noblest and oldest sport of all, are men who are expertly trained and disciplined, honed not to blink in the face of fear and injury. And if they do, to suffer the fate of the disenfranchised, the scorned, the mocked, the "coward."

Who are these men? Where do they come from? And who were the best among them—the fastest, the strongest, the toughest? Sit back and read and enjoy *The Ultimate Book of Boxing Lists* and find out who was and is the "best" in a sport that has been around for more than a hundred years—and probably will be around for another hundred or more.

BEST LINES DEFINING THE SPORT OF BOXING

Looking for a good boxing quote? Don't bother searching *Bartlett's Quotations*. Hell, there are more good boxing quotes on the walls of the men's room at Madison Square Garden than can be found in the 1,600+ pages of *Bartlett's*. We read all those pages and all we could find were two—count 'em, two—references to boxing. One came from boxing manager Joe Jacobs, who hollered after his fighter Max Schmeling lost the heavyweight title to Jack Sharkey, "We was robbed!" The other was heavyweight champion Bob Fitzsimmons' timeless, "The bigger they are the harder they fall" hidden in the footnotes. That's it—two quotes! And so to offer Mr. Bartlett some food for thought, we compiled so many prime boxing quotes that they require five different lists: lines spoken or written before (page 72), during (page 107), and after (page 205) fights; quotes on specific aspects of boxing (page 169); and these first ten lines below which provide general definitions of the sport.

"**BOXING IS SORT OF LIVE JAZZ. THE BETTER IT IS, THE LESS PEOPLE CAN APPRECIATE IT.**" Heavyweight champion George Foreman.

"**THE MANLY ART OF MODIFIED MURDER.**" Newspaper writer W.O. McGeehan.

"**A FIGHT CANNOT BE BROKEN DOWN PUNCH-BY-PUNCH AND PUT TOGETHER AGAIN MORE THAN HUMPTY-DUMPTY COULD.**" Writer-television commentator Larry Merchant.

"**BOXING IS CHESS PLAYED ON BODIES INSTEAD OF BOARDS.**" Sportswriter, novelist, screenwriter and boxing fan Budd Schulberg.

"**A BOXING MATCH IS LIKE A COWBOY MOVIE. THERE'S GOT TO BE A GOOD GUY AND THERE'S GOT TO BE A BAD GUY. AND THAT'S WHAT PEOPLE PAY FOR—TO SEE THE BAD GUY GET BEAT.**" Heavyweight champion Sonny Liston.

"**BOXING IS A CELEBRATION OF THE LOST RELIGION OF MASCULINITY, ALL THE MORE TRENCHANT FOR ITS BEING LOST.**" Writer Joyce Carol Oates.

"**BOXING IS THE ONLY SPORT YOU CAN GET YOUR BRAIN SHOOK, YOUR MONEY TOOK AND YOUR NAME IN THE UNDERTAKER'S BOOK.**" Heavyweight champion Joe Frazier.

"Boxing is just show business with blood." Heavyweight champion Frank Bruno.

"Boxing is the ultimate challenge. There's nothing that can compare to testing yourself the way you do every time you step in the ring." Champion Sugar Ray Leonard.

"There is much about jazz that relates to boxing. The improvisation, the flow, the beauty of the notes, the tempo."

Light heavyweight champion Archie Moore.

BEST BOXING NICKNAMES

William Shakespeare might have wondered: "What's in a name?" But for boxers, a nickname is a necessity. It's almost as if a fighter can't climb into the ring without one. The only boxer who didn't need a nickname was a middleweight way back in the early years of the 20th century named Ever Hammer—now there's a name that stood on its own. But other fighters have had to improvise, or let their handlers or fans or the media coin a nickname for them. From late-19th century heavyweight champ John L. Sullivan, who had no less than a half-dozen monikers—"The Prizefighting Caesar," "The Hercules of the Ring," "The Boston Strongboy," "His Fistic Highness," "The Great John L." and just plain ol' "Sully"—down through the ages, fighters have entered the ring wearing a robe, gloves, trunks and a nickname. Some have been fanciful, like "Bonecrusher" for James Smith, a name he was more known by than his given name. While others have been more mundane, with Rockys and KOs (down to, or so it would seem, KO Pectate) numbering in the hundreds. Here are what we consider the top ten nicknames in boxing history.

10. "MARVELOUS" (MARVIN HAGLER). One of the greatest of his era, Marvin Hagler originally had a name as frill-free as his style. That is, until he decided he wanted to be known as "Marvelous"—as in "awe-inspiring." So, starting in the middle of his career, he insisted on being introduced as "Marvelous" Marvin Hagler. But before his 1982 title defense against William "Caveman" Lee, one of the ABC-TV directors snapped, "If he wants to be announced as 'Marvelous' Marvin, let him change his name." And so, after dispatching of Lee in 67 seconds, Marvin headed down to the registrar's office to change his name officially to Marvelous Marvin Hagler, his nickname becoming part of his legal name.

9. "THE MANASSA MAULER" (JACK DEMPSEY). There have been several names in boxing history denoting the place of origin of the boxer—such as "The Michigan Assassin" (Stanley Ketchel), "The Pittsburgh Kid" (Billy Conn), "The Cincinnati Cobra" (Ezzard Charles), "The Fargo Express" (Billy Petrolle), as well as several alliterative nicknames like "Jersey Joe" (Joe Walcott), "The Bronx Bull" (Jake LaMotta), "The Brockton Blockbuster" (Rocky Marciano), and so forth and so on. But the first alliterative nickname that identified a geographic place of origin in an era of alliterative sports nicknames (like "The Galloping Ghost" for Red Grange and "Larrupin' Lou" for Lou Gehrig) belonged to heavyweight champion Jack Dempsey, who hailed from Manassa, Colorado, coined by no less than Damon Runyon (who hailed from the same state), who first called Dempsey "The Manassa Mauler."

8. "HAMMERIN' HANK," "HURRICANE HANK" AND "HOMICIDE HANK" (HENRY ARMSTRONG). The three simultaneous division champion with three nicknames earned them honestly with his whirlwind, non-stop attack, almost as if he were a high-speed perpetual-motion machine. Over the course of his 15-year career, this human dynamo had a recorded 174 bouts, with 145 wins and 98 knockouts—including one 53-month period (January, 1937 through May, '39) when he fought 46 times, winning all 46 bouts, among them three championships, with 39 knockouts.

7. "TWO-TON" (TONY GALENTO). In a field where many heavyweights are sculpted, Adonis-like figures (such as Ken Norton and Mike Weaver), there once roamed a heavyweight so round he resembled a beer barrel, which is what he trained on. All this laughable physical misfit accomplished on beer and a left hook from hell was 80 wins (57 by KO) and a 1939 heavyweight title shot against Joe Louis that included Galento knocking down Louis before being KO'd. Given his success and prominence, "Two-Ton" Tony Galento probably set back the cause of physical fitness another decade or two.

6. "THE MIGHTY ATOM" (JIMMY WILDE). Even before British physicists had come to completely understand the nature of the atom, the British boxing public embraced 108-pound Jimmy Wilde, the man known as "The Mighty Atom," after the Greek word for "uncuttable." All this scrawny, anemic-looking Welshman with pipestem arms and legs did during his 13-year career was win 131 bouts and knock out 99 of his opponents, his total number of KOs almost equaling his fighting weight. And he did so by being as darn-near "uncuttable" as the atom for which he was nicknamed.

5. "SUGAR" (RAY ROBINSON). Called everything from "The Greatest Fighter in Boxing History" to, at one point in his career, "The Uncrowned Champion," Ray Robinson also wore a nickname given him by his manager and trainer George Gainford. It all came about one day as a boxing writer named Jack Case was watching a young prospect and remarked to Gainford, "That's a sweet fighter you've got there." To which Gainford replied, for posterity: "Sweet as sugar." And so, "Sugar" Ray Robinson it became, a nickname many a boxer—like Sugar Ray Leonard and Sugar Shane Mosley—adopted in tribute to this all-time great after the original had hung up his gloves.

4. "THE HUMAN PUNCHING BAG" (JOE GRIM). Many's the fighter who wears a nickname proudly attesting to his prowess, like "The Michigan Assassin" (Stanley Ketchel), "Smokin'" (Joe Frazier), "Thunder" (Arturo Gatti), "Terrible" (Terry McGovern), "The Brown Bomber" (Joe Louis) and a whole list of KO-*soandsos*. But few bore the name of a loser. And loser was what Joe Grim was, one of the most-defeated boxers in boxingkind. Between the years 1901 and 1910, Grim lost almost as many fights as he appeared in, and lost them in spectacular fashion—being knocked down 20 times by Bob Fitzsimmons and 14 times against Jack Johnson, with neither able to finish him off—Grim always boasting, "I'm Joe Grim and no man can knock me out." But knock him down they did, so much so that the press labeled him "The Human Punching Bag."

3. "THE WILL O' THE WISP" (WILLIE PEP). One of the most elusive fighters in the history of boxing, Pep moved like a tap dancer with gloves on. Fighting this feath- erweight was akin to trying to catch a moonbeam in a jar or—as one of his opponents described it—like "battling a man in the hall of mirrors." This fistic genius once won a round without throwing a punch, earning Willie the nickname, "Will o' the Wisp."

2. "THE SCOTCH WOP" (JOHNNY DUNDEE). Before political correctness came into vogue, a fighter named Johnny Dundee, who fought a record 335 times during his 22-year career, was called "The Scotch Wop." But Dundee wasn't always the "Scotch Wop;" nor was he always Dundee. Born Guiseppe Carrora in Sicily, his manager, Scotty Monteith, felt that if he were to enter the ring bearing the name "Carrora," which sounded like "carrots," "people would start throwing vegetables at you." So Monteith suggested that Carrora change his last name to Monteith's Scottish hometown of Dundee, and change his first name to the English version of Guiseppe (John). The dual name change led Johnny Dundee to become known by the dual-nationality nickname, "The Scotch Wop."

1. "THE GREATEST" (CASSIUS CLAY/MUHAMMAD ALI). Long before he dubbed him- self "The Greatest," the young Cassius Clay earned two nicknames, "The Louisville Lip" and "The Mouth That Roared"—both testaments to the brash youngster who was never short of breath or *braggadocio* in describing his exploits. From the time he came back from winning the gold medal at the 1960 Rome Olympics and would stand on street corners to see how many people recognized him, the young Cassius Marcellus Clay would be "on stage." But it was as his self-advertised nickname, "The Greatest," that Clay/Ali would become known, a nickname he lived up to in the eyes of many.

MY TOP TEN ALL-TIME HEAVYWEIGHT CHAMPIONS

:: BY MUHAMMAD ALI

Note: Three-time heavyweight champion Muhammad Ali dubbed himself "The Greatest," and to many of his fans, he was. But when asked to pick his top all-time heavyweight champs, he displayed uncharacteristic humility and did not include himself, saying his name could be placed anywhere we wanted. We'll leave that to the reader and merely present those selected by Ali, ordered chronologically.

JACK JOHNSON (CHAMPION 1908-15; 105 FIGHTS, 68 WINS, 40 KOS, 10 LOSSES, 10 DRAWS, 16 NO-DECISIONS, ONE NO-CONTEST). "Defensive fighter. . . . Scientific boxer. . . . First black heavyweight champion."

JACK DEMPSEY (CHAMPION 1919-26; 80 FIGHTS, 60 WINS, 50 KOS, SIX LOSSES, EIGHT DRAWS, SIX NO-DECISIONS). "Strong. . . . Could take a punch.. . . He hit hard.. . . Good boxer."

GENE TUNNEY (CHAMPION 1926-28; 83 FIGHTS, 61 WINS, 45 KOS, ONE LOSS, THREE DRAWS, 19 NO-DECISIONS, ONE NO-CONTEST). "Great left jab. . . . Accurate left jab and right cross. . . . Straight punches. . . . Good defensive fighter."

JOE LOUIS (CHAMPION 1937-49; 71 FIGHTS, 68 WINS, 54 KOS, THREE LOSSES). "Knockout punching. . . . Fast. . . . Fought a lot."

EZZARD CHARLES (CHAMPION 1949-51; 122 FIGHTS, 96 WINS, 58 KOS, 25 LOSSES, ONE DRAW). "Scientific boxer. . . . Fast."

JERSEY JOE WALCOTT (CHAMPION 1951-52; 72 FIGHTS, 53 WINS, 33 KOS, 18 LOSSES, ONE DRAW). "Movement. . . . He would come in, then move out.. . . Fast shuffle.. . . He punched at the same time he was moving. . . . Hard to hit.. . . Good defensive fighter."

ROCKY MARCIANO (CHAMPION 1952-55; 49 FIGHTS, 49 WINS, 43 KOS, ZERO LOSSES). "Rugged.. . . Could take a punch and just keep coming. . . . He beat up on opponents' arms so they could not hold them up to defend themselves."

JOE FRAZIER (CHAMPION 1968-73; 37 FIGHTS, 32 WINS, 27 KOS, FOUR LOSSES, ONE DRAW). "Joe Frazier hit hard. . . . Brawler. . . . Just kept coming, moving forward, no matter how hard you hit him. . . . Could take a punch."

GEORGE FOREMAN (CHAMPION 1973–74 AND 1994–95; 81 FIGHTS, 76 WINS, 68 KOS, FIVE LOSSES). "Strong. . . . Hard hitter. . . . Knockout puncher. . . . Good left hook and right cross. . . . Dynamic."

LARRY HOLMES (CHAMPION 1978–85; 74 FIGHTS, 68 WINS, 43 KOS, SIX LOSSES). "Strong. . . Hard hitter. . . He beat me, didn't he?"

ROCKY MARCIANO

BOXING'S MOST COLORFUL CHARACTERS

Throughout the ages, from John L. Sullivan on, boxing has had its share of colorful characters whose out-of-the-ring exploits more than matched, and sometimes exceeded, their in-the-ring efforts. Whether by their behavior, their words or their get-ups, these 11 stood out as the most outlandish. But they are only a few of the many who have proved that not only does boxing build character, it also builds characters.

11. BATTLING SIKI (1912-25). The Senegalese light heavyweight champion earns a place on this list because he paraded around tethered to a lion—which, compared to some of his other antics, was tame.

10. JORGÉ PAEZ (1984-2003). A former circus clown, Paez continued the act in his boxing career, wearing outrageous costumes, doing flips and, on more than one occasion blowing kisses to ring-card girls as they pranced around between rounds.

9. ARCHIE MOORE (1935-63). From appearing at weigh-ins wearing tie-and-tails to publicly lobbying for a title fight with Rocky Marciano, Archie Moore was a boxing original.

8. JACK JOHNSON (1897-1932). Johnson not only flouted the establishment by becoming the first African-American heavyweight champion in 1908, he also flouted everything white society held sacred with his flamboyant lifestyle. Doing whatever he could to call attention to himself, Johnson raced fast cars—often the wrong way down one-way streets—and opened the freewheeling *Café de Champion* in Chicago, which served all comers and none of society's mores.

7. MAXIE ROSENBLOOM (1923-39). The light heavyweight champion earned his nickname "Slapsie Maxie" for his inability to clench his oft-broken fists, which forced him to resort to slap-punches. But it also fit his lifestyle outside the ring, with Maxie never letting training get in the way of his success, often partying all night before a fight and regularly mangling the English language—once responding to his manager, who was urging him to "open up" during a tough fight, with: "This guy might nail me. . . . You want me to get a 'conclusion' of the brain?"

6. RANDALL "TEX" COBB (1977-93). A pixyish, six-foot-plus heavyweight, Cobb used his rare and raw sense of humor and ability to take any and all punches to have a successful career and become a newspaperman's dream. He also enjoyed a second career as a character actor in movies like *Uncommon Valor* and *Raising Arizona*.

5. TONY GALENTO (1928-44). Looking like he had just stepped out of a Hans Christian Andersen story gone wrong, "Two-Ton" Tony Galento had the body of a butcher's block and the vocabulary of a barroom brawler, calling his opponents "bums" and promising to "moidah" them. Wrestling bears and octopi and drinking beer in preparation for his fights, Galento employed a fighting style that matched his demeanor—brawling, leaping and mixing more than an occasional head butt into his attack, then throwing a left hook from the floor—a style that earned him 80 wins and a shot at Joe Louis' heavyweight title at Yankee Stadium in 1939.

4. HECTOR CAMACHO (1980-2010). "The Macho Man" changed if not the face, then at least the wardrobe of boxing, entering the ring in outfits that made it look as if the Goodwill box had thrown up on him, wearing everything from battle fatigues to Roman headgear to Tarzan loincloths and inspiring other fighters—from Jorge Arce to Floyd Mayweather, Jr.—to try to follow, and even outdo, his fashion statements. Few could.

3. LEW JENKINS (1935-50). One of the most irresistible, irrepressible, irresponsible whackos ever to come down the boxing pike, Jenkins could climb into the ring dead drunk and throw a punch by memory to take out almost any lightweight opponent who unhappily ventured into his blurred vision. Putting the quart before the hearse, the 98-proof champion took to riding his "motorsickle" at any hour of the day or night, once even doing a "wheelie" in front of Madison Square Garden promoter Mike Jacobs before a 1941 title defense, hollering "Hey Mike! Look no hands," leaving the promoter ashen-faced and clutching at his heart.

2. MUHAMMAD ALI (1960-81). The boxing world was his stage. This playful—and boastful—fighter became the most flamboyant figure in boxing, if not the world of sports, strutting with the air of a carnival midway and adding amazing agility in the ring to his touch of theatrics outside it.

1. MAX BAER (1929-41). Baer came by the nicknames "Madcap Maxie" and "The Magnificent Screwball" honestly, as his antics and statements became the stuff of 1930s headlines. Before his title fight with Primo Carnera, Baer nonchalantly picked hairs off Carnera's chest, chanting, "She loves me . . . she loves me not." And after he lost the title in 1935 to Jim Braddock, Baer told a radio audience, "Braddock can use the title. He has three kids. I don't know how many I have."

BOXING'S DIRTIEST FIGHTS :: BY DON STRADLEY

Note: Don Stradley has written over 250 boxing stories for various magazines and websites, including *The Ring*, *Pro Wrestling Illustrated*, *Boxing Monthly* and ESPN.com. He's received numerous honors from the Boxing Writers Association of America, including its 2009 Barney Award for Best Feature. Here he offers his list of fights that gained plenty of dishonorable mentions for their displays of rule bending, cheap shots and bad behavior. We'll let Don take it from here:

A reporter once asked welterweight Fritzie Zivic to comment on his reputation as a dirty fighter. Zivic's response was as blunt as a thumb to the eye: "You're fighting, you're not playing the piano." Zivic fought during the 1930s and '40s, but he would have fit more comfortably in an earlier era, when the London Prize Ring rules provided just a slight buffer between fighters and their worst instincts. The most famous bout of the 19th century—the 1860 contest between John C. Heenan and Tom Sayer held at Farnborough, England—ended with Heenan strangling Sayer until a mob ran into the ring to break them up. Even after the Marquess of Queensberry rules were established in 1867, fighters continued to reveal their uglier sides in the ring, such as when New York welterweight Johnny Reagan used the spikes on his shoes to cut into his opponents' legs. Fighters stopped wearing spiked shoes soon after Reagan's time, but they'd find other ways to cheat.

10. JACK JOHNSON VS. "FIREMAN" JIM FLYNN, JULY 4, 1912. This heavyweight championship bout was so devoid of sportsmanship that the New Mexico State Police had to intervene. After taking a beating for five rounds, the frustrated challenger Flynn decided to accomplish with his head what he had failed to do with his fists. As if he'd turned into a hybrid—part kangaroo and part goat—the much shorter Flynn began leaping at Johnson, driving the top of his skull into Johnson's jaw. After absorbing a few of these butts, Johnson attempted to stifle Flynn by wrapping his long arms around him. Perhaps hoping to inflict as much harm as he could before being disqualified, Flynn squirmed free and continued jumping and butting. Despite numerous reprimands from referee Ed Smith and pleas from his own handlers, Flynn continued with his "flying butt" technique until the authorities stopped the fight in the ninth round. Johnson retained the title and suffered no damage to his famous golden smile.

9. STANLEY KETCHEL VS. BILLY PAPKE II, SEPTEMBER 7, 1908. When middleweight champion Ketchel offered to shake hands with Papke before the opening bell, Papke responded by firing a punch that broke Ketchel's nose. Within minutes Ketchel's eyes were puffed up like plums. He remained a blinded, pathetic figure for the rest of the fight, until Papke KO'd him in the 11th. Papke was the new champion, thanks to the most fiendish sucker punch in boxing history.

8. GENE FULLMER VS. JOEY GIARDELLO, APRIL 20, 1960. This bitter, 15-round draw remains memorable for the violent head-butting duel that took place in its fourth round. After being butted several times by Fullmer, Giardello lowered his head like a mountain ram and charged forward, splitting Fullmer's forehead open and nearly knocking him down. Referee Harry Kessler stepped in to warn the fighters and allow time for cooler, albeit bloodier, heads to prevail. The rest of the bout was marked by more generic roughhousing, but the action of the fourth round had already earned the fight a dark place in boxing history. Columnist Hack Miller observed that Kessler's clothes were eventually drenched in blood, "as if he had just killed and cleaned his first elk."

7. HARRY GREB VS. BOB ROPER, JANUARY 1, 1923. Greb was one of the dirtiest fighters of the era, but he met his match in Roper. Or was it the other way around? Their sixth meeting, fought in Greb's hometown of Pittsburgh, saw Roper go below and beyond his usual tactics, at one point choking Greb with an open glove and bending him over the ropes as if to snap him in half. The fighters paid no attention to referee Yock Henninger, who was struck several times while trying to separate them. Not even the final bell of this no-decision bout could stop them, as Greb and Roper kept swinging until several policemen leapt into the ring to break them up. Greb was temporarily suspended while Roper was banned from fighting in Pittsburgh.

6. TONY GALENTO VS. LOU NOVA, SEPTEMBER 15, 1939. Just one look at Galento's squatty frame and you knew he wasn't going to dazzle you with jabs and footwork. Galento's favorite one-two combination was a head butt followed by a thumb. Nova tried to accommodate Galento's plug-ugly style, but he lacked Galento's genius for barroom tactics. Nova finally succumbed in the 14th. *The Ring* magazine called this bout "disgraceful" and chastised referee George Blake for not disqualifying Galento.

5. TEDDY YAROSZ VS. LLOYD MARSHALL II, OCTOBER 21, 1940. Marshall started the festivities with a ball-busting shot in the first, which cost him the round. Yarosz, past his prime and overweight, resorted to eye gouging and scraping Marshall's face with the laces of his gloves. At one point Yarosz shoved Marshall to the canvas with such force that referee Red Robinson ruled it a knockdown. Yarosz tried to repeat the maneuver, but was penalized for "attempted tripping." Both fighters took turns trying to shove each other through the ropes, and Marshall lost another round for fouling. Some observers suspected the bout was a fixed job gone awry, with both fighters working hard to be disqualified. *The Pittsburgh Press* reported, "Even hardened ringsiders booed lustily in disgust." Yarosz won on points, but both fighters were suspended.

4. WILLIE PEP VS. SANDY SADDLER IV, SEPTEMBER 26, 1951. Anything resembling boxing that may have occurred during this bout was purely coincidental. Pep and Saddler had already met three times, but their distinction for being a dirty duo came from the fourth bout—a brawl highlighted by headlocks, hammerlocks and lots of old-fashioned, schoolyard tripping. Maybe these two featherweight legends were inspired by all of the pro wrestling that was on television in those days. Pep even tried to trip Saddler from behind while riding him "piggyback." Pep, who'd suffered a horrible cut over his right eye, finally quit on his stool after the ninth round. The New York State Athletic Commission revoked Pep's license and suspended Saddler.

3. RIDDICK BOWE VS. ANDREW GOLOTA, JULY 11, 1996. The echo of the opening bell was still resounding through Madison Square Garden when Golota's punches began straying way south of Bowe's beltline. Bowe retaliated with some kidney punches and a rabbit punch, which seemed to inspire Golota the way a pistol shot inspires a racehorse. Golota, whose gloves appeared magnetically guided to Bowe's protective cup, would be penalized for low blows three times during the next few rounds. When Golota landed the ultimate, pile-driving blow to the groin in the seventh, Bowe sank to the canvas. As Bowe writhed and grimaced, referee Wayne Kelly slapped Golota with a disqualification. The post-fight madness, which included one of Bowe's entourage hitting Golota's 74-year-old manager Lou Duva in the head with a cell phone and the spectators engaging in a chair-throwing riot, showed that even the seconds and the fans fought dirty in this one.

2. MIKE TYSON VS. EVANDER HOLYFIELD II, JUNE 28, 1997. The Marquess of Queensberry rules had a specific regulation against biting, which tells you a lot about fighting in the 1800s. In fact, an 1872 bout between Billy Edwards and Arthur Chambers ended when the referee disqualified Edwards after seeing bite marks on Chambers' shoulder. Edwards claimed he'd been framed, and that Chambers had actually been bitten by his own handler. Despite an editorial in *The New York Times* condemning the bout as "the downfall of pugilism," the sport not only continued, but flourished—to the point where 125 years later one of the largest pay-per-view audiences ever witnessed another famous series of bites by a boxer. During the third round of the Tyson-Holyfield rematch, Tyson chewed off the tip of Holyfield's right ear and spat it to the canvas. After a warning from referee Mills Lane, Tyson bit Holyfield's other ear, drawing a disqualification and inciting a major melee. Holyfield accused Tyson of deliberately fouling out of the fight, while Tyson claimed he was merely responding to Holyfield's butting. And once again sports editors carped about the downfall of pugilism.

1. FRITZIE ZIVIC VS. AL "BUMMY" DAVIS, NOVEMBER 15, 1940. Turning in what the United Press called "a berserk back alley performance," Davis became unhinged during this Madison Square Garden bout. Zivic had dominated the first round, putting Davis through a rigorous, three-minute demonstration of thumbs and elbows. Not interested in the finer points of dirty fighting, Davis responded in the second round by smashing left hooks into Zivic's groin. Some reporters had Davis launching as many as ten consecutive low blows. When referee Billy Cavanaugh disqualified him, the boxer known in the newspapers as "Bummy" went after Zivic again. Ringside cops struggled to pry the fighters apart while Davis' handlers brawled with sportswriters and fans threw debris into the ring. As Davis was being dragged away by security, he landed a kick to Cavanaugh's leg, either by accident, or for good measure. Davis later told Commissioner Bill Brown that he'd been blinded by Zivic's thumbs, therefore he didn't know his punches were landing so low. Brown didn't buy it. He revoked Davis' license and handed him a stiff fine. Zivic went unpunished. Perhaps Brown thought Zivic had suffered enough.

BEST BODY PUNCHERS

The body punch is the most overlooked punch in boxing. For years the body attack fell largely into disuse, as fighters went headhunting. But throughout history, some fighters have used the body attack to slow down their opponents and take away their speed or to set up their shots to the head. And then there are those who mastered the punch to the body to the point where it could get the job done itself, such as those below.

12. BILLY PETROLLE (1922-34). The man known as "The Fargo Express" would come in low in his patented crouch, bobbing and weaving his head to and fro, then use his hands like Indian clubs to the body. After feinting a right to the head, he would bury his streaking left hook into his opponent's stomach, right up to the wrist. And although Petrolle never won a title, his left hook did help him win 89 fights.

11. ROCKY MARCIANO (1947-56). "The Rock" walked into and through anything his opponents threw in his direction, wrecking them with baseball-bat swings to the arms, the midsection, the head, and just about anything else within reach. And while his right hand, his "Suzie-Q," was a punch of choice, he destroyed many of his 43 knockout victims with blasting cap shots to the body as well.

10. TONY CANZONERI (1925-39). Tony Canzoneri, or as he was familiarly called "Canzi," was an inexhaustible fighter with a cast iron chin. He could throw a lethal right-hand power punch to the jaw or swing his low-left left with equal bludgeoning effect to the body. And he did, against 176 opponents, winning 39 and knocking out 44 of them with one or the other.

9. MICKY WARD (1985-2003). A journeyman junior welterweight, Ward turned his career around by developing one of the most devastating left hooks to the body in recent boxing history. It was that left hook to the body that had Arturo Gatti lying on the floor, grimacing in pain, in their May 2002 battle-cum-war and that left hook to the ribs that took out Alfonso Sanchez in April 1997 with Sanchez on the verge of victory. Time and again, behind on the scorecards, Ward would deliver his signature punch to snatch victory from the jaws of the judges' scorecards.

8. MICKEY WALKER (1919-39). The two-division champion who, in his spare time, fought elephantine heavyweights, once said. "I belted the guts out of the best of them." And he did, his droopy-eyed look giving rise to the nickname "The Toy Bulldog," attacking his opponents almost as if obeying the exhortation of his manager Doc Kearns to "sic 'em" with a body attack that was, in large part, responsible for many of his 94 wins.

7. ALEXIS ARGUELLO (1968-95). Called *El Flaco Explosivo* ("The Explosive Thin Man"), the tall and extremely thin Arguello dealt out destruction with body punches so murderous that when he fetched Cornelius Boza Edwards a shot to the stomach, Boza Edwards lost control of his bodily functions.

6. MIKE McCALLUM (1981-97). Known as "The Body Snatcher," McCallum earned his nickname honestly, attacking the body to weaken his opponents, then sometimes doubling up on left hooks to the body to finish them off.

5. BOB FITZSIMMONS (1885-1914). The former blacksmith won the heavyweight championship in 1897 from Jim Corbett with one blow—a "solar plexus punch" to the region of the body just below the ribs. It was a patented Fitzsimmons punch, which came with a curious shifting of his feet, almost the beginning of the left hook to the body now employed by so many fighters. His left burrowed into the gullets of his opponents, both large heavyweights and smaller light heavyweights and middleweights. Fitzsimmons, fighting them all, proclaimed, "The bigger they are the harder they fall." And fall they did, 67 of them, many courtesy of "Ruby Robert's" left hook to the body.

HENRY ARMSTRONG

4. HENRY ARMSTRONG (1931-45). The man called "Hurricane Hank" was exactly that, fighting three-and-a-half minutes of every three-minute round with punches to head and body causing his opponents to suffer gentle and gradual erosion and accounting for many of the 98 knockouts.

3. SAM LANGFORD (1902-26). The man who said, "Hit him in the body and the head dies," followed his own advice throughout a career that included as many as 350 bouts, recorded and unrecorded. A short, squat middleweight-cum-heavyweight, Langford would continually press up against the numbers of his opponents, landing short, vicious punches to the body to soften them up. Harry Wills said of Langford's body punches, "When he hit me to the body, I looked behind me to see if his fist had come through the other side."

2. JULIO CÉSAR CHAVEZ (1980-2005). The legendary Mexican champion, a deity in Mexico, where his nickname "J.C." might give you some hint of his revered status, was known for his thunderous body shots, many of them landing with the sound of surf slapping shore. In his title-winning lightweight bout with Edwin Rosario Chavez practiced his own form of acupuncture, breaking down the soon-to-be-ex-WBA-lightweight champion with body shots that left Rosario standing mid-ring with his great powers reduced to barely those of respiration. And in his signature fight—his 1990 battle against Meldrick Taylor—Chavez preserved his junior lightweight title by rallying from behind for a miraculous 12th-round TKO win with two seconds to go in the fight, setting up the stoppage with wrecking-ball body shots that caused Taylor to open and close his mouth like a fish out of water.

1. TONY ZALE (1934-48). The two-time middleweight champion unleashed body punches that had the effect of a rifle butt thrust full force into his opponent's midsection. In his first fight with Rocky Graziano, Zale—exhausted and getting the bejabbers beaten out of him by "The Rock"—suddenly landed a crunching left not six inches above Rocky's waistband, sinking it almost up to the elbow, causing Graziano to sink to his haunches, gasping for breath, there to be counted out for the first time in his career.

BEST PHYSIQUES

When you consider it, boxers in the ring are basically naked except for their shorts and footwear. And while most boxers have relatively commonplace bodies, there are a few who, if they were cars, could be advertised as having "Bodies by Fisher." Here are ten who looked as if they had just stepped out of a body building magazine, along with a couple whose very presence in the ring brought "OOHS" and "AAHS" from appreciative fans—mostly those of the fairer gender.

9. JOE BUGNER (1967-99). The 6-foot-4-inch, 240-pound former British and European heavyweight champion was once described as a "Blond Adonis" by British sportswriter Hugh McIlvanney, who noted that Bugner had "the physique of a Greek statue . . . but with fewer moves."

8. MARVELOUS MARVIN HAGLER (1973-87). He wanted to be "marvelous," and with his bald head and imposing muscular physique—which looked as if you could light a match on it—he was exactly that.

7. EVANDER HOLYFIELD (1984-). Evander looked like a Black Adonis, his V-shaped body, with broad shoulders and powerful arms, sculptured by conditioning experts.

6. GEORGE FOREMAN (1969-97). Everything about "Big" George was big and impressive. A 6-foot-3-inch sequoia tree with trunks for legs and carved clubs for arms, he was as massive as he was muscular. However, that was in his first career. When George came back to the ring after a ten-year hiatus, he was big only around the middle, his physique having literally gone to "pot."

5. EMILE GRIFFITH (1958-77). As the story goes, Griffith was working in New York's Garment District, making women's hats, when his boss noticed his impressive physique—a V-shaped body with 44-inch shoulders tapering down to a 28-inch waist—and encouraged him to become a fighter.

4. MUHAMMAD ALI (1960-81). When Ali remarked on how "pretty" he was, he was referring to his face. However, he also possessed a body that could be considered "pretty" for those with an eye for smooth, toned, lithe and strong, but hardly muscle-bound physiques.

MAX BAER

3. MAX BAER (1929-41). Baer was a bear of a man, a 6-foot-2-inch muscular marvel with a 32-inch waist and broad shoulders that were called "airplane-width" in various columns, many of which—coupling his physique with his out-of-the-ring antics—called him: "The Man with the Million-Dollar Body and the Two-cent Brain."

2. KEN NORTON (1967-81). Called the "Black Hercules" for good reason, Norton looked like he stepped out of a physical fitness magazine with his powerful biceps and chiseled body. His physique was on prominent display in the 1975 movie *Mandingo*, where his body might have won him an Oscar had there been an award given in that category.

1. MIKE WEAVER (1972-2000). Weaver may have had the greatest physique of any fighter who ever stepped into the ring. Even his muscles had muscles. When he served as a sparring partner for Ken Norton, an impressive physical specimen himself who was called the "Black Hercules," Norton called Weaver "Hercules."

GREATEST BOXING IQS

It takes more than mastering every punch and every move in the boxing book to become a great fighter, advised light heavyweight champion José Torres in his 1972 bestseller *Sting Like a Bee*; you need to add "some tricks to that book." Those tricks might include weaving deception into your moves or telling lies with your punches or doing whatever it takes to outsmart and/or gain a psychological advantage over an opponent. Because, as any trainer worth his spit bucket will tell you, boxing is 50 percent psychological. And some of the greatest fighters are, not coincidentally, again in the words of Torres, "genius fighters" for their ability to gain that psychological and intellectual advantage. Here are some of the most ingenious fighters in boxing history.

10. TOMMY LOUGHRAN (1919–37) One of the pastmasters of the "Sweet Science," Loughran was in the words of Jack Johnson, "the only modern boxers I know who can really pick off punches." But Loughran was more, much more, than just a great defensive fighter, being so elusive that in his fight with Max Baer, Baer actually stopped and turned to the crowd with his arms extended and a "what-the-hell-can-you-do?" expression on his face. He also was viewed as the lineal descendant of Gentleman Jim Corbett's style of fighting, of outthinking his opponent, which extended to his timing a round in his head so that he would wind up in his own corner at the end of each round

9. JAMES J. CORBETT (1886–1903). Besides introducing "The Sweet Science" of modern boxing, Corbett also mastered the art of what was then called "getting the other man's goat." Before his historic 1892 battle with undefeated heavyweight champ John L. Sullivan, Corbett won the coin toss to select corners, then chose the corner where the previous night's winners had sat. Then, playing a game of one-upmanship, he stayed in his dressing room until the last possible second, depriving Sullivan of the time-honored champion's prerogative of entering the ring last. And during the ritualistic pre-fight instructions, Corbett—a whole century before Antonio Tarver asked Roy Jones Jr., "Any excuses tonight, Roy?"—initiated the practice of pre-fight insults by pushing his forearm against John L.'s Adam's apple and asking the ref, "Is this a foul?" All of it worked, Corbett knocking out Sullivan in 21 rounds to become the new heavyweight champ.

8. GENE TUNNEY (1915-28). Tunney's ring savvy was equal to any. Tunney began his 1926 heavyweight title fight against Jack Dempsey with a "get-acquainted" right to let Dempsey feel his power, instead of visa versa, then fought a mistake-free fight to lift Dempsey's crown. In their rematch, a year-less-a-day later, Tunney used his ring smarts to recover from the famous seventh-round "Long Count" knockdown by staying down until the referee finally got around to tolling "Nine," then backpedaling the rest of the round to evade Dempsey. And what nobody remembers: in the succeeding round, the revitalized Tunney knocked down Dempsey on his way to winning a unanimous ten-round decision.

7. ARCHIE MOORE (1935-63). "The Old Mongoose" knocked out more opponents than any other boxer, scoring as many psychological KOs as physical ones. He would arrive for weigh-ins wearing a full-length tux, talk to opponents in clichés—as he did against Tony Anthony during his light heavy defense, telling him, "You're going to be light heavyweight champion," causing Anthony to lose focus and be KO'd in the next round. He deflated Yvon Durelle by waving at him between rounds after the challenger had knocked down Moore four times, Moore later saying, "Every time I looked up, I looked into the referee's face. I got tired of looking at that man." He even used mass media manipulation, campaigning for a title shot at heavyweight champion Rocky Marciano by taking out ads in *The Ring* magazine.

6. KID McCOY (1891-1916). The inspiration for the "The Real McCoy" saying (or at least the story goes), that he was "The Real McCoy" when it came to outsmarting his opponents. He was the inventor of the "Corkscrew Punch," which, when twisted just right, could tear an opponent open, this turn-of-the-century fighter also pioneered other ways of getting under an opponent's skin. McCoy dropped tacks on the floor to gain a big advantage over a barefoot South African fighter. He distracted a French opponent with an eye for pretty members of the other gender by asking, "Who is that *mademoiselle* in the stands?"—then delivered his *au revoir* when the Frenchman turned his *tete* for a look. But perhaps his most famous trick came in his fight with Jack Wilkes, who billed himself as "the middleweight champion of the Southwest." McCoy powdered his face with a liberal dose of talcum and feigned illness in his corner before the fight. Believing his opponent weak and ill, Wilkes tried to quickly put McCoy out of his misery. But McCoy treated his would-be benefactor illy, driving a left to his solar plexus to quickly finish off Wilkes as repayment for his thoughtfulness.

5. SUGAR RAY LEONARD (1977-97). After being taken to school by Roberto Duran in their first fight, Ray demanded a rematch just five months after their Montreal battle knowing Duran partied between fights and would never let success go to his training. Moreover, Leonard came up with a strategy designed to attack Duran where he lived: in his *machismo*. He baited Duran, clowned with him—winding up with his right before attacking Duran with his left, sticking out his chin and generally frustrating Duran and his bulldog mentality. In the eighth round, Duran finally hollered out in Spanish to referee Octavio Meyran, "I won't fight that fuckin' clown!" and walked away. (And, no, Duran never said, "No mas!" Commentator Howard Cosell coined the phrase, either unable to hear what Duran hollered or unable to understand Spanish.)

4. WILLIE PEP (1940–66). Willie Pep was more, much more, than a great defensive fighter. He was also a great thinking fighter, as he proved in his second bout against the dynamite-powered Sandy Saddler. Unable to evade Saddler's punches for 15 rounds, Pep discovered when he stepped on Saddler's toes—deliberately or accidentally—that Saddler cried, "Ouch!" So all night long, he stepped on Saddler's toes on his way to winning the rematch and the featherweight title.

3. MUHAMMAD ALI (1960–81). Ali gained the psychological advantage over his opponent almost before the ink was dry on the fight contract. He'd mock them with nicknames ("The Mummy" for George Foreman, "Gorilla" for Joe Frazier, "The Acorn" for Earnie Shavers, etc., etc., etc. . .). He'd belittle his opponents in interviews and poems, then Ali would outfox them in the ring. Take for instance his change in tactics in his "Rumble in the Jungle" fight with Foreman. Seeing that he couldn't dance away from Foreman because Big George was cutting off the ring on him by placing his lead left foot between Ali's feet, forcing Ali to stand in front of him and trade, Ali resorted to the "Rope-A-Dope." He leaned against the ropes and covered up, luring George into throwing dozens of heavy-handed club punches and eventually tiring himself out in the African heat, making himself an easy target for an eighth-round Ali knockout combination.

2. JOE GANS (1893–1909). "The "Old Master" used the ring as his own private laboratory, where he made discoveries like, "If you happen to hit a man in a certain place that hurts, that is the place to hit him again. You only have to hit him half as hard there as any other place to finish him." Gans would study his opponent's style and implement his findings, as he did against Frank Erne. Having already lost to Erne, he trained for their 1902 rematch determined to put into effect something he had seen in their first fight: that when Erne started his left, he would check his opponent's reaction. If his opponent moved to block the punch, he would turn it into a hook; but if his opponent anticipated a hook, Erne would deliver a straight left. Armed with this insight, Gans planned to "shoot my right over the moment I saw the left start" And did, knocking out Erne just 100 seconds into the fight.

1. BENNY LEONARD (1911-24; 1931-32). One the smartest fighter ever to climb into the ring—if not the smartest—Leonard knew all the tricks of the trade, emphasis on the word "tricks." In his first fight against Lew Tendler—a fight in which Hype Igoe of the New York World called Leonard "the brainiest of all boxers," Tendler, one of the greatest left-handers in boxing history, hurt Leonard with a bodacious left to the midsection. As Tendler moved in for the kill, Leonard grabbed his groin and hollered, "That was a foul!" even though it hadn't been. As Tendler stopped to argue the fact Leonard added insult to his non-injury, saying to Tendler, "Stop your bellyachin' More time bought. Leonard would survive to fight another day thanks to his quick thinking. Leonard was also a brilliant thinker outside the ring, advising his stablemate Gene Tunney, who had just taken a beating-and-a-half from Harry Greb, how to beat Greb in their return bout by hitting him under his outstretched left to the heart all night, so much so that Greb complained to newspapermen after the fight that he still hurt from Tunney's shots compliments of Leonard's being able to parse his style.

BENNY LEONARD

MY TEN TOUGHEST FIGHTS :: BY SUGAR RAY LEONARD

Note: Ray Leonard more than merely filled the shoes left by Muhammad Ali, he earned the right to the nickname "Sugar Ray," originally borne by the great Ray Robinson with Robinson himself saying, "I'm gratified he's using my name." The darling of the 1976 Olympics, Ray won 36 of his 39 fights as a pro, 25 by KO, beating some of the greatest fighters of his day, including Marvelous Marvin Hagler, Wilfred Benitez, Tommy Hearns and Roberto Duran. But in the process of building his nearly all-winning record, Leonard had some tough fights—the toughest of which he ranks for us on a 10-to-1 basis.

10. Vs. Hector Camacho, March 1, 1997, Atlantic City; Third-Round TKO Loss. "He beat me . . . that SOB."

9. Vs. Floyd Mayweather, Sr., September 9, 1978, Providence, Rhode Island; 10ᵗʰ-round TKO Win. "I had bad hands . . . and he gave me trouble, though he couldn't beat me."

8. Vs. Dick Ecklund, July 18, 1978, Boston; 10-Round Unanimous Decision Win. "He was sloppy and unorthodox and gave me problems."

7. Vs. Marvelous Marvin Hagler, April 6, 1987, Las Vegas; 12-Round Split-Decision Win. "To tell the truth, I was a little nervous going into the fight. . . . But when I feinted in the first round and he cringed, covering up, I knew he was just as scared as I was and knew I'd win. . . . Tough fight."

6. Vs. Terry Norris, February 9, 1991, New York City; 12-Round Unanimous Decision Loss. "People don't give him the credit he's due. It was the first time I had fought at 154 since 1980."

5. Vs. Willie Rodriguez, May 14, 1977, Baltimore; Six-Round Unanimous Decision Win. "Only my second pro fight. . . . And he almost knocked me out with a hook."

4. Vs. Marcos Geraldo, May 20, 1979, Baton Rouge; 10-Round Unanimous Decision Win. "A tough middleweight fighter at welter. . . . Would go ten rounds with Marvin Hagler the next year, losing a close decision. . . . Bigger and stronger than anyone I had fought 'til then, very physical . . . think I damaged my eye. . . ."

3. Vs. Roberto Duran, June 20, 1980, Montreal, Canada; 15-Round Unanimous Decision Loss. "The first time I fought the wrong fight and lost. . . . But in the rematch five months later, the "No Mas" fight, I knew I'd win, especially after Ray Charles, who had sung the anthem "America," came over and hugged me before the fight and said, 'Kick his ass.'"

2. Vs. Wilfred Benitez, November 30, 1979, Las Vegas; 15ᵀᴴ-Round TKO Win. "Maybe my best performance, but I needed it against Benitez. . . . He consistently slipped my right-hand shots and countered beautifully and caught me with several shots, including one in the seventh round. . . . Told me after the fight he hadn't trained at all. . . . And afterwards I was so exhausted and dehydrated, I had to go to the hospital. . . . Years later, I visited him at his home outside San Juan and found him sitting in a chair, his eyes glazed. His mother asked him if he had recognized me and he only said, 'He beat me.'"

1. Vs. Tommy Hearns, September 16, 1981, Las Vegas; 14ᵀᴴ-Round TKO Win. "Tommy Hearns was an anomaly when it came to guys my weight, welterweight. He was just so big, so tall, so fast, and so powerful, that you couldn't make a mistake. If you made one mistake, you were . . . done."

FIVE REASONS I WON THE REMATCH AGAINST SUGAR RAY LEONARD :: BY TOMMY HEARNS

Note: Tommy Hearns ranks as one of the greatest fighters of his era. The first boxer to win world titles in four different weight classes, "The Hitman" went on to claim eight belts in six weight divisions. Able to control a fight with his long flicking jab, then end it instantly with his powerful right hand, Hearns won 61 fights (48 by KO). He beat nearly everyone put in front of him, including Hall of Famers Roberto Duran, Wilfred Benitez and Pipino Cuevas. But he never beat Sugar Ray Leonard. . . . Well, according to the judges, anyway. Leonard TKO'd Hearns in the 14th round of their epic 1981 showdown for the welterweight title. But most fans, experts, and sober and sighted folks who've watched Hearns' second fight against Leonard in 1989 agree that Tommy earned a decisive victory over Sugar Ray that night in Las Vegas. "It kinda peeved me off," said Hearns of the judges' dubious non-decision, calling it a draw. Here, Tommy offers, in his own words, the five biggest reasons he believes he won that fight.

5. "I FOUR-POSTED HIM, CONTROLLING THE FIGHT."

4. "I THREW MORE PUNCHES AND LANDED BETTER PUNCHES."

3. "I WAS AHEAD ON ALL SCORECARDS GOING INTO THE LAST ROUND AND EVEN THOUGH RAY WON THE LAST ROUND, IT WASN'T A 10-8 ROUND AS ONE SCORECARD HAD IT, GIVING HIM A DRAW."

2. "I KNOCKED HIM DOWN TWICE, HE NEVER KNOCKED ME DOWN."

1. "EVEN RAY ADMITTED, 'TOMMY WON THE FIGHT.'"

FIGHTERS WITH THE BEST JABS

The jab is the most essential punch in boxing, both offensively and defensively. It sets up a fighter for a power right (or in the case of a southpaw, a power left) and can be an important element in a fighter's defense. Although all boxers have the jab in their arsenal, few, like the ten below, have perfected it.

10. TOMMY HEARNS (1997-2006). A six-foot-one string bean with a 78-inch wingspan and arms so long that he could tie his shoestrings without bending over, Tommy Hearns used his left jab to great advantage. When he didn't have it in someone's face, as he did against Sugar Ray Leonard during the middle rounds of their first fight, he would wave it metronomically, hypnotizing his opponents who lost sight of his howitzer of a right.

9. BENNY LEONARD (1911-24; 1931-32). One of the greatest artisans ever to grace the ring, Benny Leonard used his talented left to control a fight, stabbing his opponent to the point of distraction until he could set up his dynamite-laden right. Or use it in defense to keep his adversary off him, as did against Ritchie Mitchell in their famous 1921 fight after Mitchell had knocked him down.

8. MUHAMMAD ALI (1960-81). Sometimes delivered from somewhere below his belt line, Ali's flicking left jab was far from picture-perfect. But like a snake's tongue, it came so fast and from so many different angles that his opponent could barely see it coming, much less get out of its way.

7. JIM CORBETT (1886-1903). An early proponent of the jab, Corbett used it to great effect, staving off his opponents' bull-like rushes—as he did in his heavyweight title win against John L. Sullivan and for 22 rounds against James J. Jeffries. Corbett was indeed a "master boxer" and master jabber.

6. JOE LOUIS (1934-51). No fighter ever used his left jab with such an economy of effort or efficiency of results as Joe Louis, who drew the tendrils of the octopus around his doomed opponents with his jab. The longtime heavyweight champ took out 54 opponents, almost all of them with his one-two—a left jab setting up a right hand.

5. BOB FOSTER (1961-78). Foster's left jab was a "snapping jab," one delivered with a twist that could rip open his opponent's face—as evidenced by his being the only fighter ever to cut Muhammad Ali's "pretty" face.

4. SONNY LISTON (1953-70). Everything came off Liston's left jab, a battering ram that could take his opponent's head off or set up his dynamite right, a deadly club.

3. JOE GANS (1893-1909). Known as "The Old Master," Gans is credited, along with bareknuckle champ Tom Sayers, with essentially inventing the jab. But the way Gans used his jab—employing it both defensively to blunt the attack of his opponent and offensively to set up a right hand that destroyed 85 opponents—was of his own invention and made his jab legendary.

2. LARRY HOLMES (1973-2002). Holmes' left jab was his stock-in-trade, a punch he used to subdue opponents or to set up his right or—in his fight against Ray Mercer at the grand old age of 42—to just take his opponent to school by employing his jab almost exclusively.

1. TOMMY LOUGHRAN (1919-37). Loughran's left jab was almost independent of conscious effort, a punch he used with all the stealth and guile of a pickpocket. It was that left that prompted a beaten Jim Braddock to say after his attempt to take Loughran's light heavyweight title: "Loughran? Has anybody here seen Loughran? I was supposed to fight the guy tonight . . . all I saw was his left."

MOST DEVASTATING SINGLE-PUNCH KNOCKOUTS

It's that one big punch that ends a bout thisquickly. Not an accumulation of punches, not a beat-down and stoppage, but one punch. And the bigger the fight, the bigger that one punch that ended it. Over the long history of boxing, there have been thousands of devastating single-punch knockouts. But here are, in our opinion, the *most* devastating, the ones that ended major fights in sudden and sometimes shocking fashion.

10. JIMMY McLARNIN VS. SID TERRIS, FEBRUARY 24, 1928, FIRST ROUND. Known as "The Ghetto Ghost," Sid Terris was also known as the uncrowned lightweight champion in the wake of Benny Leonard's retirement. While awaiting his shot at the title, he took on young Jimmy McLarnin, making his first appearance in New York. The result is best told in the running commentary by radio broadcaster Sam Taub: "Terris comes out fast at the opening bell . . . Terris jabs McLarnin and gets away . . . Sid leaps in with two more straight lefts . . . Terris is boxing beautifully tonight . . . McLarnin has not started a punch yet . . . Sid is in again with a straight left . . . He is fast as lightning . . . Terris leads again . . . Oy! Oy! Oy! . . . Terris is down . . . McLarnin nailed him with a right to the chin . . . There's the count . . . Seven . . . Eight . . . Nine . . . Ten . . . Oy! Oy! Oy! . . . It's all over . . . Terris is knocked out. . . ." McLarnin would go on to win the welterweight crown on another first-round knockout; Terris would go on to remain the uncrowned lightweight champion.

9. SUGAR RAY LEONARD VS. DAVEY "BOY" GREEN, MARCH 31, 1980, FOURTH ROUND. In his first welterweight title defense, Leonard fought former British and European welterweight titlist Davey "Boy" Green. But while Green had impressive upper-body strength, he also held his hands far apart, leaving himself open to a left hook. And that's exactly what happened in the fourth round as Ray hit Green with what he called "the hardest blow I've ever thrown"—a left hook from hell that resounded with all the noise of an explosion that felled five or six bystanders and laid Green endwise. Referee Arthur Mercante only counted to six before he waved it over. But he could have counted to six hundred, it taking Green that long to recover.

8. JACK DEMPSEY VS. JACK SHARKEY, JULY 21, 1927, SEVENTH ROUND. Dempsey, who had lost his heavyweight championship the previous year to Gene Tunney, wanted a warm-up fight before taking on Tunney again. What he got was more than a warm-up; it was a beating. For six rounds, Sharkey, in the words of Dempsey, "gave me living hell." In the seventh, Dempsey now fighting a desperate fight, a fistic last stand, began digging both hands into the body. Sharkey tried to tie Dempsey up, but Dempsey continued to pump his free hand to the body, four of them landing more than somewhat below the beltline. As Sharkey turned to referee Jack O'Sullivan to complain, "He's hittin' me low," Dempsey used his free hand to land his vaunted left hook to Sharkey's exposed chin. Sharkey fell to the canvas holding his groin, his head shaking feebly at the progressing ten-count. Afterwards, Dempsey said, "What was I going to do, write him a letter of apology?"

7. TONY ZALE VS. ROCKY GRAZIANO, SEPTEMBER 27, 1946, SIXTH ROUND. The first meeting between "The Man of Steel" Zale and "The Dead End Kid" Graziano was not a fight; it was a war with no survivors. Back and forth the two went at it, with Zale flooring Graziano in the first round and Graziano returning the favor in the second. The two continued to beat the bejabbers out of each other for the next three rounds, with Graziano getting the better of it. Then, in the sixth, after landing a few rights, Graziano stepped back—all the better to get a view of the damage he had administered—when an exhausted Zale leaped forward, landing a left to Graziano's stomach, sinking it all the way up to the elbow. The punch paralyzed Graziano, who lay on the canvas, gasping for air. By the time he was able to pick up the count, the fight was over, with Zale still middleweight champion.

6. TOMMY HEARNS VS. ROBERTO DURAN, JUNE 25, 1984, SECOND ROUND. Befitting his machismo demeanor, Roberto Duran dismissed Tommy Hearns for his performance against Sugar Ray Leonard, contemptuously calling him a "chicken," and leaped at the chance to face him for an upfront guarantee of $500,000. Duran's indifference to Hearns also extended to his training for the fight as he spent most of his time training on wine, women, and whoopee. And from the opening seconds of the fight his lack of training showed as all he could muster were hopeless and helpless gestures, snarling and hissing at Hearns as Hearns tee'd off with right-hand-after-right-hand, knocking down Duran in the closing minutes of the first. Then, in the second round, Hearns exploded a murderous right hand to the jaw of Duran that dropped Duran on his nose, complete with a perfect two-point landing like a plane coming to a halt. Out cold. Counted out for the only time in his career, all Duran could say of the punch was that it "shook out all the alcohol, all the women...and to the mat I went."

5. JACK JOHNSON VS. STANLEY KETCHEL, OCTOBER 16, 1909, 12TH ROUND. Middleweight champion Stanley Ketchel challenged heavyweight champion Jack Johnson in what, for all intents and purposes, was an exhibition for that new-fangled contraption, the movie camera. But not content to continue in the part of a co-star after 11 rounds of play acting, Ketchel threw a sweeping right hand that serpentined behind Johnson's neck, toppling him. Johnson leapt up, a malevolent grin on his face and, as Ketchel raced in, determined to put the final touches on his partial work, caught the oncoming Ketchel on the jaw. Ketchel fell heavily, as if poleaxed, his arms and legs outstretched in a perfect five-point star. As referee Jack Welch tolled the fatal count of ten over the fallen Ketchel, Johnson could be seen leaning against the ropes, his legs crossed, picking Ketchel's teeth out of his right glove.

4. Sugar Ray Robinson vs. Gene Fullmer II, May 1, 1957, Fifth Round. Robinson, who had lost his middleweight title to Fullmer four months earlier, avenged his loss and recaptured the middleweight crown with what to many seemed the perfect hook. Thrown, as some observers remember, while Robinson was moving backward, a deep-dish beauty of a left hook that separated Fullmer from his senses for the only time in his career and made Robinson the middleweight champ for the fourth time.

3. Bob Foster vs. Dick Tiger, May 24, 1968, Fourth Round. Bob Foster used his 79-inch reach to knock the crown off defending light heavyweight champion Dick Tiger's head with one big left hook to the jaw that traveled a short and sweet trajectory, a picture-perfect hook that belonged to the ages and knocked out Tiger for the only time in his 81-bout career.

2. Jersey Joe Walcott-Ezzard Charles. July 18, 1951, 7th Round. Thought to be "37-going on 47" by many and others suggesting "anything under fifty could be right," Jersey Joe had more chances to win the heavyweight championship than there were wrinkles on the back of his neck —of which there were plenty. But every time he had come up empty-handed, as he had twice against Joe Louis and twice against Ezzard Charles. Now he was to try his luck for a fifth time, this time against Ezzard Charles who had beaten him twice in 15-round decisions. Showing that his skills were the skills no age could destroy, Walcott landed a quick, short left hook on the inside to Charles's jaw, a punch Charles would later mournfully call "a sucker punch," making Charles one with the canvas and Jersey Joe the champion at the advanced age of 37, or so it was thought, the-then oldest man ever to become heavyweight champion.

1. Rocky Marciano vs. Jersey Joe Walcott, September 23, 1952, 13th round. For 12 rounds, defending heavyweight champion Jersey Joe Walcott had been in control of Rocky Marciano. Ahead on all-three scorecards (7-4-1; 7-5; 8-4), Walcott only had to continue delivering the voodoo he did so well and confounding Marciano for three more rounds. But with just 33 seconds gone in the 13th, Rocky landed a right hand to the jaw of the soon-to-be-ex-champion. Walcott went down, as if shot, his left arm hooked over the middle rope, a grotesque variation of a religious figure in prayer, now the ex-heavyweight champion.

BOXING'S BIGGEST PUNCHERS

The most exciting and memorable moment in boxing, if not all of sports, is the knockout. It is that explosive moment in boxing that determines the outcome of the contest, visible to all, unlike many of football's touchdowns decided by a one-yard plunge, or a hockey goal decided by an unseen shot, played and re-played in TV highlight films. And while normally the province of the bigger men, many of those in the lighter weight classes had a knockout punch that would compare with their heavyweight brethren. Because there have been so many "heavy punchers" over the long course of boxing, we have over-exceeded our limit and expanded our list to include those, through boxing history, who have been boxing's "biggest punchers."

13. JIMMY WILDE (1910-23). While the biggest punchers in boxing are usually the heavyweights, flyweight Jimmy Wilde, weighing no more than 108 pounds dripping wet, knocked out an incredible 99 men in 153 bouts, earning an astonishingly high slugging percentage of 64.7 for such a little man.

12. SONNY LISTON (1953-70). With fists larger than those of Jess Willard or Primo Carnera—15 inches in circumference—Sonny Liston was capable of virtually decap-itating his opponents with a single blow. He knocked out 39 of his 54 ring foes for a 72.2 slugging percentage.

11. SANDY SADDLER (1944-56). This skinny featherweight champ, who looked like he worked in the olive factory dragging the pimento through, had the most knock-outs of any featherweight (103), and ranks in the top ten knockout artists of all time for all divisions.

10. JOE LOUIS (1934-51). "The Brown Bomber" won his first 23 bouts, 19 by knockout, and overall scored 54 KOs in 71 bouts, including 22 KOs in 25 success-ful defenses of his heavyweight crown.

9. MAX BAER (1929-41). In the first 15 months of his career, Baer fought 27 times, winning 20 via KO, his lethal right hand accounted for 100 knockdowns in less than 100 rounds. He would go on to KO 52 of his 83 opponents, including one fatally. In 1934, Baer knocked down Primo Carnera 11 times in 11 rounds to capture the heavyweight title.

8. TOMMY HEARNS (1977-2006). The man known as "The Hit Man" was just that. Hearns won his first 17 fights by knockout and scored 48 KOs in his 67-bout career, including one over Roberto Duran to become the only man ever to KO the formidable Panamanian.

7. RUBEN OLIVARES (1965-88). This tough little bantamweight ran off 23 consecutive knockouts at the beginning of his career, then after being held to a draw in his 24th fight, ripped off another streak of 29 KOs in his next 30 fights, winning the other on a foul. Olivares' total output was 78 KOs in 104 bouts—a 75% slugging average.

6. GEORGE FOREMAN (1969-97). This Bunyanesque figure called "Big George" said after his first pro fight against Don Waldheim, "I can knock anybody out. . . . Lord, I'm tough." And he was and did, knocking out 42 of his 47 opponents in his "first career." Then coming back after a 10-year layoff, George KO'd another 26 for a total of 68 KOs in his 81 bouts for a 83.9% slugging average.

5. CARLOS ZÁRATE (1970-88). The winner of his first 23 bouts by knockout—the first 20 within three rounds—bantamweight great Zárate would record 58 KOs in 65 bouts, a slugging average of 89.23%—better than the slugging averages of Rocky Marciano and George Foreman.

4. EARNIE SHAVERS (1969-95). With a punch that could knock down tall buildings—and which Muhammad Ali said, "my ancestors back in Africa felt"—Earnie Shavers rendered 68 of his 89 opponents helpless and hopeless.

3. WILFREDO GOMEZ (1974-89). Known as "Bazooka," this small, compact king of the junior featherweight division not only defended his title 17 times with 17 knockouts, but, after a first-bout draw, ran off 41 consecutive KO victories, the most consecutive knockouts of any champion in any division.

2. ROCKY MARCIANO (1947-55). With 43 knockouts in his 49 fights for a slugging average of 87.7%, "The Rock" was devastating with his "Susie Q" right hand, leaving opponent after opponent one with the resin.

1. ARCHIE MOORE (1935-63). "The Old Mongoose" holds the all-time record for total career knockouts, which numbered anywhere from 130 to 143, depending on who was counting.

THE TEN HARDEST PUNCHES I EVER THREW

:: BY EARNIE SHAVERS

Note: Heavyweight Earnie Shavers' right hand landed with the force of a howitzer. With 68 knockouts in his 74 wins—including KOs in his first 27 fights—Shavers rightfully earned the nickname "The Black Destroyer" and was tabbed "Puncher of the Century" by the International Boxing Association. Here, he picks the 10 hardest punches he ever threw, but the list goes on as the bodies went down.

10. HAROLD CARTER (DECEMBER 4, 1978, SAGINAW, MICHIGAN; WON BY THIRD-ROUND KO). "Knocked him out in three."

9. BERNARDO MERCADO (MARCH 8, 1980, LAS VEGAS; LOST BY SEVENTH-ROUND TKO). "Good right hand . . . got up to stop me."

8. JAMES "QUICK" TILLIS (JUNE 11, 1982, LAS VEGAS; LOST TEN-ROUND DECISION). "An overhand right . . . Tillis says he's still messed up."

7. HENRY CLARK (SEPTEMBER 28, 1976, NEW YORK; WON BY SECOND-ROUND TKO). "Hit him with a good right hand in the second . . . and he went down and out."

6. HOWARD SMITH (APRIL 16, 1977, LAS VEGAS; WON BY SECOND-ROUND KO). "Caught him with a straight right. . . ."

5. ROY "TIGER" WILLIAMS (DECEMBER 11, 1976, LAS VEGAS; WON BY TENTH-ROUND KO). "Took him out with a right hand in the last round."

4. JIMMY ELLIS (JUNE 18, 1973, NEW YORK; WON BY FIRST-ROUND KO). "Caught him with a right uppercut and he was out."

3. KEN NORTON (MARCH 23, 1979, LAS VEGAS; WON BY FIRST-ROUND KO). "A right hand did it."

2. MUHAMMAD ALI (SEPTEMBER 29, 1977, NEW YORK; LOST 15-ROUND DECISION). "Hit him with a straight right over his jab in the second round . . . slowed him down."

1. LARRY HOLMES (SEPTEMBER 28, 1979, LAS VEGAS; LOST BY 11TH-ROUND TKO). "Hit him with overhand right, knocking him down. . . ."

BEST CHINS

There's an old saying amongst trainers that you "can't train a chin." Nor build one. Either you have one or you don't. And many fighters don't—like Bob Satterfield, a light heavyweight from the 1950s who, while possessing a knock-out punch made of dynamite, also possessed a chin made of china. So, if he didn't knock out his opponent, he'd be knocked out himself. Others, like those listed below, had a chin that would make Popeye proud, a "beard" that could, as they say, "take it."

10. BILLY GRAHAM (1941-55). Called the "uncrowned welterweight champion," Graham went through a 126-bout career without ever even being knocked off his feet, a distinction he shares with less than a pocketful of greats.

9. SUGAR RAY ROBINSON (1940-65). Sugar Ray was only KO'd once in his 202-bout career and that was by the heat, not his opponent. Put down on the canvas only by the likes of Tommy Bell, Rocky Graziano, and Artie Levine, Robinson always got up to win.

8. ROCKY MARCIANO (1947-55). The "Rock" went through 49 fights and only was knocked down twice—once by Jersey Joe Walcott and then, in the last fight of his career, by Archie Moore. Walcott and Moore had 164 recorded KOs between them, and both were KO'd by Marciano after he got off the canvas.

7. BARNEY ROSS (1929-38). In over 80 fights, the three-division champ was knocked down only by Jimmy McLarnin. So downright intent on remaining upright was Ross that in his last fight against Henry Armstrong, when hopelessly beaten and begged by his cornermen to quit, Ross replied: "I won my title in the ring and I'll lose it there. . . . I won't quit." And he didn't, surviving 15 rounds of brutal punishment without even going down, much less asking out.

6. RANDY "TEX" COBB (1977-93). After losing, by charitable accounts, 16 of 15 rounds to Larry Holmes in their 1982 heavyweight title fight, Randy "Tex" Cobb was asked if he would consider a rematch. Laughing at the inanity of the question, Cobb said he would agree to one, but didn't think Holmes would, because "his hands couldn't take it." But Cobb could take it, as opponent-after-opponent found out from banging their fists against Cobb's strongest point: his head, which you sometimes expected to start revolving around like Michael Keaton's in *Beetlejuice*. Holmes tried unsuccessfully to knock him out, as did Earnie Shavers, Michael Dokes, Bernardo Mercado and many other big punchers.

5. MARVELOUS MARVIN HAGLER (1973-87). The Marvelous One was only knocked down once over the course of 67 fights. And that one was not a knockdown, but a pushdown, with John Mugabi "cuffing" Hagler to the canvas in their 1986 bout.

4. MUHAMMAD ALI (1960-81). One of boxing's best trivia questions: who are the only two men to knock down Muhammad Ali? The answer: Joe Frazier and Chuck Wepner. Of course, boxing triviots know that Cassius Clay was also knocked down twice—by Sonny Banks and by Henry Cooper. But Clay/Ali used his great recuperative powers to get up from all four knockdowns and win three of those fights, losing only to Frazier.

3. KID GAVILAN (1943-58). Welterweight great Gavilan was never stopped in his 143-bout career despite going up against the best the welterweight division of the 1940s and 50s had to offer. And he was only dropped in three fights and got up to win two of those.

2. JAKE LaMOTTA (1941-54). Anyone who ever saw the movie *Raging Bull* will remember the scene where, after getting the bejabbers beaten out of him by Sugar Ray Robinson, Jake mutters, "You never knocked me down." Well, Sugar Ray didn't. In fact, the only man ever to knock down the granite-chinned LaMotta was Danny Nardico, and that came near the end of LaMotta's career.

1. GEORGE CHUVALO (1956-78). Larry Merchant once described George Chuvalo's best punch as "a left cheek to the right glove." And over his 93-fight career, George "threw" his left jaw to the right glove against some of the most fearsome punchers in recent heavyweight history—sluggers like Joe Frazier, George Foreman, Muhammad Ali and Jerry Quarry. And yet, Chuvalo was never-ever knocked down.

THE HARDEST I WAS EVER HIT :: BY GEORGE CHUVALO

Note: Canadian heavyweight George Chuvalo is a member of the World Boxing Hall of Fame. The Toronto native fought 93 fights between 1956 and 1979, including a 1965 bout against Floyd Patterson that gained *The Ring* magazine's "Fight of the Year" honors. He faced Muhammad Ali (twice), Joe Frazier, George Foreman, Jimmy Ellis, Ernie Terrell, Jerry Quarry and all the other big bangers in the heavyweight division of the 1970s. But he was never knocked down. Never. However, he was hit. And hit hard. Here, in George's words, are the times he got hit hardest.

3. MEL TURBOW. "When he hit me, for a split second I said, 'Ooooh, that was a good one. . . .'"

2. GEORGE FOREMAN. "When he hit me, my head went 'Boing!'"

1. JOEY DEJOHN. "I don't remember a thing about being hit by DeJohn, but when I saw the film clip later, I saw my legs buckle."

GREATEST CANADIAN FIGHTERS :: BY LOU EISEN

Note: Canadian boxing journalist and historian Lou Eisen serves as boxing columnist for The Fight Network. A comedian and actor in his spare time, Eisen landed the role of famed trainer Ray Arcel in the film *Cinderella Man*, starring Russell Crowe as unlikely heavyweight champion James J. Braddock. Here Lou offers his take on the ten greatest fighters to come out of the Great White North.

10. HORACE "LEFTY" GWYNNE. Olympic gold medalist at bantamweight in 1932. Pro record: 32 wins, six KOs, eight losses, two draws.

9. LOU BROULLIARD. Welterweight champion 1931-32; middleweight champion 1933. Pro record: 110 wins, 66 KOs, 27 losses, three draws.

8. JACK DELANEY. Light heavyweight champion 1926-27. Pro record: 70 wins, 42 KOs, 26 losses, three draws.

7. ARTURO GATTI. Junior lightweight champion 1995-98; junior welterweight champ 2004-05. Pro record: 40 wins, 31 KOs, nine losses.

6. LARRY GAINS. Great Depression Era heavyweight who never got a world title shot. Pro record: 114 wins, 60 KOs, 22 losses, five draws.

5. TOMMY BURNS. Heavyweight champion 1906-08. Pro record: 46 wins, 37 KOs, five losses, eight draws.

4. JOHNNY COULON. Bantamweight champion 1910-14. Pro record: 56 wins, 24 KOs, four losses, four draws, 32 no-decisions.

3. SAM LANGFORD. Elite fighter in first two decades of the 20th century who is considered by many as the greatest fighter never to hold a world title. Pro record: 167 wins, 117 KOs, 38 losses, 37 draws, 48 no-decisions.

2. GEORGE DIXON. Bantamweight champion 1890; featherweight champion 1891-97 and 1898-1900. Pro record: 78 wins, 30 KOs, 25 losses, 37 draws, nine no decisions.

1. GEORGE CHUVALO. Hard-hitting 1970s heavyweight title contender. Pro record: 73 wins, 64 KOs, 18 losses, two draws.

GREATEST LATINO BOXERS

:: BY RUBEN OLIVARES AND GENE AGUILERA

Note: A former world bantamweight and featherweight champion with devastating punching power, Mexico City native Ruben Olivares enjoyed an impressive enough career to be ranked #2 by both Bert and Teddy on their list of the all-time Greatest Mexican fighters in this book, as well as #7 in their list of boxing's all-time biggest punchers. Here, Olivares teams up with Gene Aguilera, an historian and trusted adviser to many Latino fighters, to offer a list of the ten greatest fighters from all the world's Latino countries.

10. CARLOS ZÁRATE. Bantamweight champion 1976-79. "A hard hitter. . . ."

9. JOSÉ *"MANTEQUILLA"* NAPOLES. Welterweight champion 1969-70 and 1971-75. "As smooth as his nickname...."

8. ALEXIS ARGUELLO. Featherweight champion 1974-77; junior lightweight champion 1978-80. "A tough, durable fighter. . . ."

7. OSCAR DE LA HOYA. Lightweight champion 1995-96; junior welterweight champion 1996-97; welterweight champion 1997-99 and 2000; junior middleweight champion 2001-03. "An Olympic champion and a world champion. . . ."

6. EFREN *"ALACRAN"* TORRES. Flyweight champion 1969-70. "He would have died in the ring. . . ."

5. ROBERTO *"MANOS DE PIEDRA"* DURAN. " Lightweight champion 1972-79; welterweight champion 1980; junior middleweight champion 1983-84; middleweight champion 1989. "A real brawler. . . ."

4. ULTIMINIO "SUGAR" RAMOS. Featherweight champion 1963-64. "He fought every round hard, from the opening bell to the closing bell."

3. JULIO CÉSAR CHAVEZ. Junior lightweight champion 1984-87; lightweight champion 1987-89; junior welterweight champion 1989-94 and 1994-96. "A charismatic boxer. . . ."

2. RICARDO *"FINITO"* LOPEZ. Minimumweight champion 1990-98; junior flyweight champion 1999-2002. "Great footwork."

1. RUBEN *"EL PUAS"* OLIVARES. Bantamweight champion 1969- 70; featherweight champion 1974-85. "What an educated left hand. . . ."

OSCAR DE LA HOYA

GREATEST SOUTHPAWS

Left-handed fighters were an anomaly back in the early days of boxing, most opponents refusing to fight them and most trainers refusing to train them. So most southpaws were turned around to the orthodox stance, like future greats Carmen Basilio and Oscar De La Hoya. But in more recent times, being left-handed was not viewed as a liability, and more and more fighters were allowed to keep their natural, albeit, "unorthodox" stance. Here are ten of the greatest who faced their opponents from what was once thought to be the unnatural side, the portside.

10. VICENTE SALDIVAR (1961-73). The featherweight champ from 1964-67, and then again in 1970, Saldivar won 36 of his 39 bouts with 25 KOs, meeting and beating the cream of the 1960s featherweight crop, including Sugar Ramos, Howard Winstone, and Johnny Famechon.

9. ANTONIO TARVER (1997-2009). A two-time light heavyweight champion, Tarver won 27 bouts with 19 KOs, the most famous one coming in his "No Excuses" fight against Roy Jones, Jr. in May of 2004. During the pre-fight instructions, he asked Jones, "You got any excuses tonight, Roy?" and then proceeded to knock out Jones with a bodacious straight left in the second round.

8. LEW TENDLER (1913-28). Called "Lefty Lew" and "the greatest southpaw in ring history" by none other than *The Ring* magazine's Editor and Publisher Nat Fleischer, Tendler had just 15 losses in 172 fights. The only obstacle to his establishing himself as one of the all-time greats was that he came along at the same time as lightweight king Benny Leonard. Tendler fought Leonard twice, "thrashing" Leonard, according to write-ups, but only getting a no-decision in their first meeting, then losing a decision in 1923 in their second bout—the first fight ever held at Yankee Stadium.

7. MARVIN JOHNSON (1973-87). The three-time light heavyweight champion notched 43 wins with 35 KOs, losing just six times, two of those in barnburners against Matthew Saad Muhammad.

6. MICHAEL MOORER (1988-2008). The only left-handed heavyweight champion, Moorer won 40 of his 57 bouts by knockout, including his first 26 as a light heavyweight.

5. JOE CALZAGHE (1993-2008). The longest reigning champion of the modern era, Calzaghe ruled over the super middleweight division for ten years with 21 successful defenses of his crown before stepping up to win the light heavyweight title. "The Pride of Wales" retired as world champion with an unblemished record of 46 wins and no losses—the second greatest unblemished streak behind only Rocky Marciano's 49-0.

4. TIGER FLOWERS (1918-27). His unorthodox southpaw windmill style led many observers of the time to call him "a left-handed Harry Greb." Flowers lost only 13 of his 149 bouts and in 1926 won the middleweight title, ironically from the above-mentioned Harry Greb.

3. MANNY PACQUIAO (1995-). The only boxer to win seven titles in seven different weight classes, Pacquiao was acclaimed the Boxing Writers' "Fighter of the Decade" for the first decade of the 21st Century. With a record of 51 wins and 38 KOs in his 56 fights, "Pacman" has long been acknowledged as boxing's "Best Pound-for-Pound" fighter.

2. PERNELL WHITAKER (1984-2001). One of the greatest defensive fighters of his time, or any time, Whitaker had a southpaw style that enabled him to run and hide at one and the same time, in what may best be described as a form of fistic break-dancing. A three-division champion, Whitaker posted a record of 40 wins, four losses, and one draw—and at least one of those "losses" (to Jose Luis Ramirez) and his "draw" (with Julio César Chavez) were crimes against the senses and others too numerous to mention.

1. MARVELOUS MARVIN HAGLER (1973-87). At the start of his career, Hagler was told by the boxing cynics that he had "three strikes against him"—he was "black, left-handed and good." But they were wrong on two accounts. For Hagler wasn't just "good," he was great! Or "Marvelous," if you will. And as far as being left-handed, the man known as "Marvelous Marvin" was actually a turnaround fighter. A natural right-hander, Hagler switched over to the southpaw style in order to have his power hand—his right—closer to his opponent. It was a style that worked well for Hagler, as proven by his 62 wins with 52 KOs and only three losses in 67 fights for this all-time great middleweight champion.

BEST LEFT HOOKS

The left hook has been described as "the most devastating punch in boxing," a punch unseen coming by most opponents and when delivered can end a bout prematurely. Although few can deliver a left hook with knockout power, through-out history there have been some who have, like José Napoles, Eduardo Lausse, Georgie Aroujo, Cyclone Hart, Oscar De La Hoya, Gerry Cooney, and the ten great "hookers" listed here.

10. MICKY WARD (1985-2003). Ward's left hook was a paralyzing body shot, one most vividly remembered from his first fight against Arturo Gatti when Gatti sank to the canvas in the ninth round in agony after Ward had delivered his left hook from hell.

9. TONY DEMARCO (1948-62). Nicknamed "The Miniature Marciano" by his adoring Boston fans, Tony DeMarco brought a lethal left hook with him every time he climbed between the ropes, one he had used to win the welterweight crown from Johnny Saxton in 14 rounds. Just 70 days later he would climb into the ring again to defend his newly-won title against the leather-jawed contender, Carmen Basilio. But even after batting Basilio from pillar-to-post for the first seven rounds, DeMarco ran out of gas and lost to Basilio on a KO in 12 rounds. The two repeated their two-sided pier sixer again five months later in DeMarco's hometown where he had lost just once in 33 outings. This November 1955 fight was a mirror image of their first go-round in June with DeMarco jolting Basilio time and time again with left hooks to Basilio's well-worn features, staggering Basilio in rounds five and seven with bodacious left hooks—and almost flooring Basilio for only the second time in his career in the seventh as he gave a bandy-legged impression of Leon Errol, wobbling all over the ring but keeping his feet. After eight rounds the scenario repeated itself with DeMarco looking like he was fighting in slow motion, the end coming again in the twelfth, just two seconds longer than in the first fight. Still, Tony DeMarco, who finished his career with 33 KO's, almost all courtesy of his left hook, was considered by anyone who ever saw him—especially in his two fights with Carmen Basilio—as one of the most potent left hookers ever to climb into the ring.

8. HENRY COOPER (1954-71). Nicknamed "Our 'Enry" by his adoring fans, this Englishman possessed one of the best left hooks in heavyweight history, unleashing it for most of his 27 KOs. But the one he is most remembered for was delivered on June 18, 1963 against the young Cassius Clay in the fourth round, when he caught Clay with what was called "'Enry's 'Ammer," a punch Clay later described as "making me feel as if I had gone back and visited all my ancestors in Africa." Unfortunately for Cooper, Clay came back to stop him in the next round.

7. FLORENTINO FERNANDEZ (1956-72). This Cuban middleweight used his lethal left hook to break the arm of and take out undefeated future light heavyweight champion Jose Torres on his way to 43 KOs in his 50 wins.

6. CHARLEY WHITE (1906-30). Ernest Hemingway once said, "Life is the best left hook I ever saw, although some say it was Charley White of Chicago." And those who saw Charlie White in action could only agree, White possessed one helluva left hook. With 59 KOs, almost all of them by virtue of his left hook, White was one of the leading lightweight contenders of his day, fighting for the title four times. In his title bout against lightweight champion Freddy Welsh, White had Welsh in trouble in the 11th, 12th and 13th rounds, but in each round, let Welsh off the hook. Sportswriter Hype Igoe wrote, "White is like the artist who can't resist the temptation of stepping back and admiring his incompleted work."

5. AL "BUMMY" DAVIS (1937-44). In the late 1930s a fighter named Albert Abraham Davidoff, who went by the nom-de-ring of Al "Bummy" Davis, came out of the Brownsville section of the Bronx (N.Y.) with as dynamite-laden a left hook as boxing had ever seen. It was that left hook from hell that separated Tony Canzoneri from his senses in November of 1939—the only time in Canzi's 176-bout career he had ever been KO'd. Ditto Tippy Larkin from his, and Tony Reno, Julio Galluci, Red Doty, Al Tribuani—et cetera, etc.,etc.—47 KO's in all. But perhaps his greatest left-hook knockout came in February of 1944 when he knocked out lightweight champion Bob Montgomery, knocking him down twice, the last time ending what was then the quickest knockout in Madison Square Garden history, one-minute-and-three-seconds of the first round. Unfortunately, that left hook was stilled forever when Davis was gunned down in a bar robbery in 1945, but not before Davis had used it one last time to coldcock one of the four gunman, making his total of KO's 48.

4. BOB FOSTER (1961-78). Very few punches are in the air and in the record books at the same time, but Bob Foster's left hooks were—as when he knocked the soon-to-be ex-champion Dick Tiger off his feet and onto his seat for the only time in Tiger's career; or when he landed it to the jaw of challenger Mike Quarry at the end of the fourth round in their light heavyweight title fight, leaving Quarry dead to the world, or so it was thought by all who saw the knockout.

3. JOE FRAZIER (1965-81). Frazier's left hook could fell trees and the toughest of heavyweights, including Jimmy Ellis and—in one of boxing's most memorable moments—Muhammad Ali in the 15th round of their historic first fight on March 8, 1971.

2. SUGAR RAY ROBINSON (1940-65). Robinson's left hook was but one weapon in his devastating arsenal, one he used to take out the never-before knocked down Gene Fullmer with one punch and Rocky Graziano seconds after being knocked down by Graziano

1. JACK DEMPSEY (1914-27). Before the 1923 Dempsey-Tommy Gibbons heavyweight title fight, Gibbons' manager warned his fighter to "watch out for Dempsey's left." And for good reason. It was Dempsey's left hook that had broken Jess Willard's jaw in six places, knocked Gene Tunney down for the "Long Count" and put Jack Sharkey on the canvas after he turned his head to complain to the ref about Dempsey's low blows.

NICKNAMES FOR FAMOUS PUNCHES

Almost every boxer gets a nickname while his punches usually just get named as a generic "jab" or "left hook," or maybe the occasional "flicker jab." But a few boxers gain more customized names for their punches, the nicknames sometimes coming from the fighters themselves, other times from the press, occasionally from onlookers or who knows exactly where. Here are a few of the best punch nicknames.

10. "PIVOT BLOW." An illegal punch employed by George LaBlanche in his 1889 middleweight championship fight with "The Nonpareil" Jack Dempsey. In the 32nd round, LaBlanche spun completely around and—gaining momentum, his right arm fully extended—caught the champion Dempsey with a perfectly executed "Pivot Blow." Or, more succinctly stated: he gave him the back of his hand. Dempsey went down and out cold. But while LaBlanche claimed the middleweight title by virtue of knocking out Dempsey, his "Pivot Blow" was ruled illegal and Dempsey continued to be recognized as the legitimate champion—despite, or on account of, LaBlanche's illegitimate punch and KO.

9. "ANCHOR PUNCH." The right-hand counter Muhammad Ali caught Sonny Liston with in their 1965 rematch which Ali dubbed, "The Stepin Fetchit Anchor Punch," which many of the fans never saw but was, apparently, powerful enough to knock Liston down.

8. "MARY ANN." Early 20th-century heavyweight contender Frank Moran gave this name to his knockout punch, but failed to introduce her to champion Jess Willard during their 1916 heavyweight title fight.

7. "COSMIC PUNCH." A self-appointed yoga, heavyweight contender Lou Nova called his favorite knockout blow the "Cosmic Punch." Unfortunately, it didn't serve him well in his title fight with Joe Louis, who preempted Nova's "Cosmic Punch" with ones of a more worldly nature, pummeling Nova into a sixth-round TKO.

6. "THE CORKSCREW PUNCH." A perpetual student of the game, 1890s middleweight Kid McCoy developed the "Corkscrew Punch" after watching his kitten toying with a cloth ball. Noticing that the kitten moved its paw toward the ball at an angle instead of on a straight line—punctuated by a twist at the end, sort of like the spin given a bullet by the riffling in a barrel—McCoy developed the "Corkscrew Punch," the impact of which was described by one opponent as feeling like "a telephone pole had been driven into my stomach sideways."

5. "OLD BETSY." When heavyweight Sam Langford fought at London's famed National Sporting Club, he got into a dispute with a club official who thought Langford wanted to appoint his own referee. "Tut, tut," the club official chastised him. "That will never do. The Club always appoints the referee. We positively cannot permit you to put your own referee in the ring." Langford cleared up the miscommunication by holding up his right hand and saying, "I carries my own referee with me and here it is," menacingly waving his fist—as if it was itching to deliver his devastating "Old Betsy" punch—under the nose of the official. And 117 times during Langford's career, "Old Betsy" decided the fight by KO.

4. "HAMMER OF THOR." Also called "Thunder and Lightning" (or "Toonder and Lightning"), it was the right hand thrown by Ingemar Johansson that knocked down heavyweight champion Floyd Patterson six times on the Swede's way to winning the heavyweight crown in 1959.

3. "THE BOLO PUNCH." Originated by 1930s middleweight champ Ceferino Garcia, the punch was adopted and made famous two decades later in the early days of boxing on TV by welterweight champion Kid Gavilan, who had worked in the sugarcane fields of Cuba. The punch was sort of a cross between an uppercut and a softball pitcher's underhanded delivery.

2. "THE SOLAR PLEXUS PUNCH." This punch didn't get its name from the fighter or the press, but instead from a doctor who witnessed the Bob Fitzsimmons-Jim Corbett heavyweight championship fight, won by Fitzsimmons on a punch previously known as "one to the slats" or, by bareknucklers as far back as Jack Broughton, as to "the mark." Fitz delivered it as Corbett pulled back in the 14th round from a Fitzsimmons' right. Shifting his feet and direction, Fitzsimmons put all his weight behind a left-hand smash to the midsection somewhere under the ribs where they curl away from the breastbone—an area known to medical professionals as "the solar plexus." The blow took Corbett's breath away and knocked him down. And out.

1. "SUZY Q." When trainer Charlie Goldman first saw his new protégé, Rocky Marciano, he knew he had to turn a piece of rock into a fighter. As Goldman told it, Marciano was so awkward, "We just stood there and laughed. He didn't throw a punch right. He didn't do anything right." And so Goldman changed everything. Everything except for Marciano's vaunted right-hand knockout blow, which was called his "Suzie Q"—the punch that would later nearly decapitate champion Jersey Joe Walcott and make Marciano the head of the heavyweight division.

MOST MEMORABLE ROUNDS IN BOXING HISTORY (ROUND-BY-ROUND)

In the millions of rounds in boxing history, some still echo in memory. Here are the ones, round-by-round, we think echo the loudest.

FIRST ROUND: JACK DEMPSEY VS. LOUIS FIRPO, SEPTEMBER 14, 1923. Nine knockdowns in three minutes, seven of challenger Firpo, two of champion Dempsey—including his being knocked out of the ring—in the wildest round in boxing history.

OTHER MEMORABLE 1ST ROUNDS:

FIRST ROUND: BENNY LEONARD–RITCHIE MITCHELL, JANUARY 14, 1921, JANUARY 14, 1921. Mitchell, down three times in the first round, comes back to knock Leonard down in the closing seconds of the round. Leonard, up but unsteady, beckoned Mitchell to "come on," but Mitchell, only a split second away from beating Leonard for the lightweight title, fell prey to the fake and failed to follow up his advantage. Leonard would go on to knock out Mitchell in one of the most thrilling battles in the history of the lightweight division.

FIRST ROUND: JOE LOUIS–MAX SCHMELING II, JUNE 22, 1938. Louis, the reigning heavyweight champion, avenged his only defeat two years earlier by raining vicious lefts and rights to the head and body of the helpless Schmeling, knocking him down three times and ending the fight in just two minutes and four seconds of the first round.

FIRST ROUND: ARCHIE MOORE–YVON DURELLE I, DECEMBER 10, 1958. Light heavyweight champion Archie Moore barely had time to take off his gaudy red velvet dressing gown with silver trimming before challenger Durelle whipped a right hand over the top to Moore's jaw, dropping him. Up at the count of nine on shaky legs, Moore was knocked down again by a Durelle right. This time up without a count, Moore tried to hold on, but Durelle was all over him, dropping him for the third time with still another right. Moore arose one more time and somehow got through the round, fighting largely on instinct. And although knocked down for a fourth time in the fifth, this time by a left hook, Moore managed to survive and come back to KO Durelle in the eleventh and successfully defend his title—while also adding the 127th knockout to his record, breaking the existing record for KO's

FIRST ROUND: MARVELOUS MARVIN HAGLER-TOMMY HEARNS, APRIL 15, 1985. In three of the fiercest moments in boxing history, Hagler and Hearns traded bombs, first one, then the other, as Hagler trapped Hearns on the ropes and absorbed the best Hearns had to offer as he came back with his own. It was less give-and-take than give-and-give and when the bell finally rang ending the round, a rubbery legged Hearns lurched back to his a corner, saying afterward that "the first round took everything out of me." It did those in attendance at Caesars Palace in Vegas too, most exhausted from the most exciting three minutes seen in years. And when Hagler finally stopped Hearns in the third, many boxing fans were convinced they had seen the most action-packed boxing match they had ever witnessed.

SECOND ROUND: GEORGE FOREMAN VS. JOE FRAZIER I, JANUARY 22, 1973. As ringside announcer Howard Cosell yelled, "Down goes Frazier.... Down goes Frazier," down went Frazier, hitting the canvas six times, three times in the second round. Foreman lifted Frazier off the canvas with the force of the last knockdown punch and lifted the heavyweight crown off Frazier's head.

THIRD ROUND: INGEMAR JOHANSSON VS. FLOYD PATTERSON I, JUNE 26, 1959. Challenger Ingemar Johansson landed his "Hammer of Thor" again and again, knocking heavyweight champion Floyd Patterson down six times in the third and stopping him at 2:03 of the round to win the heavyweight championship.

FOURTH ROUND: GEORGE FOREMAN-RON LYLE, JANUARY 24, 1976. In a fight for survival, both George Foreman and Ron Lyle barely survived the fourth round of their heavyweight fight. Stunned by a right early in the round, Foreman went down like a sack of potatoes, landing flat on his head, almost as if he were assuming a yoga position. He got up angry and hurt and fired a roundhouse that dislodged Lyle's mouthpiece. A left hook knocked Lyle under the lowest rope, but Lyle got up with a look that said, "Alright, now it's my turn!" And it was as a left-right dropped Foreman on his shoulder. Everyone thought it was over but the bell saved the fallen Foreman. In the fifth, with both fighters spent, they commenced pummeling each other again. Foreman, who had been challenged by his trainer Gil Clancy whether he "wanted it most," threw a left hook driving Lyle's mouthpiece out. Thirty seconds later a barrage of blows from Foreman caught Lyle in his corner and he pitched forward, there to be counted out at 2:28 of the fifth round.

FIFTH ROUND: SUGAR RAY ROBINSON VS. GENE FULLMER II, MAY 1, 1957. Sugar Ray Robinson won the middleweight title for the third time with a pluperfect left hook in his rematch with Gene Fullmer, knocking out Fullmer for the first time in his career at 1:27 of the fifth.

SIXTH ROUND: ROCKY GRAZIANO VS. TONY ZALE II, JULY 16, 1947. In a seesaw slugfest, reminiscent of their first battle a year earlier—this time a reverse mirror image with Graziano in trouble early and Zale the aggressor—Graziano overcame a closed eye to KO Zale at 2:10 of round six and then commandeered the microphone to intone his famous, "Somebody up there likes me."

SEVENTH ROUND: GENE TUNNEY VS. JACK DEMPSEY II, SEPTEMBER 22, 1927. Igniting one of boxing's longest-running controversies, Jack Dempsey knocked defending heavyweight champion Gene Tunney to the canvas for the first time in Tunney's career. In what would forever be known as "The Long Count," Dempsey delayed the ref from starting the count by standing over the fallen Tunney to admire his handiwork instead of going to a neutral corner. Tunney used the extra time to recover his senses, finally getting up at nine—or 14, depending on who was counting. Tunney survived the round, then knocked down Dempsey in the eighth on his way to a 10-round unanimous decision win.

EIGHTH ROUND: SUGAR RAY LEONARD VS. ROBERTO DURAN II, NOVEMBER 25, 1980. In what would forever be known as the "No Mas" fight (although Duran never said those infamous words), welterweight champ Roberto Duran quit midround, waving his hand at referee Octavia Meyran to indicate that couldn't take any more of Leonard's clowning and taunting.

NINTH ROUND: MICKY WARD VS. ARTURO GATTI I, MAY 18, 2002. In a war, Micky Ward floored Arturo Gatti with a left hook to the body in the ninth. Grimacing in pain, Gatti rose to take the fight to Ward for the rest of the round in one of the most exciting three minutes in boxing history.

TENTH ROUND: DIEGO CORRALES VS. JOSÉ LUIS CASTILLO I, MAY 7, 2005. In the most two-sided round since Dempsey-Firpo over three-quarters of a century before, José Luis Castillo knocked Diego Corrales down twice with left hooks, only to see Corrales rise from the canvas ashes and return the favor, catching Castillo with his own right. Corrales then hit him with a dozen murderous shots on a defenseless Castillo, trapped on the ropes, causing referee Tony Weeks to step in and put an end to the lightweight unification bout and cap one of the greatest comebacks in recent memory.

ELEVENTH ROUND: MUHAMMAD ALI VS. RON LYLE, MAY 16, 1975. With Ron Lyle ahead on all the scorecards going into the round, heavyweight champion Muhammad Ali rallied with 30 unanswered punches to stop the challenger in one minute and eight seconds of the eleventh to retain his title.

TWELFTH ROUND: JACK JOHNSON VS. STANLEY KETCHEL, OCTOBER 16, 1909. With Jack Johnson out of so-called "worthy" contenders for his heavyweight crown and the "Great White Hope" campaign having developed no hope or hopes at all, one man came forward to challenge Johnson: middleweight champion Stanley Ketchel. Although standing only five feet nine inches tall and weighing all of 154 pounds, Ketchel was thought to have a chance to wrest the heavyweight championship from the African-American champion for the "White race." After 11 rounds of what charitably could be called sparring, Ketchel met Johnson leaping in with a sweeping right hand which serpentined around the back of Johnson's neck. Johnson lost his balance and toppled towards the canvas, holding himself up with an outstretched left glove. Johnson jumped up and, as Ketchel raced in to put the finishing touches on his partially completed work, Johnson caught the incoming Ketchel on the jaw. Ketchel fell heavily, as if poleaxed. The momentum of his effort carried Johnson through and over the stricken Ketchel, forcing him to stumble on the fallen form. He hurriedly jumped up and, picking two of Ketchel's teeth out of his right glove, stood, his legs crossed with one hand on the ropes, the other on his hip, as referee Jack Welsh unnecessarily tolled ten over Ketchel. Asked later how he felt being knocked down, Johnson answered: "Far better than Ketchel did 30 seconds later."

THIRTEENTH ROUND: ROCKY MARCIANO VS. JERSEY JOE WALCOTT I, SEPTEMBER 23, 1952. Well ahead and just needing to last just nine more minutes to successfully defend his heavyweight title, Jersey Joe Walcott inexplicably backed into the ropes, where, as he came off them, got caught with as hard a punch as he'd ever been hit with—a short right by Marciano that sent him slowly down to the canvas, his arm hooked over the ropes, dead to the world, the ex-champion.

FOURTEENTH ROUND: AARON PRYOR VS. ALEXIS ARGUELLO I, NOVEMBER 12, 1982. In the greatest fight in junior welterweight history, the two combatants went at each other for 13 rounds, both landing bodacious shots that would have felled ordinary fighters. Finally, in the 14th after the two traded punches in the middle of the ring, Arguello left an opening and Pryor filled it with an overhand right, then landed a fusillade of punches—too many to count—driving the defenseless Arguello into the ropes, where referee Stanley Christodoulou finally called a halt to the onslaught.

FIFTEENTH ROUND: LARRY HOLMES-KEN NORTON, JUNE 9, 1978. In a fight for the WBC portion of the heavyweight champion, Larry Holmes and Ken Norton had waged a fight with more plot turns than could be found in a Russian novel with first one, then the other taking control of the action. And going into the fifteenth and final round, the scorecards were dead even. The fifteenth and deciding round was, quite simply, the most violent finale in heavyweight title history with skill and finesse irrelevant. With both fighters too weary and damaged to do anything but stand in front of each other and take turns using each other's head as a fungo ball, first it was first Norton, then Holmes whalloping the bejabbers out of one another. Holmes somehow found the strength for a final rally with but a minute to go which decided the fight and the championship for Holmes, two judges giving him the last round and a split decision win—based on the last round.

OTHER MEMORABLE 15TH ROUNDS:

FIFTEENTH ROUND: JAKE LAMOTTA VS. LAURENT DAUTHUILLE, SEPTEMBER 13, 1950. In what looked like the last three minutes of LaMotta's reign as middleweight champion after losing almost every round of the previous 14 to challenger Laurent Dauthuille, LaMotta staged a last-second comeback worthy of a Phileas Fogg, catching Dauthuille with a deep-dish beauty of a left and then assailing him with an assortment of lefts and rights which felled the challenger over the bottom rope with one long, looping left where he was counted out with only 13 seconds to go in the fight.

FIFTEENTH ROUND: MIKE WEAVER-JOHN TATE, MARCH 31, 1980. For 14 rounds John Tate was in total command of his fight with Mike Weaver, landing everything he threw. Weaver, on the other glove, had only connected with one punch of any note, a left hook in the 12th which caught Tate's attention, but little more. But with less than a minute to go in the one-sided fight, Weaver threw another left hook and this one caught Tate flush, toppling him like a fallen tree, there to be counted out with but 45 seconds to go in the fight, ending Tate's five-month reign as heavyweight champ and beginning his own.

GREATEST OLYMPIC BOXERS

Boxing remains one of the few Olympic sports in which professionals are not allowed to compete. But the Olympics have long provided a proving ground for future professional greats. Starting with future welterweight champion Jackie Fields, who won gold in the 1924 Paris Olympics, such future professional greats as Floyd Patterson, Nino Benvenuti, Cassius Clay, Joe Frazier, George Foreman, Sugar Ray Leonard, Michael Spinks, Mark Breland and Oscar De La Hoya have used their Olympic gold as a step towards the professional ranks. But there have also been Olympic gold medalists who have not matched their Olympic success with success in the pros, like Otto von Porat, Henry Tillman and Jerry Page. On the other side of the equation, there have been those who came up less than golden in their quest for an Olympic title, like Wilfredo Gomez and Eder Jofre, who later enjoyed professional careers that were pure gold. And then there are those who lived in Communist countries who never got a chance to test themselves in the pro ranks. Disregarding what their futures held, we selected the Top Ten Olympic boxers whose efforts in the Olympics were 24-karat.

10. JERZY KULEJ. The Polish light middleweight scored a rare repeat, winning gold at the 1964 Tokyo and the 1968 Mexico City Olympics.

9. CASSIUS CLAY. The 18-year-old American started building his reputation as "The Greatest" at the 1960 Rome Olympics, stopping Yan Becaus of Belgium in the second round, then defeating 1956 Olympic middleweight champion Gennady Shatkov of Russia and Australian Tony Madigan by unanimous decision before beating three-time European champion Zbigniew Pietrzykowski of Poland in the light heavyweight final.

8. OLIVER KIRK. Winner of both the bantamweight and featherweight gold medals in the 1904 St. Louis Olympics, the American remains the only boxer to claim two titles in one Olympics.

7. GUILLERMO RIGONDEAUX. The seven-time Cuban national bantamweight champion won gold in the 2000 and 2004 Olympics. Rigondeaux defected, then returned to Cuba, but was barred from boxing again on the Cuban national team by Fidel Castro. So he defected again and turned professional.

6. HARRY MALLIN. He was called the "unroasted human beef of Old England" for a reason; the reason being that while defending his Olympic middleweight crown at the 1924 Paris Olympics Mallin met one Roger Brousse in the quarterfinals. After the decision came down 2-1 in favor of Brousse, Mallin showed the referee fresh teeth marks on his chest, which further examination proved that Mallin had definitely been bitten by his French opponent. Brousse was disqualified, clearing the way for Mallin to go on to win his second Olympic gold.

5. FLOYD PATTERSON. The sensation of the 1952 Helsinki Olympics, 17-year-old American middleweight Floyd Patterson breezed through his first four fights. Watching him, columnist Red Smith wrote, "he confuses opponents with an impetuous style, lunging forward to throw the first blow, sometimes misses with that opening punch. He doesn't mind, because he has six or seven hands with which to follow up." Using what Smith called "his beautiful hands," Patterson KO'd his Romanian opponent in just one minute and fourteen seconds of the first round to win the gold medal. Patterson's performance inspired former New York's boxing commissioner, Eddie Egan, to say, "I think he could take Ray Robinson right now."

4. ANGEL HERRERA. In a 1976 Montreal Olympics dominated by American fighters this Cuban won featherweight gold with a second-round knockout, then moved up to the lightweight division for the 1980 Moscow Olympics and won gold with a third-round KO.

3. FÉLIX SAVÓN. Savón won three heavyweight golds while dominating all but one fight—his 1992 Barcelona Olympics bout against American Darnell Nicholson. Trailing 4-1 after the first round and 8-6 after two, Savon dominated the third and final round to pull out a 13-11 victory vs. Nicholson, then went on to cruise to a 14-1 win in the final.

2. TEÓFILO STEVENSON. Stevenson won three Olympic super heavyweight titles, using his stinging left jab and powerful right to knock out Americans Duane Bobick in 1972 and John Tate in 1976. In the 1980 super heavyweight final Stevenson won a decision over Soviet Pyotr Zayev who ran around the ring for three rounds to "earn" the distinction of becoming the only Olympic boxer to go the distance with the Cuban super heavyweight. Stevenson may have well won a fourth gold medal if the Cubans had not boycotted the 1984 Games in Los Angeles.

1. LASZLO PAPP. Winner of three Olympic gold medals—the light middleweight championships in 1952 and 1956 and the middleweight championship in 1948—Papp turned pro in 1957 at the age of 31 after gaining permission from the Hungarian authorities to become the first boxer from a Soviet Bloc country to box professionally. He had an undefeated career, winning the European Middleweight Championship before Hungary's communist government barred him from boxing for the world championship.

GREATEST BRITISH FIGHTERS :: BY GARETH DAVIES

Note: Gareth Davies has been writing about sports for the U.K.–based Telegraph Media Group since 1993, with his articles appearing regularly in their daily and Sunday newspapers and on their website. He currently serves as their boxing reporter. Of this endeavor, he writes: "The Top Ten of all time is a subject which could occupy many days and nights and a huge quantity of argument and counter-argument. Put more people together discussing it and it would become an endless task. In short, like two bald men fighting over a comb, picking a Top Ten, like the judging of boxing itself, will always be subjective based on what we've seen, what we've read, what times we've lived through and—whether we like it or not—sometimes the opinions of others. From a list that, at times, also included Nigel Benn, Freddie Mills, Chris Eubank, and Ricky Hatton, these final ten came out after much deliberation, in a quasi-order of merit as follows":

10. JOHN CONTEH (1971-80). The WBC light heavyweight champion from Liverpool was so good he was even talked of as a possible opponent for Muhammad Ali. Beautiful puncher, great athlete.

9. HOWARD WINSTONE (1959-68). The featherweight from Merthyr Tydfil, Wales, lost the tips of three fingers on his right hand in an accident while working as a teenager in a toy factory, but it did not prevent him from winning 61 of 67 professional fights. His left became his main weapon. The WBC featherweight champion lost only two of his first 59 fights.

8. RANDOLPH TURPIN (1946-64). The name resonates in British sporting circles even today. There is a statue of "Randy" Turpin in the market town of Warwick. He defeated the world middleweight champion Sugar Ray Robinson on July 10, 1951, on a 15-round decision and became a national hero overnight, the equivalent of Ricky Hatton today. Two months later Turpin lost the crown to Robinson by a tenth-round TKO at the Polo Grounds in New York.

7. JOE CALZAGHE (1993-2008). Great record and one of the few to retire undefeated and walk away at his peak and on his own terms. The nights on which he defeated Mikkel Kessler and Jeff Lacy in Cardiff and Manchester were testimonies to his greatness and showed he had a champion's heart.

6. PRINCE NASEEM HAMED (1992-2002). Promoter Frank Warren told me Hamed was the most talented fighter he had ever worked with. Hamed was pure box office. The featherweight lit up in front of a crowd and a camera gave him an energy that transformed him. For a small man, the power he generated was staggering. Physically, he was something of a magician. No wonder he once made his ring walk sitting on a magic carpet.

5. LENNOX LEWIS (1989-2003). A late bloomer, Lewis took the traditional route to Olympic gold, followed by a long path to becoming undisputed heavyweight champion. He was the first of the great "super heavyweights" who could move, box, and punch athletically. The only gray clouds over his career are the fact he faced Mike Tyson well after the American's prime and that he never met Riddick Bowe in his professional career.

4. JACKIE "KID" BERG (1924-45). Judah Bergman came from London's East End. In 1931, he moved to the U.S., where he won 64 out of 76 fights and was trained by the legendary Ray Arcel. He fought between lightweight and welterweight. Outside the ring, he was reputed to have had an affair with Mae West and a long friendship with Jack Spot, the East End Jewish mobster.

3. KEN BUCHANAN (1965-82). Probably the best British boxer in my lifetime to this point. Efficient, teak-tough, the world lightweight champion fought the best. He even had the privilege of headlining at Madison Square Garden one night with Muhammad Ali on the undercard. In fact, that night the organizers had overlooked Ali and he had not been assigned a dressing room. Angelo Dundee, Ali's trainer, popped his head around the door of Buchanan's dressing room to ask to share it. As a joke, Buchanan took a piece of chalk and marked a line down the centre of the room. "Stay on your side," he said, as the camps collapsed in laughter.

2. JIMMY WILDE (1910-23). Unbelievable record, with seven years as world champion. "The Mighty Atom," hewn from Welsh miner's stock in the Rhondda Valley, stands as arguably the greatest flyweight in history. Retired in 1923, after losing to Pancho Villa, the first Filipino world champion.

1. TED "KID" LEWIS (1909-29). No question he comes out on top. Born Gershon Mendeloff in a gas-lit tenement in London's East Side, he started for the Judean Boxing Club and went on to become the world welterweight champion. Yet after twenty years as a boxer, incredibly he became a bodyguard to Oswald Mosley, the fascist turned Nazi. Famously, Lewis struck Mosley and his henchmen after discovering he was anti-Semitic.

BOXING'S TOP TECHNICIANS

Some boxing virtues—like quickness and the ability to take a punch—can mostly be traced to genetics. But technical abilities are just as important, and can only be gained through long hours of training. These guys not only learned the technical aspects of the fight game, they pretty much perfected them through practice and by applying them in the ring.

12. KEN BUCHANAN (1965-82). Considered the greatest boxer ever to come out of Scotland, Buchanan was a smart fighter with a classic left jab. He posted a record of 61-8 with 27 knockouts, winning his first 33 professional bouts and claiming the world lightweight title from Ismael Laguna in 1970.

11. WILLIE PASTRANO (1951-65). A technical master in the ring, Pastrano used his excellent jab and elusive defense to outpoint Harold Johnson to win the world lightweight championship in 1963. He held the title for two years. Winning most of his fights by decisions, Pastrano established a record of 63-13-8, with just 14 of those victories by knockout.

10. JAMES J. CORBETT (1886-1903). Known as "Gentlemen Jim," this Californian became a national star when he stopped the heralded heavyweight champion John L. Sullivan in the 21st round of their seminal 1892 title bout. Corbett, with Professor Mike Donovan in his corner, introduced a more scientific and technical style of fighting to the heavyweight class, using movement and footwork to avoid Sullivan and making more use of the jab. Ahead of his time, Corbett ushered in a new, more technical era in the sport.

9. BILLY CONN (1934-48). The light heavyweight champion of the world from 1939 to 1941, Conn gave up the title to fight heavyweight champion Joe Louis. Known for his hand speed and his defense, Conn proved to be the more skilled fighter in the ring against Louis, and led on all scorecards through 12 rounds. But in round 13, Conn, a smart fighter, made the dumb move of trying to knock out Louis, and instead was knocked out, losing his bid to become the heavyweight champion. He didn't often make mistakes, though, compiling a record of 64-12-1 with 15 knockouts over his career.

8. JACK DELANEY (1919-28; 1932). The 1920s light heavy champ, Jack Delaney, had a complete bag of tricks at his disposal: a superb ring grace, uncanny judgment of distance and an artistic ability to thwart his opponent which, when coupled with a rapier-like left and a precision right cross, enabled him to beat some of the best fighters of his era, including Maxie Rosenbloom, Tiger Flowers, Tommy Loughran, and Paul Berlenbach.

7. ARCHIE MOORE (1935-63). The light heavyweight champion for longer than any in history, Archie Moore is primarily known as a knockout artist, as attested to by his having 145 knockouts amongst his 199 wins. But Moore scored as many knockouts psychologically as he did physically, outsmarting his opponents with all the wiles and instincts of a fencing master. Rowing with muffled oars, Moore would peer out from behind his crossed-arm "Armadillo" curtain, make a slight insouciant move and then, BAM!, score with his devastating right hand. Other times he would half-talk and half-punch his opponents into oblivion, controlling them and the tempo of the fight with his wits and his fists.

6. TOMMY LOUGHRAN (1919-37). Light heavyweight champion in 1929, Loughran was considered a master at footwork and a superb counter puncher. Over the course of his career, Loughran used his superior technical skills to defeat 96 opponents— including Jim Braddock, Harry Greb and George Carpentier—and even gain a heavyweight title shot against Primo Carnera in 1934.

5. PACKEY McFARLAND (1904-15). It was once said that the only time opponents ever laid a glove on Packey McFarland was when they touched gloves with him before a fight. Cool and calculating, McFarland performed his own ring wizardry when moving at top speed or when on the defensive—his forte an ability to hit an opponent with accuracy when on the retreat. Although never a champion, McFarland lost only one bout in his 104 fights between 1904 and 1915, fighting all the great lightweights, welterweights and middleweights of his time. Perhaps the greatest compliment ever paid him was that by British lightweight champion and world welterweight claimant Matt Wells who, after being outpointed by McFarland and asked by his Cockney trainer, Dai Dollings, "Why didn't you 'it 'im, Matt?" said, "Ah couldn't 'it that bloke with a 'orsewhip."

4. GENE TUNNEY (1915-28). A master boxer with a powerful punch, Tunney could analyze the strengths and weaknesses of any opponent and exploit them, as he did with Jack Dempsey in their first fight, employing something he saw Georges Carpentier do in an earlier fight against Dempsey, by landing a straight right in the opening seconds and controlling the fight for 10 rounds to win the heavyweight title. Or in attacking Henry Greb in their rematch by constantly hitting him under the heart to debilitate his former conqueror. After meeting Tunney for the fifth time and getting the worse of it, the great Greb was to say, "I'm through fighting Gene Tunney. There's one man I never want to meet again," going on to explain why he believed Tunney was one of the greatest technicians of all time.

3. WILLIE PEP (1940-66). A featherweight who began fighting in 1940, Pep applied his advanced technical skills and superior defensive abilities to become the world titleholder just two years later. He would hold the belt until he was knocked out by Sandy Saddler in 1948 in the first of their four epic battles. Pep was known for his fast hands and great footwork with his style once described as "tap dancing with boxing gloves." He would go into the ring 241 times over his 26-year career, amassing a record of 229-11-1 with 65 knockouts.

2. BENNY LEONARD (1911-24; 1931-32). Known as one of the smartest fighters ever to step into the ring, Leonard was the lightweight champion from 1917 to 1925, and would compile a career record of 183-19-11 with four no decisions and 70 knockouts. Leonard was a speedy technician who often tried to psych out his opponents, talking to them while fighting in the ring. Born and raised in the Jewish ghettos of New York, Leonard was known as "the Ghetto Wizard" and is said to have learned his skills fighting on the streets.

1. SUGAR RAY ROBINSON (1940-65). Considered by many as the greatest pound-for-pound fighter in boxing history, Robinson was as smooth a ring technician as the sport has ever seen. He combined a lightning quick jab with the power to put opponents away with both hands, even while moving backward. He once declared, "Rhythm is everything in boxing. Every move you make starts with your heart, and that's in rhythm or you're in trouble." Over a 25-year career, Robinson fought all the greats of his time—Jake LaMotta, Carmen Basilio, Gene Fullmer, Henry Armstrong and Rocky Graziano among them. He used his dazzling technique to score 173 wins and 108 knockouts.

BEST PRE-FIGHT LINES

Cassius Clay may have raised pre-fight talk to a new level in the 1960s and then taken it a few steps further in the 1970s as Muhammad Ali. But he didn't invent the stuff. Pre-fight trash talk and brash predictions have been spewing out of fighters' mouths since before the invention of the mouthpiece. Here are ten of the most brazen, significant and—in some cases—misguided pre-fight quotes over the decades from boxers and, in one case, a journalist who became part of a fight he was covering.

"THEY'RE TWO BIG GUYS. IF SOMEBODY GOES THROUGH THE ROPES, I HOPE IT'S DEMPSEY. AT LEAST HE'S LIGHTER THAN THAT TRUNK, FIRPO." *New York Times* sportswriter Jack Lawrence, before the 1923 Jack Dempsey-Luis Firpo fight, during which Dempsey actually went through the ropes, landing atop Lawrence's typewriter.

"I'LL MOIDAH DA BUM." Heavyweight challenger Tony Galento, before his 1939 fight against champion Joe Louis, who KO'd Galento in the fourth round.

"THAT FAG WON'T LAST A ROUND." Heavyweight champion Sonny Liston, before his 1964 fight with Cassius Clay, who beat Liston so badly that he forced Liston to quit in his corner after the sixth round.

"FEET BROUGHT ME IN AND FEET WILL BRING ME OUT." Light heavyweight champion Battling Levinsky, in a rumored boast before his 1918 non-title fight against Jack Dempsey, at the end of which Levinsky was carried feet–first out of the ring following a third-round KO by Dempsey.

"LEON SPINKS IS SO UGLY THAT WHEN A TEAR ROLLS DOWN HIS FACE, IT ONLY GETS HALFWAY DOWN, THEN IT ROLLS BACK." Three-time heavyweight champion Muhammad Ali, on rival Leon Spinks, who upset Ali to win the title in 1978, with Ali winning the rematch later that year.

"THAT'S ALRIGHT, CHAPPIE, YOU'LL ONLY HAVE TO CLIMB THEM ONCE TONIGHT." Heavyweight champion Joe Louis, after his trainer Jack Blackburn complained that he didn't know if his heart condition would allow him to climb the stairs to the corner in-between rounds for his upcoming 1942 fight against challenger Buddy Baer, whom Louis knocked out in the first round.

"YOU'RE NOTHING MORE THAN OVERSTUFFED SALAMI AND WHEN I GET THROUGH WITH YOU, YOU'LL THINK YOU'VE BEEN THROUGH A MEAT GRINDER." Challenger Max Baer to heavyweight champion Primo Carnera at the weigh-in before their 1934 championship fight, which Baer won, knocking down Carnera 11 times.

"HE CAN RUN, BUT HE CAN'T HIDE." Heavyweight champion Joe Louis, before his 1946 title fight against the smaller and faster Billy Conn, who was tracked down and knocked out by Louis in the eighth round.

"THESE ARE MY REFEREES." Early 20th-century midleweight/heavyweight Sam Langford, holding up his fists after being told that the British Board of Boxing Control had its own referee for his upcoming fight, which Langford's "referee" won by knockout.

"I LOOKED ACROSS THE RING AND REALIZED I WANTED TO GO HOME EARLY." Heavyweight Max Baer, on his reactoin to seeing Joe Louis in the opposite corner before being KO'd in four rounds.

"THE BIGGER THEY ARE, THE HARDER THEY FALL."

Heavyweight champion Bob Fitzsimmons, before his 1899 title defense against challenger Jim Jeffries, who outweighed him by 39 pounds. Jeffries felled Fitzsimmons in the 11th round.

GREATEST RIVALRIES

Throughout history there have been great rivalries, those oil-and-water rivalries that sparked memorable confrontations, like those below.

11. BARNEY ROSS VS. JIMMY MCLARNIN VS. TONY CANZONERI. More than a rivalry between two fighters, this engulfed three of the era's top boxers, all great and each representing a different ethnic constituency—Ross an icon for Jews, McLarnin a standard bearer for the Irish and Canzoneri, the pride of Italians. Together, they gave their fans something to cheer about and a lot to remember, battling one another in three intersecting series with lightweight, junior welterweight and welterweight championships won and lost in great fights that made everything else in the 1930s pale in comparison.

10. HENRY ARMSTRONG VS. BABY ARIZMENDI. In a West Coast rivalry involving two of the most popular Los Angeles battlers of the 1930s, Armstrong and Arizmendi locked horns six times, with Arizmendi winning the first three on decisions and Armstrong taking the next two on decisions, then evening the score in defense of his recently-won welterweight title in the final confrontation in their exciting rivalry.

9. SUGAR RAY LEONARD VS. TOMMY HEARNS. Although they only fought twice, the Sugar Ray Leonard and Tommy Hearns rivalry was one of the most storied in recent boxing history. Their first fight in 1981—called "The Showdown" for the unified welterweight championship—was one of the most anticipated fights in welterweight history, one with more eddies and flows than could be found in the most turbulent waters. It ended with Leonard, behind on points, stopping Hearns in the 14th round. Their rematch eight years later was ruled a "draw," albeit most observers—and Leonard himself—thought Hearns had won.

8. STANLEY KETCHEL VS. BILLY PAPKE. This rivalry was a blood rivalry, literally. Ketchel successfully defended his middleweight title against Papke with a 10-round win in June 1908. Three months later, the two met again. But when Ketchel extended his hands to Papke before the fight, he got a murderous right to the nose in return. Down four times in the first round and beaten to a bloody pulp, Ketchel managed to hang on for 11 rounds, the blood on his trunks testimony to his bravery. Finally, even raw courage wasn't enough and Papke prevailed on an 11th-round KO. With the words "shake hands and come out fighting" now a part of boxing's tradition as a result of Papke's unfriendly gesture, Ketchel came back just 80 days later to settle his debt of violence, dispatching Papke in 11 rounds, then beat him again the next year to more than even the score.

7. MARCO ANTONIO BARRERA VS. ERIK MORALES. In a Mexican turf war, with Barrera representing megalopolis Mexico City and Morales standing up for small-town Tijuana, these two multiple champions fought each other three times—for pride, bragging rights and title belts in three different weight classes. Morales won the brutal first bout in February of 2000 for the super bantamweight championship. Two years later, Barrera took Morales' WBC featherweight title, then grabbed his rival's super featherweight belt two years after that. All three fights went the distance and led to close decisions, with the first and third bouts earning "Fight of the Year" honors from *The Ring* magazine.

6. IKE WILLIAMS VS. BOB MONTGOMERY. It was a classic grudge rivalry with enough bad blood to satisfy Dracula. The two first fought in 1944 in a unification match for the lightweight title, with Montgomery stopping Williams in the 12th round. Their dislike for one another, stemming from Williams having thrashed a friend of Montgomery's, continued to simmer for another three years. Then on the night of August 4, 1947, it all came to a head when the two met again, this time with Williams administering an ass-whuppin' and stopping Montgomery in half the time, six rounds, to win his rival's lightweight title.

5. TED "KID" LEWIS VS. JACK BRITTON. These two 1920s welterweight champions fought each other 20 times in 12 different cities over a period of five years. The final score of their traveling road show: Britton four wins to Lewis' three, with one draw and 12 no-decisions.

4 TONY ZALE VS. ROCKY GRAZIANO. In a post-World War II rivalry that lit up boxing's skies, these two middleweights fought each other in a trilogy that remains one of the most vicious ever. There was no animosity, no grudge, Graziano even saying, "I like Tony Zale, but I'm gonna kill him." But you couldn't tell it from their ring wars, with the 1946 and 1947 installments named "Fight of the Year" by *The Ring* magazine and still remembered as two of the greatest fights—fights for survival—in ring history.

3. SUGAR RAY ROBINSON VS. JAKE LAMOTTA. In 1943, LaMotta handed Robinson his first-ever ring loss after 40 consecutive wins, one of them over LaMotta the previous year. But three weeks later in the same ring, Robinson gained revenge, winning a lopsided 10-round unanimous decision. They would go on to fight a total of six bouts, Robinson winning five—including the famous "St. Valentine's Day Massacre" fight on February 14, 1951 when Robinson stopped LaMotta in the 13th round to win the middleweight title. LaMotta would later say, "I fought Sugar Ray so many times it's a wonder I didn't get diabetes."

2. Sandy Saddler vs. Willie Pep These two magnificent fighters' greatness intersected for four years back in the late forties and early fifties when they held annual affairs that could have doubled as get-togethers of two warring Irish clans. Four times the human eraser known as Sandy Saddler and the "Will o' the Wisp," Willie Pep, engaged in epic feats of arms, legs, and virtually every other anatomical appurtenance known to boxingkind as they answered each other's insult to the Marquess of Queensberry with one of their own, using each other as 126-pound throw rugs with Saddler winning three of their four featherweight donnybrooks.

1. Muhammad Ali vs. Joe Frazier. There has never been a more famous pairing that Muhammad Ali and Joe Frazier. It's as if they were linked together permanently, always connected by a hyphen, impossible to say the name of one without the other. Together these two greats gave boxing fans three fights and 41 rounds filled with nonstop action and great thrills. But underneath their three fights was an undercurrent of resentment on Frazier's part who was hurt by Ali's constant calling him "ignorant," "ugly" and worst of all, "Uncle Tom," a resentment that boiled over before their third fight, "The Thrilla In Manila," when, after Ali called him a "gorilla in Manila," Frazier said, "It's real hatred...I didn't want to knock him out, I want to take his heart out." It was that third match, the rubber match in a trilogy—that had Frazier winning the first one on March 8, 1971, a decision by Ali in their second, a non-title bout three years later—that would be one of the classic fights of all time, a fight Ali called "the closest thing to death," with Frazier's corner stopping the bout before the 15th round. And although Ali was to win two out of their three match-ups, the two would forever be one historical entry, Ali-Frazier, the hyphen between their two names as permanent as the memories they gave.

JOE FRAZIER (LEFT) vs MUHAMMAD ALI IN THEIR FIRST TITLE FIGHT AT MADISON SQUARE GARDEN, 1971.

BOXING'S BEST BROTHER COMBINATIONS

:: BY STEVE FARHOOD

Note: Steve Farhood serves as a fight analyst for Showtime. During his 32-year association with boxing, he has written for *Boxing Monthly* and maxboxing.com and served as editor-in-chief of *The Ring* and *KO* magazines. Author of the book, *Boxing: The 20th Century*, Steve has also worked as a correspondent for ESPN, CNN, SportsChannel and *Tuesday Night Fights* on the USA Network. The Brooklyn native claimed the Sam Taub Award for Excellence in Broadcast Journalism in 2002 and was named First Vice President of the Boxing Writers Association of America. The youngest of four Farhood brothers, Steve offers his take on boxing's top ten fraternal orders.

10. MARV, STEVE, AND AL ALBERT. Marv called fights for NBC, Steve for Showtime and Al for the USA Network. Need more? My father-in-law was Steve's high school golf teacher.

9. DONALD AND BRUCE CURRY. In the mid–1980s, welterweight Donald was the best fighter in the world. Bruce was a big puncher who briefly held the junior welter title.

8. ORLANDO AND GABY CANIZALES. Both were bantam champs, Hall of Famer Orlando for much longer.

7. ABE AND MONTE ATTELL. Featherweight great Abe is best known for helping fix the 1919 World Series. Monte briefly reigned at bantamweight.

6. TERRY AND ORLIN NORRIS. Junior middleweight champ Terry humbled Sugar Ray Leonard. Orlin was an underrated cruiserweight champ and a top ten heavyweight.

5. WLADIMIR AND VITALI KLITSCHKO. They both ranked number one at heavyweight. That's more than enough to land here.

4. KHAOSAI AND KAOKOR GALAXY. The only twins to win world titles. Khaosai was the greatest junior bantam ever. (In case you were wondering, they were named after nightclubs.)

MIKE GIBBONS

TOMMY GIBBONS

3. TOMMY AND MIKE GIBBONS. Tommy lost to heavyweight champ Jack Dempsey, but beat Harry Greb and Georges Carpentier. Middleweight Mike was just as good.

2. LEON AND MICHAEL SPINKS. Leon shocked Ali and Michael was one of the better light heavies ever. Both won Olympic gold medals and heavyweight titles.

1. JUAN MANUEL AND RAFAEL MARQUEZ. Awesome credentials: multi-division champs, great pound-for-pounders, future Hall of Famers.

GREATEST ITALIAN-AMERICAN FIGHTERS

:: BY GEORGE RANDAZZO

Note: George Randazzo founded the Italian American Boxing Hall of Fame in 1977 in Elmwood Park, Illinois, to raise money for a local Catholic youth program. The venture proved so successful Randazzo expanded it a year later into the Italian American Sports Hall of Fame, which moved into a larger location in Chicago's Little Italy 12 years later. His son Marc fought as a successful light heavyweight for a decade and suffered only one loss—in a 1995 world title bout. A guest on ESPN's *Sports Century* and at a White House dinner, George Randazzo remains chairman of the Italian American Sports Hall of Fame and a respected authority on Italian–American boxing greats. Here, he looks into that crowded field and picks out his top dozen all-time Italian-American fighters.

12 (TIE). PETE HERMAN (1912-22) AND SAMMY MANDELL (1920-34). Born Pete Gulotta, Herman notched 69 wins and reigned as world bantamweight champion from 1917-20 and again in 1921. Mandell scored 82 wins and held the world lightweight title belt from 1926-30. Their records speak for themselves and both were great champions.

10 (TIE). LOU AMBERS (1932-41) AND SAMMY ANGOTT (1935-50). These two great lightweight champions both enjoyed long careers and were great boxer-punchers who each scored over 80 wins. Ambers held the world lightweight title belt from 1936-38 and 1939-40, while Angott wore it in 1940 and again from 1941-44.

8. ROCKY GRAZIANO (1942-52). Tremendous puncher and colorful fighter who reigned as middleweight champion from 1947-48.

7. JAKE LaMOTTA (1941-54). "The Raging Bull" was world middleweight champion from 1949-51. He had tremendous heart, and his epic fights with Sugar Ray Robinson speak for themselves.

6. JOEY GIARDELLO (1948-67). If you wanted a shot at the middleweight title, you had to go through Joey Giardello. The uncrowned champion for years finally became the middleweight champion in 1963 by beating the great Dick Tiger and held the title until 1965.

5. CARMEN BASILIO (1948-61). The onion farmer from Canastota, New York was only 5'6" but won titles from the likes of Johnny Saxton and Sugar Ray Robinson.

He held the world welterweight title in 1953 and from 1955-57, then wore the world middleweight belt from 1957-58.

4. JOHNNY DUNDEE (1910-32). Born in Sicily, Dundee relocated to New York and became one of the first Italian Americans to win a world title, serving as featherweight champion from 1923-24 and junior lightweight champ from 1921-23 and 1923-24.

3. ROCKY MARCIANO (1947-55). The heavyweight world titleholder from 1952-56, Marciano remains boxing history's only undefeated heavyweight champion with a 49-0 career record that included 43 knockouts. What else can you say?

TONY CANZONERI

2. TONY CANZONERI (1925-39). One of boxing's immortals of the 1920s and 30s, Canzoneri had great punching power and fought the very best of his time. He reigned as world featherweight champion in 1928, wore the world lightweight crown from 1930-33 and 1935-36, and held the world junior welterweight title from 1931-32 and in 1933.

1. WILLIE PEP (1940-66). Born Gugliermo Papaleo in Connecticut, he changed his name to Willie Pep and transformed himself into a master boxer, ruling as world featherweight champion from 1942-48 and 1949-50.

MOST EXCITING FIGHTERS

The word "exciting" is defined by Noah Webster as the quality of something which "arouses" or "stirs up" or "kindles" the emotions. And nothing "arouses" or "stirs up" or "kindles" the emotions of the fight fan more than an exciting fighter, be it for their performance, their hyperventilating activity or their style. Here are the ten fighters who have given boxing fans the most excitement in the ring over the years.

10. BOB SATTERFIELD (1945-57). A leading heavyweight contender of the early 1950s, Satterfield was picked as one of the 100 greatest punchers of all time by *Ring* Magazine. With 50 wins, 35 of those by KO, and 25 losses, 12 of those KO'd by, Satterfield either knocked out his opponent or was knocked out by his opponent—as witnessed by his fight with Rex Layne whom he knocked down in the first round only to be KO'd in the eighth.

9. JOE FRAZIER (1965-76; 1981). Joe Frazier's savage style of boxing and the small pieces he left behind of himself in almost every one of his fights made for pure excitement. No matter the opponent, Frazier's plain vanilla style of wading into the blazing guns of his adversary made for exciting action and great fights.

8. ARUTRO GATTI (1991-2007). Nobody, but nobody, was ever in more exciting fights than the boxer called "The Human Highlight Reel." Gatti came back time and time again after almost being destroyed to turn the tables on his tormentor, as he did against Gabriel Ruelas, Wilson Rodriquez, and Micky Ward, a record four times participating in *Ring* magazine's "Fight of the Year."

7. ROCKY GRAZIANO (1942-52). Seemingly always down to his last chance against improbable odds and somehow surviving, as he did against Tony Zale in their second fight, Graziano described his style as that of "a guy who liked to swap punches with a guy." And in most of his 53 knockouts he came back, as he did to knock out Charley Fusari in the tenth and final round after losing the first nine and twice KO'ing Freddie "Red" Cochrane in the tenth of losing battles.

6. AARON PRYOR (1976-90). A pinwheel out of control, "The Hawk" fought with total abandon for three-and-a–half minutes of every three-minute round with the confidence that repels bullets. The cornerstone of his career was his brutal, 14-round donnybrook with Alexis Arguello in 1982 when he took punches from the three-time champion and came back with all the energy of a ferret on 10 cups of cappuccino.

5. BEAU JACK (1939-55). A dynamic, non-stop puncher who fought like someone who stopped runaway trains in complete disregard of his own safety, Beau Jack appeared in 21 Madison Square Garden main events (including three in one month), the most of any fighter in the Mecca of Boxing's long history, drawing more than 336,000 fans who paid to watch his exciting style.

4. BOBBY CHACON (1972-88). Every Chacon fight was a melodrama. His brutal wars with Bazooka Limon and Cornelius Boza-Edwards were memorable—in his fourth fight with Limon in 1982, he scored a knockdown in the final seconds to win and in his 1983 fight against Boza-Edwards, with ringside announcer Marv Albert calling for the referee to stop the fight to save Chacon, he came back to win.

3. STANLEY KETCHEL (1903-10). With a ferocious attacking style and a murderous punch, Stanley Ketchel, aka "The Michigan Assassin," was one of the most exciting fighters of the early 20th century. Many's the time, without looking back to see the comatose form of the fighter he had just destroyed lying on the canvas, the victorious Ketchel would vault the ropes and run down the aisle to his dressing room, so sure was he of the knockout power of his punch.

2. HENRY ARMSTRONG (1931-45). A perpetual motion machine, Armstrong ran over his opposition, suffocating them with punches. In one 29-month period—from January of 1937 through May of 1939—Armstrong fought 46 times, winning all 46 with 39 knockouts while claiming world titles in three different weight classes (featherweight, lightweight and welterweight). Small wonder they called this overachiever "Hurricane Hank."

1. JACK DEMPSEY (1914-27). Pure and simple, Jack Dempsey mainlined excitement for hundreds of thousands of post-World War I sports-starved fans who crowded into outdoor arenas hoping they could see his lightning strike at any second. The first great sports hero of the 20th century, Dempsey's popularity ushered in "The Golden Age of Sports," his exploits in the ring matching the excitement of the 1920s.

FASTEST HANDS

A boxer's hands—whether large like Dempsey's, or small like LaMotta's—are his basic tools of the trade. But no matter their size, several fighters have been able to employ them in a faster-than-fast manner, working their hands like a magician, practicing their own form of legerdemain. Here are some of boxing's most prominent hand-speed merchants.

12. WILLIE JOYCE (1937-47). A 1940s lightweight out of Chicago, Joyce unfortunately came long in the lightweight era of Ike Williams, Beau Jack, and Bob Montgomery. Still, it was with a left jab, one of the best in boxing, delivered with Gatling gun speed, that left Joyce's mark. And 71 wins on the plus side of his ledger.

11. FLOYD MAYWEATHER, JR. (1996-). His punches are almost imperceptible to the human eye as he delivers blindingly fast counters and straight rights both economically and efficiently, one punch at a time.

10. HECTOR CAMACHO (1980-2010). Although known more for his flamboyance and outfits, "The Macho man" also possessed a pair of the fastest hands seen in recent years. In his one-round stoppage of John Montes in 1983, not only did neither Montes nor the referee see his knockout punch, the ref didn't even see Camacho grab Montes head and pull it down into his punch, that's how fast Camacho was.

9. BEAU JACK (1939-55). Jack flailed away with both hands, throwing a smorgasbord of punches, hooks, crosses and just about everything imaginable with either hand, always following his corner's shouted command to: "Rip 'em all the time!"

8. MANNY PACQUIAO (1995-). Coming at his opponents like a buzzsaw, the left-handed "Pacman" throws a blurring number of punches almost faster than the eye can see, overwhelming his opponent as he did versus Oscar De La Hoya or with one unseen pluperfect knockout punch, as he delivered from out of the blue against Ricky Hatton. "Pacman" registers off-the-charts punch counts, Miguel Cotto saying after his fight with Pacquiao, "He was so fast, I couldn't see his punches coming."

7. MUHAMMAD ALI (1960-67; 1970-81). One of the most innovative fighters in history, the then-young Cassius Clay imitated the style of many fighters, one of whom was his idol, Sugar Ray Robinson. And often when the young Cassius was shadow-boxing or sparring, he would acknowledge his debt to Robinson by executing a Robinson-like jab with verbal "bam . . . bam . . . bam. . . ." But it was not only his jab, Ali could do it all, coming at his opponent from anywhere with quick punches, as he did against Sonny Liston in their second fight in Lewiston, Maine, with a punch so fast that half the fans in the audience never saw it. Nor did Liston.

6. ROY JONES JR. (1989-2010). Called "a genius fighter" by Budd Schulberg, Jones was a genius with his hands, able to get away with lead right hands to the body and throw one-two's that became one-two-three's ,-four's, quicker than the proverbial quick brown fox that jumped over the fence.

5. WILLIE PEP (1940-66). Pep was so fast at throwing his own form of rat-a-tat-tat punches that one of his opponents, Kid Campeche, said, "Fighting Willie Pep is like trying to stamp out a grass fire."

4. HENRY ARMSTRONG (1931-45). A non-stop punching machine, Armstrong would suffocate opponents with his blinding hand speed, throwing punches in bunches *asfastasyouycanreadthis.*

3. SUGAR RAY ROBINSON (1940-65). Known for his fast flurries, none were faster than the relentless rain of punches Robinson unleashed in his 1951 rematch with Randy Turpin when, according to one ringside observer, he landed 30 punches in 25 seconds in the 10th round to win the fight and regain his middleweight crown.

2. FLOYD PATTERSON (1952-72). From the very first time Patterson stepped onto the world stage at the tender age of 17 for the 1952 Helsinki Olympics, he had what Red Smith described as "faster paws than a subway pickpocket." It was an asset Patterson would eventually parlay into a world heavyweight championship.

1. SUGAR RAY LEONARD (1977-97). With lightning-fast fists that seemed almost a blur, Sugar Ray Leonard was faster than fast, as he demonstrated by stealing rounds in his classic 1987 fight against Marvin Hagler by "rat-a-tatting" the "Marvelous One" in the last 15 seconds of every round.

BEST FOOTWORK

Some boxers put their best feet forward, looking as light as cucumber sandwiches as they move around the ring, always with a tacit and tactical understanding of where they are and what they have to do to win. Here are a few of the greatest footmen in boxing history.

12. WILLIE PASTRANO (1951-65) Willie Pastrano was one of the most disingenuous users of footwork ever seen in boxing. He could stutter-step, deke his opponents out of their jocks by feinting and then go the other way, or turn left-handed in midstep without losing a beat and get away with it, always one step ahead of his opponent whether they be middleweights, light heavies or elephantine heavyweights, able to dispose of the unfair disadvantage of weight with his footwork.

11. KID GAVILAN (1943-58). The Cuban "Keed" rumba'd his way through fights to a Latin beat as he moved in and out, the soles of his shoes barely touching the canvas. He would sometimes even mimic his opponents' moves, shifting—without breaking step—into a left-handed stance if they were southpaws, or into a flat-footed stance, all the better from which to throw his famous bolo punch.

10. BILLY CONN (1934-48) With his speed of foot Billy Conn took the measure of no less than ten men who held titles at one time or another—from A to Z: Fred Apostoli, Melio Bettina, Young Corbett III, Vince Dundee, Solly Kreiger, Gus Lesnevich, Babe Risko, Teddy Yarosz, Tony Zale and Fritzie Zivic. But it was the one fight Conn came close enough to touch the hem of Lady Fortune, his first fight with Joe Louis, and lost, that cemented his claim to fame. For 12 rounds the smaller Conn, continually on the move, tormented Louis with his footwork, retreating and stopping only long enough to hook his left into Louis' face or throwing punches while on the retreat, all the while dancing away from Louis and staying out of danger. It was only when he decided to slug it out with "The Brown Bomber," betraying his well-laid battle plan, that Conn met defeat. But for 12-plus rounds Billy Conn had put his two best feet forward in one of the greatest displays of footwork in boxing history.

MUHAMMAD ALI

9. JERSEY JOE WALCOTT (1930-53). Walcott was an old sand dancer who backpedaled, side-stepped, and forward-shuffled to his own rhythm in a befuddling array of moves, liberally sprinkled with decorous retreats and embellished shifts and sways—all designed to frustrate his opponents and disrupt their rhythms.

8. PARNELL WHITAKER (1984-2001). Pernell Whitaker was a fistic breakdancer, one who always looked like he had taken a four-way cold tablet and had to move three different ways to catch up with it. His was a style that enabled him to run *and* hide at one and the same time.

7. TOMMY LOUGHRAN (1919-37). The light heavyweight champ was a firm believer in the precept: "They have to hit me to hurt me . . . and they can't hit me." Practicing the "Manly Art of Self-Defense," Loughran was a lineal descendant of James J. Corbett's school of scientific boxing, even using his footwork to move the fight into his own corner at the end of each three-minute round so that he could just sit down at the bell and make his opponent walk all the way across the ring.

6. BENNY LEONARD (1911-24; 1931-32) True to his motto "Hit and not be hit," Benny Leonard could use his speed afoot to go through an entire fight with his slicked-down, brilliantined hair intact, proudly running his hand through his hair after every fight and announcing, "I never even got my hair mussed." Leonard was at his most impressive brushing back his hair, hitching up his trunks, and circling his adversary, all the time using what he called his "mental energy" and his footwork to set up his opponent for the kill.

5. MUHAMMAD ALI (1960-81). Ali brought an amazing physical grace to the ring, something never seen in the heavyweight division. His footwork matched his hand speed as he 'floated like a butterfly' to the heavyweight championship and into boxing lore.

4. JOHNNY DUNDEE (1910-32). This all-time great featherweight moved with the agility of a fistic Nijinsky—always up on his toes, pirouetting in the middle of the ring, ricocheting off the ropes and bouncing up and down in jumping-jack motions that looked like a combination of ballet entrechats and leaping left hooks.

3. SUGAR RAY ROBINSON (1940-65). His footwork something rarely seen before or since, Robinson practiced tap dancing with gloves on, moving around the ring with grace and style, giving his opponents countless looks and feints, but little to hit.

2. SID TERRIS (1922-31). Known as "The Ghetto Ghost" Sid Terris's move afoot could take your breath away, as it did so many of his opponents. One of the greatest lightweights in an era of great lightweights, the 1920s, Terris was called by *The Ring* magazine, "the speediest fighter of his generation." And by the *New York Times*, "a fighter with remarkable speed and cleverness." Cus D'Amato remembered him once virtually defying the laws of gravity by jumping off the canvas and landing three jabs before descending back to earth.

1. WILLIE PEP (1940-66). Known as "The Will o' the Wisp," Pep gave his fans and his foes a run for their money, literally. Willie practiced reverse polarity, making opponents chase his shadow until they realized it was impossible to hit something they couldn't find, his moves making him as hard to catch as lightning in a bottle.

MOST AWKWARD FIGHTERS

Throughout boxing's long history, many "classic" fighters have come along who could rightfully be called descendants of such great practitioners of the "Sweet Science" as Gentleman Jim Corbett and Benny Leonard. On the other glove, there have been those who couldn't be judged by their style, there being little or no evidence of it. These guys rank as the most awkward boxers through the ages, whether their awkwardness came from their clumsiness or their comical antics.

10. GENE FULLMER (1951-63). Gene Fullmer was strong and sturdy and could box when he had to, as he did against Dick Tiger and Carmen Basilio. But, at other times, his "style," if you could call it that, was barreling into his opponent, head down as if checking to see if his zipper was broken, giving his opponents, as he did Ray Robinson, a fit and the words "ring science" a bad name.

9. PRINCE NASEEM HAMED (1992-2002). Although he didn't hold the original copyright for unorthodoxy, Prince Naseem Hamed perfected it, leaping in with right-hand leads, falling to one side or another to get an angle, and generally doing everything one is not supposed to do, at least according to the boxing style textbook. And yet his power came from his speed and unorthodox and awkward moves.

8. PRIMO CARNERA (1930-46). A former circus strongman, Carnera never quite got the hang of boxing, though he didn't really have to, many of his fights being fixed. In unfixed fights, he would turn his back on his opponents when hit, step on their feet, or grab them in bear hugs between trying to throw punches.

7. VIC DARCHINYAN (2000-). Darchinyan has a style that looks like a crab siding up to his prey. And yet, he boasts an impressive knockout record and even has a championship belt to his credit.

6. RANDY TURPIN (1946-58; 1963-64). Blocking punches with his shoulders hunched around his ears, and taking them on his elbows, and heavily-muscled arms ("He always looked more like a heavyweight than a middleweight," said Sugar Ray Robinson who fought him twice), Turpin combined that with an unusual pull-back maneuver to keep from being hit cleanly. It was an awkward defensive style that gave Sugar Ray so much trouble and took him almost 25 rounds to solve before he finally was able to stop Turpin in the 10th round of their rematch.

5. RAY "WINDMILL" WHITE (1958-74). A Los Angeles area favorite, White brought comic relief to his fights, sometimes even throwing punches from behind his back.

4. EMANUEL AUGUSTUS/BURTON (1994-). A showman of the first order, Emanuel Augustus (who changed his last name from Burton in 2001) has his own style, which he calls "string puppet dances." He likes to dance around the ring and spin away from clinches, several times being penalized by referees with little or no sense of humor.

3. OSCAR BONAVENA (1964-76). A barrel-chested, do-anything-you-can-do-to-win fighter, Bonavena, in the words of trainer Angelo Dundee, "threw punches from out his ass."

2. TOMMY "HURRICANE" JACKSON (1951-61). As one writer put it, "If I described Jackson as different, that would be an understatement." Jackson, who looked like a marionette whose strings had been cut, less fought his opponents than "surrounded" them—throwing punches, many of them slaps, with boundless energy, sometimes with both hands at once.

1. GYPSY JOE HARRIS (1964-68). When it came to style, Gypsy Joe Harris threw away the boxing textbook, his movements requiring decoding. Curtis Cokes, welterweight champion, who fought and lost to Harris in a non-title bout, said of Harris' "style": "He don't have a style, he just stands there and acts the monkey." And his trainer, Willie Reddish, trying to describe Harris' improvisational approach to boxing—including holding his arms at his side, employing a Jersey Joe Walcott walk-away-and-turn-back-and-punch offense, and slipping and sliding away from punches by almost contortionist means—could only say, "He don't make plans, 'cause he don't know what he gonna do till he do it." Yet for all his eccentric, almost bizarre behavior in the ring, Harris compiled a record of 24 wins and only one loss, that loss coming in his last fight, against ex-welterweight and middleweight champion Emile Griffith after Harris nonchalanted his way to a 10-round loss. After that fight, taking an eye test for his next fight, it was found that Gypsy Joe had been fighting his entire career with but one eye, blinded in a childhood accident, and was barred from boxing despite his almost all-winning record.

BOXING'S MOST CONTROVERSIAL FIGHTS

Some fights don't end definitively, but live on as controversies, their final bells acting as an opening bell for arguments that last not for rounds, but for decades. Here are but ten of the many fights that led to verbal bouts outside the ring as lively as and much longer-lived than the physical bouts inside the ring that raised their points of contention.

10. LUIS RESTO VS. BILLY COLLINS, JR., JUNE 16, 1983. The Resto-Collins fight was on the undercard of a Roberto Duran-Davey Moore main event on a night when "unloaded" gloves became the center of a controversy. A journeyman fighter, Resto was matched against the up-and-coming Collins, an undefeated welterweight being groomed for bigger and better things. Unbelievably, Resto, a fighter not known for his power, smashed and bashed up Collins' face, welting it in several places and closing his eye on his way to a unanimous 10-round decision. But officials discovered that Resto's trainer, Panama Lewis, had removed the horsehair from his fighter's gloves, making them rock-hard. Resto and Lewis were sent to prison for their malfeasance. Collins suffered permanent damage to his eyesight during the bout and was forced to retire from boxing. Then, in a tragic ending to the episode, Collins died the following year in a car accident many believed to be a suicide.

9. JOEY GIARDELLO VS. RUBEN "HURRICANE" CARTER, DECEMBER 14, 1964. The controversy did not begin in the ring, where Giardello clearly won a 15-round decision by "sticking" Carter with his left jab all night long after a quick start by Carter, with even Carter admitting afterwards, "He won the fight." The debate arose 35 years later due to the fight's depiction in the movie *The Hurricane*, which portrayed the decision for Giardello as an act of racial bias against Carter. Giardello instituted legal action to remedy the misrepresentation, forcing producers to add a footnote to the movie indicating that he had won the fight and racism was not the basis for the decision. In the opinion of some, the controversy cost early Oscar favorite Denzel Washington the Best Actor Award for his portrayal of Carter.

8. PRIMO CARNERA VS. JACK SHARKEY II, JUNE 29, 1933. Many suspected that Carnera's record was padded with fixed fights. But the mammoth Italian, known as "The Ambling Alp," still gained a title shot against heavyweight champion Jack Sharkey in 1933 at the "Graveyard of Champions"—the Long Island Bowl, where no champion had ever successfully defended his belt. The two had met two years before, with Sharkey winning a 15-round decision, knocking down Carnera twice and saying, "The big lug will be tough when he learns how to fight." In the early going of their rematch, it looked as if Carnera still hadn't learned, as Sharkey outmaneuvered, outboxed, and outhit his lumbering foe. Then, in the sixth, Carnera used his nearly

60–pound weight advantage to push Sharkey into the ropes, where he threw three sweeping punches that looked like they came from the third row. With Sharkey looking dazed, Carnera knocked the champion down with what seemed, to many in the crowd like a phantom uppercut. And out. The dubious KO spurred suspicion that Carnera was a fraud and Sharkey just one more of his set-up "victims."

7. BATTLING SIKI VS. GEORGES CARPENTIER, SEPTEMBER 24, 1922. France's national hero Carpentier defended his light heavyweight title in front of his adoring public at the Velodrome Buffalo Arena in Paris against the fighter called "The Singular Senegalese," Battling Siki. Few thought that Siki would make much of a showing, especially after he was knocked down by Carpentier in the first round. Carpentier then made the mistake of toying with his opponent, allowing Siki to come back with a fierce attack. In the sixth, Siki's offense intensified and he hit Carpentier with several hard shots to the body and knocked him down with a hard left hook. The champ's legs got caught up in the ropes as he fell and, without a count, referee Henri Bernstein disqualified Siki for "tripping and throwing." The decision seemed so unjust that the French crowd protested angrily and the judges awarded the fight and the title to Siki.

6. JACK DEMPSEY VS. JACK SHARKEY, JULY 21, 1927. Having lost his title to Gene Tunney the previous year, Jack Dempsey ignored overtures from promoter Tex Rickard for a quick rematch and opted instead for a "tune-up" fight against a top contender to see if he "still had it." That top contender was Jack Sharkey, who dominated the fight, piling up points as Dempsey was visibly shaken time and time again, his legs failing to meet the obligation they had sworn to fulfill. Sharkey, who had staggered Dempsey in the fifth, came out for the seventh aggressively, determined to end the fight. Dempsey shot in two low blows and, in the ensuing clinch, Sharkey turned his head to complain to the referee. That was all Dempsey had to see. He whipped over his patented left hook and Sharkey went down, out to the world, despite his corner's protest of a foul. As Dempsey said afterwards, "What was I going to do, write him a letter of apology?"

5. JAMES "BUSTER" DOUGLAS VS. MIKE TYSON, FEBRUARY 11, 1990. The so-called "Baddest Man on the Planet," Mike Tyson met 42-to-1 underdog Buster Douglas in what looked to all like a walkover. It was, but the one doing the walking was Douglas, who fought the fight of his life, dominating the "invincible" champion and reducing him to a pitiful figure crawling around the mat and groping for his mouthpiece as he was counted out in the 10th round. Tyson enjoyed one big moment during the fight—an uppercut that floored Douglas in the eighth round. That flash knockdown became the subject of controversy, with promoter Don King claiming Douglas was down for more than ten seconds and invoking the Tunney-Dempsey "Long Count" (see #1 on this list) as justification for his demand that Tyson still be ruled the champion by virtue of an eighth-round KO. And, for a short while he got the WBO and WBA to agree. However, by the next morning a firestorm of protest had broken out and both alphabet-soup organizations backtracked, declaring that, despite the controversy, Buster Douglas was their new champion.

4. MAX SCHMELING VS. JACK SHARKEY I, JUNE 12, 1930. Schmeling met Sharkey for the final fight to determine the successor to heavyweight champion Gene Tunney's vacated title. For three rounds Sharkey controlled the fight, even staggering Schmeling in the third. In the fourth Sharkey let go a left hook to the body just as Schmeling suddenly stood up straight to deliver a left hook to Sharkey's head, causing Sharkey's punch to land palpably south of the border. Schmeling went down holding his groin and referee Jim Crowley, not having seen the punch, decided against starting the count and instead consulted with the judges. One judge, Harold Barnes, told Crowley he'd seen Sharkey's punch stray low. Meanwhile, the bell ending the fourth had rung and Schmeling's corner had lifted their charge and literally dragged him back to his corner. At the bell to start the fifth, Sharkey raced across the ring, but referee Crowley restrained him from getting at the still-writhing Schmeling seated on his stool. Crowley then made boxing history by ruling that the heavyweight championship of the world had been decided on a foul, awarding the belt to the fallen Schmeling. The result was upheld by the New York State Athletic Department in a 2-1 vote, but remains controversial to this day.

3. MUHAMMAD ALI VS. SONNY LISTON II, MAY 25, 1965. The rematch of their heated first fight when Liston, for reasons still unknown, quit on his stool before the seventh round, was, if possible, even more controversial. The interim between the two bouts featured Ali publicly declaring his conversion to Islam and changing his name from Cassius Clay, along with rumored threats from both the mob and Black Muslims. Then, as Alice said, it just got "curiouser and curiouser." With the opening bell, Liston took off after the elusive Ali, chasing him around the ring, but not landing a punch. Every time Liston led with his jab, Ali wasn't home. Then, as Liston reached for Ali on the ropes with a long left, Ali countered with a right over the top—a punch he later described as his "Stepin' Fetchit Anchor Punch." All of a sudden, there was Ali standing over the fallen Liston, screaming, "Get up, sucker . . . " with referee Jersey Joe Walcott tugging at him, trying his mightiest to pull Ali away and direct him to a neutral corner. Slowly, Liston climbed back to his feet. But Walcott, who had never administered a count, was called over to the press section by *The Ring* magazine publisher Nat Fleischer, who told him that Liston had been down for more than ten seconds. So apprised, Walcott walked across the ring and broke up the two fighters, who were now back to battling, and held up Ali's arm in victory. The timekeeper added to the confusion, ruling that the time was one minute when it was longer . And the crowd, adding to strangeness of the scene, sent up a chant of "Bullshit. . . . Bullshit." To this day, nobody is sure of what really happened.

2. AD WOLGAST VS. JOE RIVERS, JULY 4, 1912. Wolgast was making the first defense of his newly-minted lightweight title against a challenger known as "Indian Joe" Rivers. The seesaw battle exhausted both men, especially Wolgast, who had threatened to "retire" after the 12th round before being dissuaded by his corner. After wobbling out for the 13th, Wolgast met the onrushing Rivers and clung to him like a shipwreck survivor. He sent a left into Rivers' groin just as Rivers threw a picture-perfect left-right to Wolgast's jaw. Both men fell, with Rivers dropping first and Wolgast falling on top of him. As referee Jack Welch went over to view the two fallen fighters, screams of "Foul! Foul!" rang throughout the Vernon, California, open-air arena. Welch ignored the cries and began counting over the two, lifting Wolgast from the top of the pile. Welch tucked the drooping Wolgast under his arm and tolled the fatal "ten" over the fallen Rivers, then raised Wolgast's limp arm in victory. The angry crowd stormed the ring and the police were called in to quell the riot as Welch bolted from the ring. Long after the fight had ended, the crowd was still there, shouting, threatening, and arguing amongst themselves.

1. GENE TUNNEY VS. JACK DEMPSEY II, SEPTEMBER 22, 1927. Known simply as "The Long Count" fight, the second Tunney-Dempsey fight was a moment that will never be fully explained. Was Tunney down for the count of "nine" or was he down for over 14 seconds? The controversy began when Tunney crumbled to the floor in the seventh round under a fusillade of Dempsey punches. Referee Dave Barry's arm came down at the count of "one" as soon as Tunney's fanny struck the canvas. But as his arm began its descent for the count of "two," he chanced to notice that Dempsey was standing over Tunney like an avenging angel, waiting for Tunney to get up so that he could powder him again. Barry stopped counting and motioned Dempsey to go across the ring to a neutral corner, as both fighters had agreed to in a pre-match stipulation concerning knockdowns. But Dempsey was having none of it. Finally, Dempsey made the concession and hied himself to a neutral corner, but it was the nearest corner, not the farthest. So Barry again waved him over and only when Dempsey had obeyed did he begin his count again—at "one." Tunney finally stirred and got up at Barry's count of "nine" (actually about 14.5 seconds) and spent the rest of the round running away from Dempsey, then went on to win a unanimous ten-round decision. But the controversy still runs on.

GREATEST FAN FAVORITES

It takes more than a good-guy persona, big knockout victories, winning title belts, signing autographs, and talking about how much he appreciates his supporters for a fighter to become a fan favorite. As this list demonstrates, sometimes the bad and even baddest guys get cheered like the good guys by the public—and not just by their hometown partisans. Boxing fans across the world and throughout the ages have embraced fighters with such a wide variety of personality and pugilistic traits that no formula exists for determining a fan favorite. All you can do is list the boxers whom fans have embraced most fanatically and marvel at their dissimilarities.

12. MANNY PACQUIAO (1995-). The first fighter ever to win seven world championships in seven different weight classes, Pacquiao rose through the ranks to become the most decorated and internationally celebrated fighter of his time. A crowd favorite for his furious fighting style, Pacquiao was named the 2000-09 Fighter of the Decade by the Boxing Writers Association of America. His three fights against Erik Morales made him a star attraction, and subsequent wins over Ricky Hatton and Oscar De La Hoya made him an even bigger star, plus a lot of money. The total revenue for his De La Hoya fight was reportedly close to $17 million, making it the second most lucrative bout in boxing history. A native of the Philippines, Pacquiao's acclaim made him so popular that in 2010 he was elected to that nation's House of Representatives.

11. HENRY COOPER (1954-71). Sir 'Enery Cooper was the British, European and Commonwealth heavyweight champion and probably the most popular fighter in England's rich boxing history. He gained international attention with his two fights against Muhammad Ali, the first filling England's Wembley Stadium in 1963 when Ali still went by the name Cassius Clay. Cooper knocked Clay down near the end of the fourth round, with Clay likely saved by the bell, but Clay came back in the fifth round to stop a bloodied Cooper. They fought a rematch in 1966 after Clay had become Muhammad Ali and heavyweight champion, this time at Arsenal Stadium in London, where Ali won again. Cooper retired in 1971 with a record of 40-14-1, with 27 knockouts. He became the first two-time winner of the BBC Sports Personality of the Year award, and is only one of three people to claim the honor more than once. Cooper remained popular and in demand for television and radio appearances in retirement, and was even knighted in 2000.

10. JOHN L. SULLIVAN (1879-92). The last bareknuckle heavyweight champion and the first heavyweight champion during the era when fighters started wearing boxing gloves, Sullivan became the first American sports hero, his dynamism and swashbuckling heroics mirroring the age. Stories about Sullivan didn't end at the three-mile limit, but continued far out to sea. And his name was so famous that fans were known to brag, "Shake the hand that shook the hand of the great John L." Considered the first sporting event to receive national press attention, the Sullivan-Jake Kilrain fight in 1889 put professional prizefighting, as it was then called, on the American sports map. Sullivan remained a celebrity in retirement in various roles as an actor, speaker and special guest for public appearances.

9. OSCAR DE LA HOYA (1992-2008). A star before he even fought his first professional fight, Oscar was a popular Mexican-American from Los Angeles known as the "Golden Boy" when he won the lightweight gold medal for the United States at the 1992 Olympics. He made his professional debut with a first-round knockout in November 1992, then two years later at the age of 20 won his first world title by stopping World Boxing Organization junior lightweight champion Jimmi Bredahl. He would go on to win nine more world championships in five weight classes, defeating 17 world champions along the way, including Julio César Chavez, Pernell Whitaker and Ike Quartey. His good looks and pleasant personality made him a crossover star and he remains the all-time leader in pay-per-view revenue, bringing in $610.6 million on 12.6 million buys from 18 events.

8. MIKE TYSON (1985-2005). "Iron Mike" or "The Baddest Man on the Planet" was a force of nature who dominated the heavyweight division in the 1980s with knockout power that made him one of the biggest attractions in America. He won his first 19 professional fights by knockout, ending 12 of them in the first round. In 1986, he became the youngest heavyweight champion in history at the age of 20 years, four months and 222 days when he knocked out WBC champion Trevor Berbick in the second round. He would go on to win all three major heavyweight titles and capture the attention of the world with his ferocious style. His appeal transcended boxing, as evidenced by his perpetual presence in all types of media outlets. But Tyson's popularity in the ring peaked with his 91-second knockout of Michael Spinks in 1988. Soon after, Tyson's notoriety began to bring him intense negative attention outside the ring, including fallout from an interview with Barbara Walters on ABC's *20/20* in which he admitted to beating his wife Robin Givens and the coverage of his rape conviction in Indiana in 1992. Tyson would emerge from prison three years later more famous than ever and reclaim the heavyweight title in 1996, only to lose it later that year to Evander Holyfield. His increasingly bizarre behavior outside the ring and even inside (he was disqualified for repeatedly biting Holyfield's ear in their 1997 rematch) still made him a fan curiosity, if nothing else.

7. ROBERTO DURAN (1968-2001). Called "Hands of Stone" for his punching power, Duran became a fan favorite for his ferocious brawling style. He is generally considered one of the greatest lightweights of all time, with a record of 62-1 in that weight division. The Panamanian native followed his illustrious lightweight career by winning titles in three more weight classes, including the middleweight championship in 1989—more than 20 years after his professional debut. Duran fought in some of the biggest fights of the 1980s and gained perhaps his greatest victory when he bested Leonard in Montreal in 1980 to win the welterweight title. His enduring popularity allowed him to keep fighting until 2001, when he retired as only one of two fighters to have boxed in five different decades.

6. SUGAR RAY LEONARD (1977-97). Flashing his fighting skills and ebullient personality at the 1976 Montreal Olympics, Leonard captured the light welterweight gold medal, the admiration of the country, and the attention of influential TV commentator Howard Cosell. With Leonard tabbed by ABC Sports President Roone Arledge as a rising star and potential heir to Muhammad Ali as boxing's biggest attraction, the network broadcast his professional debut in 1977. He would go on to win the welterweight title in 1979 and serve as the centerpiece of the biggest fights of the 1980s—in bouts against Roberto Duran, Tommy Hearns and Marvin Hagler. Leonard came out of one of his several retirements in 1987 to defeat Hagler, the reigning middleweight champion, and would eventually retire with a record of 36-3-1 with 25 knockouts, having won world championships in five different weight classes and earning more than $100 million.

5. JULIO CÉSAR CHAVEZ (1980-2005). A Mexican fighting legend during his 25-year career and six-time world champion in three weight divisions, Chavez established a reputation as a brutal puncher and engaged in some of the biggest bouts of his era. His 1990 epic win over Meldrick Taylor is considered the "Fight of the Decade" for the 1990s. He would draw more than 130,000 fans in 1993 for his fifth-round knockout of Greg Haugen in Mexico City and nearly 60,000 for his controversial draw with Pernell Whitaker at the Alamodome in San Antonio.

4. JACK DEMPSEY (1914-27). Dempsey belongs in a class with Babe Ruth, Red Grange, Bobby Jones and Bill Tilden as one of the American sports heroes responsible for the onset of the "Golden Era of Sports" in the 1920s. Dempsey was heavyweight champion from 1919 to 1926. With punching power and an aggressive style making him a fan favorite, his fights established new attendance standards. His bout against Georges Carpentier in 1921 in Jersey City drew 91,000 fans to earn the first million-dollar gate. Two years later at New York's Polo Grounds, an estimated 85,000 fans watched Dempsey get knocked through the ropes by Luis Firpo, then saw Dempsey climb back into the ring to knock out Firpo. Dempsey lost his title to Gene Tunney in 1926 in Philadelphia before a reported 120,557 fans—one of the largest crowds ever to attend a sporting event.

3. Benny Leonard (1911-24; 1931-32). Lightweight great Benny Leonard carried the banner for the whole of the Jewish community, his excellence of achievement stirring a profound pride amongst his fellow Jews, his every triumph theirs. As Budd Schulberg remembered: "The Great Benny Leonard," with emphasis on the word "Great," Leonard was "our champ who was doing with his fists what the Adolph Zukors and William Foxes were doing in their studios and in their theatres . . . fighting the united efforts of the goyim to keep them in their ghettos." Throughout his eight-year reign as lightweight champion, from 1917 to 1925, all of New York flocked to see his fights—Leonard headlining the first card at the new Madison Square Garden and the first championship fight at the new Yankee Stadium. When he retired, Major Jimmy Walker, speaking for all New Yorkers, said of Leonard, "He left the ring finer and better than he found it."

2. Joe Louis (1934-42; 1946-48; 1950-51). Joe Louis was accorded a special place in the hearts of boxing fans for his annihilation of Max Schmeling in 1938, setting back the cause of the so-called Master Race and bringing joy to millions of Americans, both black and white. But to call Joe Louis just a fighter is not to understand the times. Nor the man. For no heavyweight champion so captured the fancy of the public, fan and non-fan alike, as this son of an Alabama sharecropper who wore his crown with dignity and bore the hopes of millions on his shoulders.

1. Muhammad Ali (1960-81). The most popular fighter and perhaps the most popular athlete to walk the planet, Ali's fame spread from his Olympic gold medal victory in Rome in 1960—when he was known by his given name of Cassius Clay—to his stunning upset of fearsome heavyweight champion Sonny Liston in 1964. He fell out of favor with many after that fight when he changed his name to Muhammad Ali and joined the Nation of Islam. He became a pariah when he refused to be drafted during the Vietnam War and was stripped of his title and exiled from boxing from 1967 to 1970. But with his return and subsequent trilogy against Joe Frazier and historic win over George Foreman in Zaire in 1974 to regain the heavyweight title Ali became celebrated worldwide.

MOST MENACING NICKNAMES

While some fighters' nicknames, like those of Willie "The Worm" Monroe and Bobby "Boogaloo" Watts, hardly inspire fear, others can make some opponents all eye-twitchy and wondering, "What the hell am I doing getting into the ring with him?" Here are ten of the most menacing nicknames to come down boxing's long pike.

10. "THE CALIFORNIA GRIZZLY BEAR" (JIM JEFFRIES). Heavy-pawed Jeffries imposed early hibernation on the notable likes of Bob Fitzsimmons and Gentleman Jim Corbett while defending his world heavyweight title from 1899-1904.

9. "VIOLENT" (ELMER RAY). Heavyweight contender Elmer "Violent" Ray fought from 1935-49, delivering a knockout portion of his nickname to 70 opponents. He won 51 "Battle Royales"—brutal all-against-all fights in which ten men enter the ring and fight until only one is left standing. "Violent" was the one left standing in 51 of them. Even heavyweight champ Joe Louis wanted no part of Elmer Ray.

8. "THE BLACK TERROR" (BILL RICHMOND). A bareknuckle fighter from 1804-15, Richmond gave nightmares to numerous opponents between 152 and 168 pounds.

"THE BLACK TERROR"

7. "THE MICHIGAN WILDCAT" (AD WOLGAST). Lightweight champion from 1910-12, Wolgast mauled rival Battling Nelson so badly in their 1910 rematch that the referee stopped the fight when the near-blinded Nelson took up his fighting stance facing a ring post. (Ace Hudkins, who fought lightweight to light heavyweight from 1924-32, was known as "The Nebraska Wildcat.")

6. "THE BROCKTON BLOCKBUSTER" (ROCKY MARCIANO). During his all-winning, 49-fight career that culminated with a heavyweight championship reign from 1952-55, Marciano knocked the blocks off 43 opponents, including greats Joe Louis, Jersey Joe Walcott, Archie Moore and Ezzard Charles.

5. "HATCHETMAN" (CURTIS SHEPARD). A heavyweight contender from 1938-49, Shephard chopped down 32 foes—including future light heavyweight champion Joey Maxim in the first round of their 1943 bout for the only KO loss in Maxim's 115-fight career.

4. "HOMICIDE HANK" (HENRY ARMSTRONG). Armstrong, who held the featherweight, lightweight and welterweight belts in 1938, put 97 foes six feet under for a ten count.

3. "THE BEAST" (JOHN MUGABI). Junior middleweight champion from 1989-90, Mugabi stampeded 39 KO victims in his 42 winning fights.

2. "THE BARBADOS DEMON" (JOE WALCOTT). The original Joe Walcott sent 59 opponents to hell for a ten-count and reigned as world welterweight champion from 1901-04 and again in 1906.

1. "THE MICHIGAN ASSASSIN" (STANLEY KETCHEL). The future middleweight champion ran away from his Michigan home at the age of 12 and made his living in Montana as a bouncer and traveling bareknuckle fighter while still a teenager. All but three of his 53 wins in official fights came by knockout. (Paul Berlenbach, light heavyweight champion from 1925-26, was known as the "Astoria Assassin" and Larry Holmes, heavyweight champion from 1978-85, was called "The Easton Assassin.")

MOST INTIMIDATING FIGHTERS

It takes more than a nasty nickname and an impressive pre-fight glare to intimidate most fighters. The most intimidating boxers possess a certain mysterious and frightening quality arising from a combination of characteristics that no one can quite put his finger on, but their very presence in the ring left their opponents shuddering from their hair gel to their shoe bottoms. Almost every fighter tries to be intimidating, but these ten succeeded in the worst way.

10. BOB FOSTER (1961-78). This long, angular light heavyweight was so intimidating that he had to take on heavyweights, no light heavyweight wanting a piece of him. It took him eight years until he could get a shot at the light heavy title—and then only after his managerial team agreed to fight for no purse.

9 RON LYLE (1971-95). The sinister-looking Lyle had, by his own admission, been "to hell and back," having spent seven-and-a-half years for second-degree murder at the Colorado State Penitentiary where, during a prison fight, he was pronounced dead on the operating table. His take-no-prisoner eyes and wicked-looking Fu Manchu beard gave him the appearance of an otherworldly creature whose face could be seen pressed against the window on Halloween.

8. MARVELOUS MARVIN HAGLER (1973-87). His shaven head and championship scowl made Marvin Hagler more menacing than "Marvelous." George Foreman once said that Hagler looked like a "double-hard bastard."

7. ROBERTO DURAN (1968-2001). Any fighter with a nickname as fearsome as "Hands of Stone" is going to intimidate some opponents. Add to that a death-defying stare and a total distain for the rules of the ring and this personification of *machismo* was one scary hombre to almost everyone he faced.

6. ELMER "VIOLENT "RAY (1935-49). Anyone nicknamed "Violent" would tend to be intimidating by virtue of their name alone. But combined with the nickname Elmer Ray had a résumé that would back up his inclusion on any list of intimidating fighters. For not only had he participated in those brutal all-against-all fights called "Battle Royals," winning 51 of them by KOing his other nine opponents—once with one hand tied behind his back—but he also participated in another sport few would ever dare, alligator wrestling. With a record of 86 wins, 70 of those by KO, and 50 of those wins coming in consecutive bouts, it was little wonder that Ray was so intimidating that several of the top heavyweights of his day, including Tami Mauriello and Arturo Godoy sidestepped him and Joe Louis wanted no part of him in exhibition matches.

5. JOE LOUIS (1934-42; 1946-48; 1950-51). The devastating punching, cold, distant stare and mere presence of "The Brown Bomber" left several of Louis' opponents looking for the first train going south even before the opening bell had sounded. For references, see King Levinsky—the 23rd consecutive victim at the beginning of Louis' career; he had to be pushed out of his corner at the opening bell, literally shaking in his boots.

4. MIKE TYSON (1985-2005). Tyson's fearsome aura began early in his career with a reign of terror as he knocked out opponent-after-opponent in brutal and devastating fashion. He fueled that aura with his stark appearance as he entered the ring, no socks, no robe and merely a sweatshirt with the neck cut open, all the better to scare the bejezus out of his opponents. And his reputation as "The Baddest Man on the Planet" grew with each devastation and bizarre act, with Tyson sneering at his opponents and putting the fear of Tyson in them—one of his victims, Bruce Seldon, so frightened he fell from the first Tyson near-miss.

3. STANLEY KETCHEL (1903-10). Ketchel came by his nickname "The Michigan Assassin" honestly, coldcocking 50 of his 66 opponents. What would have been a straight smile on a face belonging to a normal human became instead an off-centered sneer on Ketchel's face, which—when accompanied by the guttural sound he made with every punch he threw—gave him a Renfield-esque quality. With hate in his heart and murder in his eyes, Ketchel fought every fight with a "trespassers-will-be-prosecuted" mentality, intimidating the best, and the worst, of them.

2. JACK DEMPSEY (1914-27). Teeth bared, swarthy face with a perpetual five-o'clock shadow bearing in on his opponents, Jack Dempsey fought with an animal instinct, an inner fury, and a lust for battle, some 60 of his opponents, including those he fought in exhibitions, never hearing the bell ending the first round. And in those pre-"go-to-a-neutral-corner" days, he would stand over those he floored like an avenging angel of death, ready to beat them down to the floor once again when they arose. Small wonder Harry Greb, arguably the greatest middleweight of all time, said, "I'd like to fight Dempsey, but only for six rounds. After that, he'd kill me." Many of Dempsey's opponents went into the ring fearing the same thing.

1. SONNY LISTON (1953-70). Sonny Liston practically made a science out of initiating fear in the hearts and minds of his opponents. Entering the ring wearing a floppy hood, staring out from under it like some character from the Netherworld, Liston's searing eyes cast a laser-like look that could cause his opponents to curl up like a burnt piece of toast. In short, Sonny Liston was the meanest "Muthah" on the boxing block and wanted everyone to know it.

MOST FRAGILE CHINS

As the actor Ian Holt, playing the role of track coach Sam Massabini in the movie "Chariots of Fire," said, "You can't put in what God has left out." And that truism is as true in boxing as it is in track, maybe even more so when it comes to chins. For a good chin—or, as it is called in the trade, a "beard"—is something no trainer, no matter how gifted, can teach. Throughout boxing history many's the fighter, both the talented and untalented, who has possessed a "glass chin," one which has proved to be their undoing. Here are but a few of those whose opponents were in constant danger of being hit by flying glass.

10. ROMEO ANAYA (1967-80). The WBC bantamweight champion for less than three months during 1973, Anaya holds the record for being knocked out more times (14) than any other boxing champion in history.

9. JOE BECKETT (1912-23). A British heavyweight titlist, Beckett was a straight stand-up fighter, or, according to write-ups of the time, "a man who had the disinclination to stand erect." Winner of 17 fights (13 by knockout), Beckett was also the designated hittee no less than seven times.

8. TIPPY LARKIN (1935-52). While the 1940s junior welterweight champ had a reputation for being a clever ring general, winning 137 fights, he also had a reputation for fragility, acknowledging it later by saying, "I was virtually unbeaten as a boxer. I beat the best boxers, but I had trouble, a poor chin. I could do all in a ring but take a punch." It was something he exhibited by being knocked out 10 times, three times having to be carried to his corner after being KO'd by Lew Jenkins, Henry Armstrong, and Beau Jack. Even in fights he won, like his fight against Willie Joyce, he was knocked down three times.

7. FRANK BRUNO (1982-96). Bruno was a powerful-looking heavyweight with something less than a powerful chin. As sportswriter Jim Murray described him: "Frank Bruno has a chin of Waterford crystal. It gives rise to the old adage that people who live in glass jaws shouldn't throw punches."

6. BOMBARDIER BILLY WELLS (1910-25). The British Empire heavyweight champion and first holder of the Lonsdale belt, Wells was knocked out 11 times, one of his conquerors, Frank Moran, saying, "Billy Wells was all chin from the waist up."

5. BOB SATTERFIELD (1945-57). Boxing's high-wire act, Satterfield was a hard-hitting heavy who either knocked out his opponent or was knocked out himself, losing 13 fights by KO.

4. JULIUS FRANCIS (1993-2006). Called "the well-respected professional punch-bag" by one British journalist, Francis was so little thought of that one newspaper had their logo emblazoned on the soles of his shoes for his fight against Mike Tyson and got their money's worth, with Francis going down five times in a fight that lasted just over four minutes.

3. FLOYD PATTERSON (1952-72). Although he won 55 fights and twice held the heavyweight title, Patterson is best remembered for having been one with the canvas no less than 13 times in heavyweight championship fights.

2. PHIL SCOTT (1919-31). A British heavyweight who was knocked out so many times he became a punchline, inspiring the nickname "Phainting Phil" and one writer to observe, "Scott kept collapsing whether hit fair or foul." Scott's favorite tactic was to leap into the air to ensure that an opponent's body blows landed below the beltline, then, in an over-the-top injury exaggeration, flop onto the floor in his best soccer-foul imitation, grabbing his groin, and writhing in mock pain until the referee ruled he had "won" on a foul—something which occurred no less than six times, thanks to his theatrics.

1. SYLVESTER WILDER (1971-81). This Ohio heavyweight set the all-time Guinness record for being knocked out: 29 times in his 50-bout career.

FIGHTERS WITH THE MOST "HEART"

Call it heart, call it toughness, call it whatever you want. Just know that it's the singular quality that distinguishes those fighters with the ability to dig deep and overcome anything. Over the course of boxing history there have been some boxers with enough heart to jump-start the Tin Man, fierce in their determination to win at any cost. Here are those who have shown the most heart down through the years.

12. JUAN MANUEL MARQUEZ (1993-2009). The quintessential Mexican warrior, Juan Manuel Marquez, copying the words from a once-popular song, could "Pick himself up, dust himself off, and start all over again," as he did in the first fight with Manny Pacquiao. Knocked down three times in the first round, Marquez picked himself up, dusted himself off, and came back to fight to a draw many believed he won. In his fight against Juan Diaz, Marquez sustained an early beating from the "Baby Bull," but like a true warrior held his ground and came back to knock Diaz out.

11. JAKE LaMOTTA (1941-54). The man nicknamed "The Bronx Bull" was more than that; he was a fighter with the heart of a thoroughbred trapped inside the body of a mule. And he fought like all three, challenging anyone to knock him off his pins. In the 1951 fight known as "The St. Valentine's Day Massacre" in which LaMotta lost his middleweight title to Sugar Ray Robinson, he withstood Robinson's murderous assault. As he sagged against the ropes, one could almost hear the sound of metal fatigue. But in a scene made famous by the movie *Raging Bull*, Jake still had the pride and heart to shout at his tormentor: "You never knocked me down, Ray."

10. BATTLING NELSON (1896-1917). Jack London called Battling Nelson, "The Abysmal Brute," and the fighter simply known to most as "Bat" held the same position in boxing as the Piltdown Man once did in anthropology—a genetic link, spanning two boxing worlds, the world of the rough-and-tumble and the more civilized world of modern boxing. With a skull three times as thick as the normal cranium, Nelson could absorb enormous amounts of punishment, always coming in and willing to take two or three or four or whatever was needed to land one club-like punch to any exposed area he could find. "The Durable Dane" once suffered a broken arm in the middle of a 15-rounder and later begrudgingly said, "It made me somewhat cautious and kept me from winning by a knockout."

9. BARNEY ROSS (1929-38). Ross fought with a resolution unseen since the early days of boxing, showing no fear of any man. His bona fides were many as he met every fighter worth his mouthpiece during his ten-year career. But perhaps the greatest testimony to his toughness and heart came in his last fight ever. Hopelessly beaten, his reflexes as dead as his chances, he was begged by his cornermen to quit, to let them thrown in the sponge. His reply was that of a true champion, "I won my title in the ring and I'll lose it there . . . I won't quit!"

8. HARRY GREB (1913–26). The 1920s middleweight champion known as "the Pittsburgh Windmill" would walk through minefields to get at his opponents, his face often bearing witness to his having sustained a destructive fusillade of blows, giving him the look of a loser in a razor fight. Still Greb lost only eight of his recorded 294 bouts, a feat made even more unbelievable by the fact that when he died on the operating table at the age of 33 it was discovered he had fought the last part of his career with sight in only one eye.

7. EVANDER HOLYFIELD (1984–). Evander could no more be discouraged than ice welded or steel melted. Driven by that ramrod certainty that comes from knowing you are capable of triumphing over anything and everything through sheer determination, he fought on, no matter the odds or the circumstances. In the tenth round of his first fight with Riddick Bowe, Holyfield came back from a beatdown that had referee Joe Cortez perilously close to stopping the fight, staggering the much-heavier Bowe by round's end.

EVANDER HOLYFIELD

6. ROCKY MARCIANO (1947-56). No fighter was ever more aptly nicknamed "The Rock" than Rocky Marciano, as indestructible as any in history. Marciano would walk into—and through—thousands of hard, clean, jolting shots in the manner of a human steamroller to get at his opponent. In the first fight against Jersey Joe Walcott Marciano took everything Walcott threw—including being knocked down in the first round and jumping up at the count of four "because I was more mad at myself than hurt"—and coming back and coming back, proving that not only did he have the chin of granite but a boxing heart to match.

5. MICKEY WALKER (1919-35). "The Toy Bulldog" feared no man. He would fight anyone, anywhere, anytime. His fistic ambitions knowing no weight bounds, Walker alternately fought light heavyweight and heavyweight bouts while defending his two titles, welterweight and middleweight, in his spare time. Giving away height, weight and reach, the bulldog-tough Walker met them all, beating top-notchers like Paolino Uzcudun and Johnny Risko and fighting a draw with future heavyweight champion Jack Sharkey. His campaign amongst the heavyweights finally came a cropper against Max Schmeling, who battered him unmercifully. But when his manager, Doc Kearns, signaled for the referee to stop the fight after the eighth round, saying, "I guess this was one we couldn't win," Walker, spitting blood, snarled, "Speak for yourself. . . . You were the one who threw in the sponge, not me."

4. AND 3. JOE JEANNETTE (1904-22) AND SAM McVEY (1902-21). It's well-nigh impossible to separate these two members of the black "Murderer's Row" of the first two decades of the 20th century who fought on the other side of "the color line," and fought one another innumerable times because they were denied fights with white fighters. In one of the greatest and goriest fights in the storied history of great fights, Jeannette and McVey met in a "fight to the finish" in 1909, with McVey knocking down Jeannette 27 times and Jeannette returning the favor by knocking down McVey 11 times. Jeannette finally won when McVey retired in his corner after 49 rounds, his right eye closed and his left reduced to a slit. That's heart with a capital "H."

2. ARTURO GATTI (1991-2007). Gatti was always able to come back from the edge of disaster in the ring, fighting all the harder when hurt. His face a magnet for every punch thrown by his foes, his body a human punching bag, Gatti would always dig deep no matter what and go back on the attack with blows of fire-inducing ferocity.

1. CARMEN BASILIO (1948-61). Carmen Basilio had enough heart to kick-start the tin man—and add the strawman and the cowardly lion as well. A true warrior, he wore all his marks like a Heidelberg dueling academy graduate, his face bearing more stitches than a baseball. When Ray Robinson sneered at him during the pre-fight instructions before their first fight to scare him, Basilio just laughed, just as he laughed at every challenge and punch thrown his way, determined as he was to get at his opponents with dogged, indomitable courage.

BEST LINES DURING FIGHTS

Delivered in the heat of a battle with so many other things to focus on, great lines improvised by fighters, cornermen and journalists during big fights may rate as the most impressive rhetorical feat in all of boxing. Here are ten of the best.

"IF YOU HIT ME AGAIN AND I FIND OUT ABOUT IT, YOU'RE IN BIG TROUBLE." Heavyweight champion John L. Sullivan, to one of his outclassed opponents.

"WHO DO?" Former heavyweight champ Joe Louis, serving as a TV commentator, after his co-announcer said that one of the fighters didn't like punches to the body.

"IT'S ALRIGHT, HE'S NOT GOING TO BE COMING AROUND HERE AGAIN." Fighter Sam Langford, to his opponent's corner after hearing them shouting out instructions.

"YEAH, AND YOU'RE DEALING WITH A BETTER CLASS OF PEOPLE, TOO." Sportswriter Eddie Schuyler, at ringside for fights at the Marion, Ohio Correctional Institute, to fellow writer Red Smith, after Smith said to him, "Gee, I feel safer here than I did at Yankee Stadium," where Smith had his pocket picked during the Muhammad Ali-Ken Norton III fight.

"YOU'RE BLOWING IT, SON." Angelo Dundee, to Sugar Ray Leonard in the corner before the 13th round of the first Leonard-Tommy Hearns fight, in which Leonard rallied to knock out Hearns in the 14th.

"DOWN GOES FRAZIER. . . . DOWN GOES FRAZIER." TV announcer Howard Cosell, broadcasting the George Forman-Joe Frazier bout in Kingston, Jamaica, after Frazier went down for one of six times.

"YEAH, BUT HE DOESN'T SEEM TO KNOW WHAT TO DO WITH IT." Sportswriter Heywood Broun, at ringside for the Max Baer-Primo Carnera fight, to fellow sportswriter Grantland Rice, after Rice said, "The big guy (Carnera) can sure take it."

"HOW MANY GUESSES DO I GET?" Heavyweight Chuck Wepner, after being knocked down and asked by the referee how many fingers he was holding up.

"YOU'RE WHITE, HELP ME!" Randy "Tex" Cobb, to referee Steve Crosson, during his fight against heavyweight champion Larry Holmes.

"TELL YOUR GOD, HE'S IN THE WRONG HOUSE TONIGHT." Joe Frazier, in "The Fight," the first of his three bouts against Muhammad Ali, after Ali told him, "God says you're going to lose tonight."

BOXING'S MOST TWO-SIDED FIGHTS

Philosophers, diplomats and folk singers may urge us to consider both sides of a dispute or question. But boxing matches are often relatively one-sided affairs. Not these dozen, which featured great drama and back-and-forth action, with both fighters gaining the upper hand and the winner remaining in question to the end.

12. MATTHEW SAAD MUHAMMAD VS. MARVIN JOHNSON II, APRIL 22, 1979. Both fighters played big parts in the golden age of light heavyweights of the late 1970s and early 1980s. A fan favorite due to his aggressive style and ability to take punishment, Saad Muhammad (when he was still known as Matthew Franklin) knocked out Johnson in the 12th round of their first fight in 1977. But Johnson came back to win the World Boxing Council light heavyweight crown from Mate Parlov the next year, then looked to gain revenge against Saad Muhammad in a rematch the following spring. Like many of Saad Muhammad's fights, this was an all-out ring war. The challenger was beaten and bleeding and almost blinded from cuts above both eyes when he knocked Johnson out in the eighth round to win the championship.

11. BOBBY CHACON VS. CORNELIUS BOZA-EDWARDS II, MAY 15, 1983. These two super featherweights engaged in two memorable contests, but the second one in particular stands out. Boza-Edwards defeated Chacon for the World Boxing Council's super featherweight crown in 1981, stopping him in the 14th round. In their 1983 rematch, Chacon—bloody and seemingly beaten—came back to win a hard-fought decision despite many ringside commentators calling for the bout to be stopped earlier to keep Chacon from taking so much punishment.

10. LARRY HOLMES VS. KEN NORTON, JUNE 9, 1978. Larry Holmes was best known as Muhammad Ali's sparring partner until he emerged as a heavyweight contender with a win over Earnie Shavers in March 1978. Three months later, Holmes faced Ken Norton, the man who had once beaten Ali. Norton had been declared World Boxing Council heavyweight champion after Leon Spinks had chosen to fight a rematch with Ali instead of facing a mandatory challenge against top-contender Norton. His first defense came against Holmes at Caesars Palace in Las Vegas. Days before the fight, rumors emerged that Holmes had suffered a torn left tricep muscle in workouts. But Holmes was sharp with his left jab right from the start of activity and dominated the early rounds. Norton came back in round eight with a series of head and body blows that hurt Holmes. The two engaged in tremendous back-and-forth exchanges for much of the rest of the fight. They put on a show in the 15th round—considered by many to be one of the greatest final rounds in heavyweight history—slugging away until Holmes got the better of Norton to win the round and the title on a split decision.

9. ALEXIS ARGUELLO VS. ALFREDO ESCALERA I, JANUARY 28, 1978. A Puerto Rican boxing legend, Escalera was the reigning World Boxing Council featherweight champion, successfully defending his title ten times before facing hard-punching rising star Alexis Arguello in a classic brawl in Bayamon, Puerto Rico that came to be called "The Bloody Battle of Bayamon." The two fighters traded blows for 13 rounds until Escalera, with a broken nose and cuts above his eyes, was stopped by Arguello. They met again in a 1979 rematch and Escalera built up a lead on the judges' scorecards for 12 rounds before being knocked out by Arguello in the 13th round.

8. GEORGE FOREMAN VS. RON LYLE, JANUARY 24, 1976. The great sportswriter Red Smith called this 1976 Caesars Palace brawl "the most two-sided battle of heavyweights in recent memory." It was Foreman's first fight since losing the heavyweight title to Muhammad Ali. Lyle had come out of a Colorado state prison to establish himself as one of the hardest punchers in the division, knocking out another claimant to that title, Earnie Shavers, the previous year. Lyle showed his power early in the first round when he rocked Foreman, but Foreman came back to return the favor, rocking Lyle and winning the next two rounds. Then came the epic fourth in which Lyle sent Foreman to the canvas with a right hand. But Foreman got up and landed his own right that knocked Lyle under the ropes. Lyle came back with a combination that put Foreman down again, and he might have been counted out save for the bell. The two brawlers came out punching in the fifth round, with Foreman landing a left hook that sent Lyle's mouthpiece flying. Big George followed with a barrage of blows in the corner and Lyle pitched forward on his face to end the mayhem at 2:28 of the fifth.

7. MICKY WARD VS. ARTURO GATTI I, MAY 18, 2002. Ward was a tough veteran junior welterweight who labored in relative obscurity for much of his career until he faced fan favorite Arturo Gatti in an epic battle in Atlantic City. Neither man held a title at that point, but both fought as if they were battling for the greatest-fight-in-history title. The style of both fighters—straight ahead and take a punch to deliver one—proved a recipe for a thrilling brawl. Ward was known for his brutal left hook and he put Gatti down with a shot to the body in the ninth round, going on to win a majority decision. They met two more times over their careers, and both fights were nearly as dramatic with Gatti prevailing in both.

6. DIEGO CORRALES VS. JOSÉ LUIS CASTILLO I, MAY 7, 2005. Corrales, the World Boxing Organization lightweight champion, met Castillo, the World Boxing Council titleholder, for what proved to be *The Ring* magazine's "Fight of the Year." Corrales and Castillo stood right in front of each other, trading blows at a remarkable pace until Castillo knocked Corrales down twice in the 10th round. But each time he was knocked down Corrales spat out his mouthpiece and beat the extended count. Then he came back with a right hand shot that stunned Castillo. He backed Castillo against the ropes with a vicious attack that resulted in a 10th round TKO. They would meet six months later in a rematch that Castillo won on a fourth-round knockout, with a third fight cancelled when Castillo failed to make weight.

4. AND 5. CARMEN BASILIO VS. TONY DEMARCO I AND II, JUNE 10, 1955 AND NOVEMBER 30, 1955.

These two welterweights met in two historic battles, both of which deserve spots on any list of the greatest two-sided fights in history. Basilio won the first bout and the welterweight belt with a 12th-round technical knockout. Their rematch was considered one of the greatest fights that DeMarco's hometown of Boston had ever hosted. DeMarco dominated the fight from the opening bell, but was cut above the eye in round two, the result of a head butt—the same round in which Basilio broke his left hand. DeMarco kept coming and appeared to be on the brink of victory in the seventh round when he staggered Basilio with a left hook. But Basilio managed to keep his feet despite staggering around the ring in a bandy-legged impression of Leon Errol. Basillio came back to gain the upper hand and then in the 12th landed a series of devastating combinations that put DeMarco down twice to end this classic Pier Sixer at 1:54 of the round, only two seconds longer than it had taken Basillio to win their first brawl.

3. MUHAMMAD ALI VS. JOE FRAZIER III, OCTOBER 1, 1975.

Hyped as "The Thrilla in Manila," the third fight in the Ali-Frazier trilogy proved to be their most dramatic and brutal. In the searing Philippine heat, Ali dominated the early rounds but Frazier turned the tide in the middle rounds, banging on Ali's body and keeping up a frenzied pace that seemed to wear Ali down. Frazier finally began to slow down in the 11th round when Ali found a reserve of energy, landing a series of hard combinations that caused Frazier's face to swell. By the 14th, Frazier's right eye was virtually swollen shut and he could no longer see Ali's punches coming. Before the start of the 15th, Frazier's trainer Eddie Futch stopped the fight over Frazier's protests, refusing to let his fighter take more of a beating. Ali collapsed in his corner, raising questions over whether he would have been too exhausted to come out for the final round. It was an epic finale to one of the greatest rivalries in all of sports—a fight Ali later called, "The closest thing to death."

2. MARVELOUS MARVIN HAGLER VS. TOMMY HEARNS, APRIL 15, 1985.

While most Americans were home practicing do-it-yourself muggings by filing their income taxes, two men entered the ring at Caesars Palace to mug each other in an all-out war. In one corner was the defending middleweight champion Marvelous Marvin Hagler, undefeated in nine years and defending his title for the 11th time. In the other stood challenger Tommy Hearns, who, after losing to Sugar Ray Leonard four years before, had won eight fights since and now had a 41-1 record with 34 KO's. But while most pundits had predicted that if there was going to be a knockout, it would most likely be by Hearns, Hagler had other ideas, determined to "cut Tommy

Hearns down like a tree." Racing from his corner at the bell, Hagler threw a lethal right in the direction of Hearns, who ducked under it. Within seconds Hagler had forced Hearns into the ropes, but it was Hearns who was having the better of it, landing 10 booming right hands, one of which cut Hagler's forehead and momentarily stunned him. But Hagler took a step backward and came in again, fists flying as the two practiced rock-'em-sock-'em target practice on each other for the rest of the round. At the end of the furious first, Hearns felt his legs begin to betray him, feeling, as he later said, "the first round took everything I had." After a much-slower second, with Hearns trying to box and stay away from the pursuing Hagler, the third opened with Hagler switching to right-handed and again bombarding the retreating Hearns. Suddenly referee Richard Steele stepped between the two and escorted Hagler to the corner to inspect his bleeding forehead. When asked if he "could see," Hagler replied, "I'm hitting him, aren't I?" The doctor wiped off the cut and waved at Steele to let the action continue. And within seconds Hagler connected with a hard right, driving the rubbery-legged Hearns half across the ring, then with another equally hard right, dropping him to the canvas. And even though Hearns struggled to his feet at the count of nine, referee Steele wrapped his arms around the wounded Hearns, ending the brawl at 2:31 of the third round, eight minutes-plus of war.

1. JACK DEMPSEY VS. LUIS "ANGEL" FIRPO, SEPTEMBER 14, 1923. The legendary American heavyweight champion known as "The Manassa Mauler" went up against an Argentine challenger dubbed "The Wild Bull of the Pampas" in a brawl in which they lived up to their nicknames. Each knocked down the other with their first punch, with Dempsey going on to put Firpo on the floor a remarkable seven times in the first round. But Firpo kept getting up, and later in the round, pinned Dempsey against the ropes and landed a combination of hard blows that sent Dempsey flying out of the ring and onto a press table where Dempsey hit his head on a typewriter. Dempsey appeared on his way to being counted out, but climbed back into the ring at the referee's count of nine despite nearly 20 seconds elapsing since he went down and out of the ring. (Sportswriter Bugs Bair was to write: "If the Dempsey-Firpo fight had been held on a barge, Firpo would have been champion because Dempsey would have drowned.") Dempsey survived the round and went on to knock out Firpo in the second to put an end to their brief but legendary bout.

MOST FAMOUS DRAWS IN BOXING HISTORY

A draw, to paraphrase a line from football's Duffy Daugherty, is like kissing your sister. Of course, to some fighters—fighting out of town against a local favorite—a draw is the equivalent of a win. Only it's not quite the same thing. Throughout the course of boxing history almost every fighter has had one "D" on his record, whether earned or not. Here are some of the most famous ones.

11-10. ABE ATTELL VS. OWEN MORAN I & II, JANUARY 1 AND SEPTEMBER 7, 1908. Featherweight champion Attell and challenger Moran battled to a 25-round draw on New Year's Day of 1908. San Francisco promoter Jim Coffroth, anxious for a "do-over," signed them to fight nine months later, but added one promotional fillup: he scheduled the rematch for 23 rounds. And wouldn't you know it? The two fought to another, albeit two rounds shorter, draw in the rematch.

9. GENE FULLMER VS. JOEY GIARDELLO, APRIL 20, 1960. Middleweight belt holder Fullmer and challenger Giardello spilled a lot of blood, most of it bad, as a result of head butts and punches. After 15 brutal rounds, the judges ruled that the two battering rams had fought to a draw.

8. TOM SAYERS VS. JOHN C. HEENAN, APRIL 17, 1860. In the first international boxing match between American and British champions, the two battled to a 42-round "draw," with police finally storming the ring to save the two exhausted and half-blinded fighters.

7. JACK JOHNSON VS. BATTLING JIM JOHNSON, DECEMBER 19, 1913. Convicted of violating the Mann Act (for "immoral" behavior), heavyweight champion Jack Johnson fled the United States and chose to defend his title in Paris against Battling Jim Johnson in the first world heavyweight title bout between two African-Americans. The fight was ruled a "Draw" in the 10th round after champion Johnson broke his arm, an injury that would have cost him his crown under U.S. rules back then.

6. MARVIN HAGLER VS. VITO ANTUOFERMO, NOVEMBER 30, 1979. Not yet called "Marvelous," Hagler was marvelous in every respect against middleweight champion Antuofermo. Except in the eyes of the judges in Vegas, where the one-eyed man is king. Hagler didn't get the decision.

5. SUGAR RAY LEONARD VS. TOMMY HEARNS II, JUNE 12, 1989. Eight years after their classic first fight, Leonard and Hearns got it on again in a bout hyped simply as "The War." And it was, with Hearns knocking down Leonard twice—in the third and 11th rounds. Needing a KO to win, Leonard came on in the 12th and final round to rake Hearns with punch-after-punch, getting a rare 10-8 round without a knockdown on one judge's scorecard to gain a draw. Leonard later admitted, "Tommy won the fight."

4. LENNOX LEWIS VS. EVANDER HOLYFIELD, MARCH 13, 1999. Despite clearly outpointing Holyfield, the best Lennox Lewis could get was a draw. One judge's scorecard—that of Eugenia Williams—was so out of line with the other two judges' cards that it prompted local and state investigations of the decision.

3. PERNELL WHITAKER VS. JULIO CÉSAR CHAVEZ, SEPTEMBER 10, 1993. In the words of *Sports Illustrated* writer Bill Nack, "Pernell Whitaker put on one of the most dazzling ring performances in recent years" against Chavez, who spent 12 rounds bewildered and groping for his opponent, only to have the judges rule the fight a draw. The *Sports Illustrated* cover line was "Robbed" and *Boxing Illustrated*'s read: "If you think this fight was a draw, don't buy this issue." The next week, as Whitaker's manager, Lou Duva, walked down New York's Broadway, a beggar with sunglasses and tin cup wearing a "Blind" sign told him, "Lou, anyone could see that Whitaker won that fight."

2. JAMES J. CORBETT VS. PETER JACKSON, MAY 21, 1891. Known as "The Black Prince," Jackson had long been denied a shot at the heavyweight championship, then held by John L. Sullivan, who drew the "color line" and proclaimed, "I will not fight a Negro. I never have and never will." But future champion James J. Corbett agreed to take on Jackson in the first fight in America conducted under the Marquess of Queensberry Rules. Corbett was soon to discover, "He was shifty and fast. And I thought I was fast!" For 28 rounds, the two tried everything in their arsenals to no avail. Then, in the 29th and 30th rounds, Corbett went on the attack, but Jackson weathered the storm and from there on it was a contest of sheer endurance. Finally, after 61 rounds, the referee stepped in and called it "No Contest," ending the battle between the two exhausted greats.

1. HENRY ARMSTRONG VS. CEFERINO GARCIA, MARCH 1, 1940. Henry Armstrong had staked more claims to titles than an Alaskan claim jumper, winning the featherweight, welterweight, and lightweight titles in that order. Now he was attempting to add the middleweight belt to his already crowded beltline. But rumor had it that if Armstrong didn't knock out the reigning champion Garcia, then the 10-round bout would be called a "draw." He didn't and it was, ending Armstrong's quest to win four of the eight boxing titles then in existence.

MY FAVORITE FIGHTERS TO DRAW :: BY BILL GALLO

Note: Bill Gallo began working at the *New York Daily News* in 1941 as a copy boy, eventually becoming a popular columnist and cartoonist—jobs he continued performing for the paper into the second decade of the 21st century. During his storied career, Gallo has gained numerous honors, including the James J. Walker Award from the Boxing Writers Association and a 1998 Lifetime Achievement Award from the National Cartoonist Society, which also gave Bill its Best Sports Cartoon of the Year Award ten times. A 2001 inductee into the International Boxing Hall of Fame, Gallo has appeared as a guest on *The Charley Rose Show* and numerous other television programs. Here, Bill gives us a list of the 11 fighters who have made the sports cartoonist portion of his career the most fun.

11. JOE LOUIS.

10. ROCKY GRAZIANO.

9. JAKE LaMOTTA.

8. MAX SCHMELING.

7. FLOYD PATTERSON.

6. TONY CANZONERI.

5. CARMEN BASILIO.

4. PRIMO CARNERA.

3. MUHAMMAD ALI.

2. JACK DEMPSEY.

1. FRITZIE ZIVIC.

FRITZIE ZIVIC
HAD A FACE
LIKE AN
IRONING BOARD

FLATTEST NOSES

In days of old, boxers like Jem Walsh wore their cauliflower ears in much the same way Heidelberg dueling champions wore their scars, as badges of honor. In fact, stories had it that heavyweight Max Baer, in order to show that he was a boxer, wanted sparring partners to hit him on the ears so he could look like a champion. Today, a fighter is more identified by his flattened nose than by his cauliflower ears. Here are some of those who could appear in a police line-up and be immediately picked out as "pugs" with much more than a pug nose, but a flattened one.

10. Trainer Freddie Brown.

9. Heavyweight Randy "Tex" Cobb.

8. 1950s-era Middleweight Paddy Young.

7. 1920s Junior Welterweight Champion Mushy Callahan.

6. Bantamweight and Trainer Charley Goldman.

5. 1920s Featherweight Champion Bat Battalino.

4. 1950s Featherweight Champion Hogan "Kid" Bassey.

3. 1940s Flyweight Champion Rinty Monaghan.

2. 1980s and 90s Super Middleweight Doug DeWitt.

1. 1940s Welterweight Champion Fritzie Zivic.

TAKE-TWO-TO-GIVE-ONE FIGHTERS

Certain fighters don't have to be looked for—they're always right there in front of their opponents, ready, willing, and more than able to take anything thrown in their direction, hoping their opponents will get tired from hitting them or hurt their hands. If they were lawyers, they could plead: "The Defense Rests!" If baseball players, they would be catchers. For that is what they are, boxing's catchers, those fighters who take two (or three or four or more) punches to land one.

10. FRANKIE DEPAULA (1962-69). A barroom brawler who made every fight a fistic version of a shootout at OK Corral, Frankie DePaula would wade straight in, bobbing and weaving but open to any punch thrown by his opponent, intent on just one end: landing his own punches. In his fight against Dick Tiger, he knocked down Tiger who returned the favor. And in his title bout versus Bob Foster, he clubbed Foster to the canvas early in the first round but Foster more than evened the score with three first-round knockdowns. It was always thus with DePaula, punish or perish—the winner the one left standing.

9. RON STANDER (1969-82). Stander once said, "I'll fight any living human being and most animals if the price is right." And he did, fighting right into their strength, eating punch-after-punch, never backing down. In his fight with Earnie Shavers, Stander took a frightful beating for four rounds until Shavers, either tired or bored using Stander's head for fungo practice, collapsed in the fifth. And against Joe Frazier, in a fight his wife said was like entering "a Volkswagen in the Indianapolis 500," Stander kept coming forward, eating left hook after left hook, gallantly taking everything Frazier could throw until the fight was stopped on cuts.

8. MICKY WARD (1985-2003). A lunch-pail type of fighter, Micky Ward would stand on the inside taking any and all punishment just to land his paralyzing left hook to the body. In several of his fights he would take a licking and keep on ticking, as he did in his fights with Arturo Gatti and Emanuel Burton—three times participating in *Ring* Magazine's "Fight of the Year."

7. GENE FULLMER (1951-63). Gene Fullmer's style was no style at all, consisting of merely barreling into his opponent with his head down as if he were checking to see if his zipper were open or fulfilling a death wish to be hit. An inartistic fighter imbued with animalistic drive and guts, Fullmer would take anything his opponent had to deal out and then launch his own offensive, consisting mainly of swarming all over his opponents, giving them little or no chance to move or catch the license plate of the truck running over them.

6. TEX COBB (1977-93). Almost as if he were paying tribute to John L. Sullivan's line to an opponent—"If you hit me again and I find out about it, you're in big trouble"—Tex Cobb would stand there, his head swiveling around like Michael Keaton's in "Beetlejuice," taking dozens of punches while awaiting his turn to retaliate. Sometimes there would be a carload of them, as in his fight against Larry Holmes when, after taken almost two dozen unanswered punches, he turned to the referee and shouted, "You're white, help me!"

5. BATTLING NELSON (1896-1917). "The Bat" was more like "The Battee," his style that of a human punching bag, barreling into the wheelhouse of an opponent, ready to take three or four blows merely to land one. Studied by scientists, Nelson was found to have a skull three times the normal thickness of any skull analyzed up to his time, all the better to absorb enormous amounts of punishment.

4. GEORGE CHUVALO (1956-78). The Canadian heavyweight champion's best punch, according to writer-commentator Larry Merchant, was "a left cheek to the right glove." (see page 47) And to Muhammad Ali, Chuvalo was "one of the toughest men I ever faced." In his 93 fights against the likes of Ali, Joe Frazier and George Foreman, the granite-chinned Chuvalo was never-ever knocked down.

3. ARTURO GATTI (1991-2007). Called "The Human Highlight Reel," Arturo Gatti would be blasted, bombarded, beaten and any other concussive word you can come up with, then miraculously come back to return the favors to his tormentor, as he did in successfully defending his super featherweight title against Wilson Rodriguez and in his four *The Ring* magazine's "Fight of the Year" bouts—his wars versus Gabriel Ruelas and Ivan Robinson, plus two of his three wars versus Micky Ward.

2. JOE GRIM (1899-1913). A turn-of-the-last-century middleweight, Grim fought anybody and everybody in his 134-fight career—from Jack Johnson and Bob Fitzsimmons to the original Joe Walcott and Philadelphia Jack O'Brien. "He was," wrote one sportswriter, "so wide open a blind man could hit him," and came by his nickname, "The Human Punching Bag" honestly, setting the less-than-revered record for most times knocked down in a fight, hitting the canvas 14 times against Jack Johnson and 20 times courtesy of Bob Fitzsimmons. And yet none of them could finish him. Nor could most of the fighters he faced, as Grim suffered only six knockouts in over 130 (and maybe as many as 300) fights. And after every fight, the proud Grim would stand mid-ring and shout, "I am Joe Grim! Nobody can knock me out!"

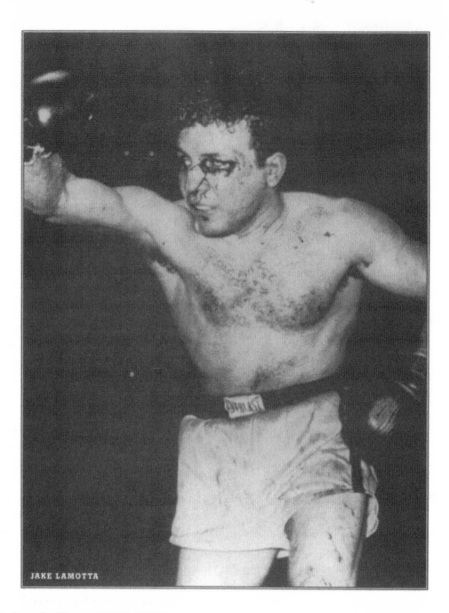

JAKE LAMOTTA

1. JAKE LaMOTTA (1941-54). "The Raging Bull" took a "knock-the-stick-off-my-shoulder" approach, challenging every opponent to knock him off his pins. Time and again, LaMotta would take furious combinations from his opponents— sometimes even playing "possum" to lure his opponent into his trap—then retaliate. Even in the face of his battering and beating by Sugar Ray Robinson in their famous "Saint Valentine's Day Massacre" fight, there was no unconditional surrender by LaMotta to undeniable facts as he absorbed Robinson's barrages like a sponge.

MOST FAMOUS ROCKYS

"Rocky" has been associated with, among other things, geographic areas (the Rocky Mountains), ice cream (Rocky Road) and cartoons (*Rocky and Bullwinkle*), while also being used as a synonym for adjectives (hard, stubborn, rigid, etc.). But it's most often associated with boxing—most specifically, with boxers' names. Here are the ten Rockys most known for the association.

10. ROBERTO "ROCKY" DURAN*. Qualified here with an asterisk (*), Duran wore a robe proclaiming himself to be "Rocky" Duran for his 1972 lightweight title-winning fight with Ken Buchanan.

9. GARY "ROCKY" RANDALL. An American lightweight of the 1950s and 60s, Randall fought 150 times, mostly in his native Southeast, once losing to Sugar Ray Robinson.

8. JUAN CARLOS "ROCKY" RIVERO. An Argentine middleweight of the early 1960s, he fought Don Fullmer, Hurricane Carter (in Carter's last fight), Florentine Fernandez (three times), Jose Gonzales (twice), and Joey Giardello (twice—once when Giardello had Rocky Graziano in his corner and Rivero had Rocky Marciano in his).

7. RICARDO "ROCKY" JUAREZ. A super featherweight best known for his two 2006 battles with Marco Antonio Barrera, the first of which was originally declared a draw, but later changed to a split-decision win for Barrera.

6. RICK "ROCKY" LOCKRIDGE. A junior welterweight champion who fought from the late 1970s to the early 90s, Lockridge won the title in 1984 by knocking out Roger Mayweather in one round. Over the course of his career, he fought many of the top-notch fighters in his weight division, including Wilfredo Gomez, Cornelius Boza-Edwards and Julio César Chavez.

5. ATTILIO "ROCKY" CASTELLANI. A ranking middleweight in the 1940s and 50s, Castellani fought and defeated many of his era's other top middleweights, including Joey Giardello, Gil Turner, Ernie Durando, Ralph "Tiger" Jones, Harold Green, and Tony Janiro.

4. ROCKY KANSAS. One of the first fighters to adopt the name "Rocky," the boxer born Rocco Tozzo won 64 fights and the lightweight title during a career spanning from 1911 to 1932.

3. ROCKY GRAZIANO. Born Thomas Rocco Barbella, Graziano was a "rock-'em-sock-'em" fighter who earned his Rocky nickname. He fought more than 80 times between 1942 and 1952, registering 52 knockouts and becoming a huge fan favorite in the early TV age of boxing. This former Dead-End kid even inspired a big Hollywood biopic, one of the best boxing movies ever, entitled *Somebody Up There Likes Me* after his famous comment following his winning the middleweight title from Tony Zale in 1947.

2. ROCKY BALBOA. Through the original Oscar-winning film *Rocky* in 1976 and five sequels, "reel-life" Rocky, Sylvester Stallone, made the name "Rocky" synonymous with the sport.

1. ROCKY MARCIANO. The man born Rocco Francis Marchegiano became known simply as "The Rock." With an all-winning record in his 49 fights—the second-most famous streak number in sports, behind only Joe DiMaggio's 56 (as in consecutive-game hitting streak)—Marciano was to his followers the only fighter worthy of the name "Rocky."

OTHER FILM HEROES I WISH I WOULD HAVE INSPIRED

:: BY CHUCK WEPNER

Note: For his first title defense after re-winning the heavyweight championship in 1974 from George Foreman, Muhammad Ali chose a journeyman named Chuck Wepner, who was better known for his nickname, "The Bayonne Bleeder," than for his fistic record of 30-9—two of those losses coming at the hands of Jerry Judge and Randy Neumann. With prefight predictions ranging from a walkover to the challenger starting to bleed somewhere between "O Say" and "Can You See?", and even magager Al Braverman saying, "The whole world's a mismatch," Wepner shocked the boxing world by putting Ali down in the ninth round. After the knockdown, Wepner went back to his corner, crowing to his manager, Al Braverman, "Get in the car . . . we're going to the bank . . . we're rich." But Braverman, who had seen Ali rise from the canvas with that "if-you-ever-dreamed-of-beating-me-you'd-better-wake-up-and-apologize" look in his eyes, hollered at Wepner, "You'd better turn around 'cause he just got up and he's pissed!" For the rest of the fight, Ali battered and bloodied Wepner, who came out of the bout with a broken nose, but a moral victory by falling just 19 seconds short of going the 15-round distance. Before the fight Wepner had bought his wife a negligee, telling her that she "would be sleeping with the champ tonight." When he returned to his hotel room after the fight, he found her sitting on the edge of the bed in her new nightie, asking, "Is Ali coming to our room or am I going to his?" Wepner's brave performance served as the inspiration for the creation of *Rocky* by Sylvester Stallone, something Stallone readily admitted. Here, Chuck comes up with a list of other movie heroes he wishes he could have served as the inspiration for, saying, "I wouldn't mind being any of these guys."

11. AL PACINO IN *HEAT*.

10. ERROL FLYNN IN *GENTLEMAN JIM*.

9-8. GARY COOPER AND BURT LANCASTER IN *VERA CRUZ*.

7. SYLVESTER STALLONE IN *RAMBO*.

6. BURT LANCASTER IN *LAWMAN*.

5. JOHN WAYNE IN *THE QUIET MAN*.

4. CLINT EASTWOOD IN *DIRTY HARRY*.

3. STEVE REEVES IN *HERCULES*.

2. CHARLES BRONSON IN *HARD TIMES*.

1. VICTOR MATURE IN *SAMSON AND DELILAH*.

TOP BOXING MOVIES

Ever since Thomas Edison staged a made-for-the-cameras fight between then-heavyweight champion James J. Corbett and Peter Courtney at his Orange, New Jersey studio back in 1894 in one of the first "moving pictures" ever made, boxing has been a movie staple. In fact, more films have been made about boxing than any other sport, because, in purely cinematic terms, it is easier to frame two people in conflict on the screen than to encompass the sometimes complex dynamics of a team game. Over the century-plus since Edison's first boxing film, the movie industry has produced some "reel" great fight films—from Buster Keaton's *The Battling Butler* (1926) to *The Champ* (1931) with Wallace Beery to *The Set-Up* (1949) with Robert Ryan. Here are our Top Ten.

10. *FAT CITY* (1972). As much a story about the lonely, empty life of the urban poor as a boxing movie, *Fat City* portrays a washed-up 31-year-old boxer, played by Stacy Keach, with limited expectations (once saying, "Before you get rollin', your life makes a beeline for the drain").Worn down by his bleak existence, he encourages a younger man, played by Jeff Bridges, to enter the fight game. Their story offers new insights on the oft-explored American theme of "second chances," as two men look to boxing as a way out of their dead-end lives.

9. *CHAMPION* (1949). Based on a story by Ring Lardner, *Champion* details the dark rise and fall of Midge Kelly (Kirk Douglas), a young, down-on-his-luck wanderer who reluctantly enters the ring to pick up some spare change and soon punches his way to the top, stepping over opponents and friends on his way while falling under mob influence. In the end, after taking a brutal beating in a championship fight, Midge hears the radio announcer say, "Kelly's through. . . . He's totally washed up. . . . We're getting a new champion tonight." Midge miraculously gets off the canvas and, turning the tide with a volley of damaging punches, knocks out the challenger. Afterwards, a delirious Midge shouts: "Those fat bellies with the big cigars aren't going to make a monkey out of me. I can beat 'em. . . . You know I can beat 'em . . . " and then collapses, dead from a brain hemorrhage.

8. *THE GREAT WHITE HOPE* (1970). This fictionalized biopic of African-American heavyweight champion Jack Johnson (called "Jack Jefferson" in the movie) captures how Johnson, unbeatable in the ring, was pursued and ultimately beaten by a racist white society and power structure outside the ring. The film hints that he was finally forced to take a dive in a fixed championship fight to a "White Hope," though history would not support the claim. Nevertheless, James Earl Jones' portrayal of Jefferson/Johnson is dazzling and powerful.

7. SOMEBODY UP THERE LIKES ME (1956). Based on the autobiography of legendary middleweight champion Rocky Graziano, the film casts Paul Newman in his breakthrough role as the young Graziano, a budding hoodlum who battles his way out of the dark streets of New York City's East Side, where, as a shop owner tells him, most of the old gang members have ended up "crippled, in prison, or dead." Graziano's journey takes him to the top of the middleweight mountain, his redemption aided by the love of his wife Norma (played by Pier Angeli). At the end of the film, Newman says to Norma, "You know I've been lucky. . . . Somebody up there likes me." Mrs. Graziano, looking out at his victory parade, answers, "Somebody down here, too."

6. GENTLEMAN JIM (1942). The gentleman of the title is Gentleman Jim Corbett, the heavyweight champion of the world in the 1890s. Errol Flynn took time off from war-winning efforts in the year following the attack on Pearl Harbor to play the suave, brash fighter. An excellent amateur boxer, Flynn turns in a great performance while showing off perhaps the best moves in boxing movie history (only Robert Ryan comes close in *The Set-Up*). The film also presents an interesting look at the colorful turn-of-the-20th-century boxing scene, with a blue-collar, boisterous Irish family of Corbett's ready to do battle (to the oft-heard shout of "The Corbett's are at it again!") with anyone who doesn't think their Jim is the greatest boxer in the world. Ward Bond does an admirable job playing John L. Sullivan, and in the final scene of the film, the once-proud brawler comes to congratulate his scientific conqueror, Corbett, in a movie moment that marks the end of one boxing era and the beginning of another.

5. REQUIEM FOR A HEAVYWEIGHT (1962). A former contender and now beaten-up heavyweight named Mountain Rivera (Anthony Quinn) comes to the final days of his 17-year-career after losing to a young up-and-comer played by future heavyweight champion Cassius Clay. Told he should retire because any more fights could cause him to go blind, Rivera seeks other employment, going to a sympathetic social worker, played by Julie Harris. However, his manager, Maish (Jackie Gleason), has lost money on Rivera's last fight (Maish bet his fighter wouldn't go past four rounds, but Rivera lasted seven) and now must pay back the bookie, "Ma Greeny." Maish books Rivera as a pro wrestler, making him wear a Native American costume as a gimmick. But the proud Rivera, who, "never took no dive for nobody," rebels at wrestling in fixed fights. After Maish is beaten by Ma Greeny and her thugs, Rivera relents and enters the wrestling ring in the final sequence of this sad and powerful drama. The film also features boxers Jack Dempsey, Barney Ross, Gus Lesnevich, Willie Pep, and Rory Calhoun.

4. ROCKY (1976). This low-budget, sentimental Cinderella-in-boxing-trunks story became a sentimental Cinderella-in-a-tuxedo story, taking Best Picture honors at the

Academy Awards. Sylvester Stallone, a small-time character actor, wrote and starred in the film about Rocky Balboa, a small-time Philadelphia club fighter who gets a one-chance-in-a-million fight for the heavyweight belt against the champion Apollo Creed. Balboa tells his painfully shy girlfriend, Adrian (Talia Shire), that he's a boxer because "I can't sing or dance." Amazingly, Rocky proves he's not "just another bum from the neighborhood" in the title fight, losing the knock-down-drag-out battle on a split decision. But he became a star in the process, as did Stallone and his Rocky Balboa character, who went on to earn hundreds of millions of dollars at the box office and inspire five sequels.

3. *THE HARDER THEY FALL* (1956). Humphrey Bogart, in his last role, plays Eddie Willis, an out-of-work newspaperman who takes a job from mobster Nick Benko (Rod Steiger) to "sell" a weak-jawed, untalented giant of a boxer named Toro Moreno. Budd Schulberg's screenplay, a tale of the darker side of boxing that prevailed back in the 1930s when Primo Carnera (the prototype for Toro Moreno) became heavyweight champion, takes its title from former heavyweight champ Bob Fitzsimmons' famous line: "The bigger they are, the harder they fall." And fall Moreno does, losing to Buddy Brannen, played by Max Baer, who knocked out Carnera for real as well as reel back in 1934 for the belt. When Willis goes to collect Toro's share of the purse for his losing effort to Brannen, it turns out to be less than $50 "after expenses" from a million-dollar gate. The movie closes with Bogart's Willis typing a manifesto calling for the abolition of boxing, an ending lifelong boxing fan Schulberg didn't include in his original screenplay and fought against, but to no avail.

2. *BODY AND SOUL* (1947). Not to be confused with the 1981 film of the same name with Jayne Kennedy, Leone Isaac Kennedy and Peter Lawford, this classic stars John Garfield as Charlie Davis in what may have been a film about the life of welterweight great Barney Ross. Charlie turns to boxing after his father is killed in an attempt to earn money for his family and falls in with a promoter with mob ties. He begins to live the high life, turning his back on his friends and his ideals. In his final fight, Charlie has promised to take a dive, but regains his self-respect and wins in a knockout in the last round. Afterwards, the crooked promoter approaches Charlie and says, "What makes you think you can get away with this?" To which Charlie replies, "What are you gonna do? Kill me? Everybody dies." Cinematographer James Wong Howe captured the fight action by skating around the ring on roller skates to give the fights a new, more flowing and realistic look.

1. *RAGING BULL* (1980). The uncompromising, brutal look at the life of former middleweight champion Jake LaMotta captures his rise, fall and ultimate redemption. The superb Robert DeNiro mirrors the rage, the violence, the paranoia and jealousy of the real LaMotta, winning the Academy Award for Best Actor for his performance in this brilliant Martin Scorsese film.

BOXING'S GREATEST RING GENERALS

Ring generalship, often invoked as one of the criteria for judging a round, can at times seem so vague a metric that even General George S. Patton couldn't define it. Like an empty glass, it is defined by whatever you put in it. And yet, when you see it, you know it, as when a fighter exhibits the ability to completely control his opponent and the round itself. Here are the fighters who best exemplified that indefinable quality known as "ring generalship."

10. WILLIE PASTRANO (1952-65). One of the most underrated fighters of his era, Pastrano was a throwback to the fighters of yesteryear, a clever and elusive fighter who, like Willie Pep (see #3 on this list), earned the nickname "The Will o' the Wisp."

9. ROBERTO DURAN (1968-2001). Duran proclaimed ownership over his opponents by barreling straight into their wheelhouse and delivering a devastating punch. And yet, his defensive skills enabled him to control his opponent and the fight, which, when combined with his courage and aggressiveness (read: *machismo*), made him an overall ring general.

8. PHILADELPHIA JACK O'BRIEN (1896-1912). Patterning all his moves after those of his idol, James J. Corbett, O'Brien could deliver a quick, stinging jab, throw a right hand behind it and move out of trouble, controlling both the fight and his opponent. With only six losses in 179 bouts against fighters from heavyweight down to lightweight, O'Brien picked his opponents clean with his own brand of ring generalship.

7. RICARDO LOPEZ (1985-2001). Although only a minimumweight and light flyweight, Lopez packed the punch of a heavyweight, knocking out 38 of his opponents. But it was his overall ability that captured the attention of the fans and the press. Dan Rafael, then of *USA Today*, enthused, "He did everything right . . . excellent skills . . . great power." Lopez was, to many, the best pure boxer of his generation.

6. SUGAR RAY LEONARD (1977-97). With superior hand speed, well-defined moves, a schoolbook jab, and the ability to outthink any opponent, Leonard proved he had it all in his fight against Wilfred Benitez when he outthought and outfought one of the greatest defensive fighters of his era, stopping him in the 15th round.

5. BARNEY ROSS (1929-38). With one of the best defenses in the sport and all-around boxing ability equal to any—all underwritten with a punch—Ross could adapt to any method of attack. A student of the game, Ross could make any fighter look bad, embarrassing his opponent by controlling him.

4. JAMES J. CORBETT (1886-1903). The man who put the word "science" into the "sweet science," Corbett's technical virtuosity, speed and cleverness would mark the beginning of scientific boxing, with everything before his appearance in the ring relegated to B.C. (Before Corbett).

3. WILLIE PEP (1940-66). Known for his almost impenetrable defense, Willie Pep possessed an uncanny ability to anticipate an opponent's blows and parry them. His virtuoso performance came on the night of July 25, 1946 against a tough featherweight southpaw named Jackie Graves. All Pep did that night was win a round without throwing a punch, switching to southpaw to mimic the left-handed Graves, dancing, weaving, giving head feints, shoulder feints and feint-feints. As sportswriter Dan Riley wrote, "He made Jim Corbett's agility look like a broken-down locomotive. He made even Sugar Ray Robinson's fluidity look like cement hardening. Never has boxing seen such perfection!"

2. BENNY LEONARD (1911-24; 1931-32). Leonard was the prototype of the master boxer/puncher. He combined masterful technique, pinpoint accuracy and speed. Little wonder that the boxing experts of his day thought him to be the greatest all-around boxer.

1. SUGAR RAY ROBINSON (1940-65). The man originally called "Sugar" was flawless, almost seamless. He could deliver a knockout blow while going backward; his left hand, ever at the ready, was purity in motion; his footwork superb; his hand-speed and leverage unmatchable; his power lethal. In short, he was the sweetest practitioner of "The Sweet Science", its five-star general when it came to ring generalship.

BOXING'S MOST OVERLOOKED "BIT" PLAYERS

Although the boxers take center stage, managers, promoters, trainers and other supporting players play an important role in almost everything they accomplish. Some of these "bit players" have achieved prominence, yet their contributions remain unknown to even the most dedicated boxing fan. Here are but a few who played an important but overlooked part in the history of the sport.

11. ANGELO DUNDEE. Most cornermen have something to say to their fighters between rounds. Sometimes it's meaningful advice; often, however, it's empty clichés. Angelo Dundee specialized in the meaningful stuff. In the first Cassius Clay-Sonny Liston fight, Clay came back to his corner after the fourth round complaining, "I can't see, Angelo . . . my eyes are burning." And then, trying to take off his gloves, the anguished Clay screamed, "Get them off! I can't see. I want the whole world to see there's dirty work afoot." But the calm Dundee held him down, saying, "You can't fight without gloves. . . . Sit down!" Angelo washed out Clay's eyes, then half-lifted his fighter off the stool to show the referee he was alright and propelled him back into the ring, shouting, "This is for the big one son, the world championship. . . . Now get the hell out there . . . AND RUN!" A distressed and vulnerable fighter less than a minute before, Clay was inspired by Dundee to regain his composure and to win the fight and the championship that launched the legend of Cassius Clay/Muhammad Ali. Dundee remained the cornerman for Clay/Ali for most of the rest of the fighter's legendary career, and did the same for Sugar Ray Leonard, telling Sugar Ray, "You're blowing it, son" before the 13th round of his classic fight against Tommy Hearns, which Ray won in the 14th.

10. JAMES W. "BODY" JOHNSON. As a little-known member of the Shelby, Montana Chamber of Commerce, Johnson came up with the idea of making his small Montana oil town "the next Tulsa of the West" by hosting a heavyweight championship fight. At first a mere publicity stunt, the much ballyhooed showdown between heavyweight champion Jack Dempsey and challenger Tommy Gibbons took flight on its own, soon entangling Shelby in a financial fandango that would bankrupt the town and put, it was rumored, three banks out of business. Dempsey would carry the fight and win a 15-round decision and his manager, Doc Kearns, would carry away over $250,000, leaving challenger Gibbons with little except the bumps and lumps of battle. And as for the rumor that three banks had closed their doors as a result of the fight, all Kearns, could say, in the true manner of a hustler, was: "It was not three . . . it was four!"

9. PETER COURTNEY. Courtney was the co-star of the first movie showing fighters in action in a six-round exhibition bout between heavyweight champion James J.

Corbett and the aforementioned Courtney, an amateur. The fight was staged at Thomas Edison's Kinetographic Theatre, known as the Black Maria, a movie studio painted black, both inside and out, that could be revolved on its base to follow the sun. Courtney was knocked out in the sixth and earned $250 for his efforts—along with a place in history that September day in 1894.

8. "DUMB" DAN MORGAN. Morgan came by his nickname dishonestly, being as wise as the old owl he resembled. He traded in his managerial robes for those of an "advisor" to heavyweight challenger Jim Braddock for his 1935 battle with champion Max Baer. Knowing Baer's proclivity for two-legged wildlife, Morgan planted a beautiful, bleached blonde in the front row for the Baer-Braddock fight, telling her to hike up her skirt, spread her legs and wave at Max Baer throughout the fight. And "Madcap Maxie" responded to the lure of a blonde seated ringside seeking to make his acquaintance by waving back at her most of the 15 rounds. In the process, he also waved goodbye to his championship belt, as Braddock jabbed his way to victory over the distracted Baer.

7. NAT FLEISCHER. In the first round of the second Muhammad Ali-Sonny Liston fight, Ali caught Liston flush with a swift, straight right that put Liston flat on his back. As Liston lay there, Ali stood over him, shouting, "Get up and fight, sucker." Referee Jersey Joe Walcott tugged at Ali, trying to steer him to a neutral corner without bothering to administer a count to the fallen Liston. By the time Walcott had moved Ali to a neutral corner, a hurt Liston had gotten back to his feet. But Ali was right back on top of him, throwing punches from every angle. With the battle still raging on one side of the ring, Nat Fleischer, the editor and publisher of *The Ring* magazine, was on his feet on the other side, waving his arms and hollering at Walcott, "It's over . . . it's over . . ." Walcott finally heard Fleischer and walked across the ring and stuck his head through the ropes to talk to Fleischer, who told him that, although no count had been given, Liston had been down for more than ten seconds. With that, Walcott walked back across the ring, where Liston—having finally regained his feet—was trying to cover up from Ali's punches. Walcott broke up the fighters and raised Ali's hand in victory.

6. ARTHUR BRISBANE. The executive editor of William Randolph Hearst's publishing empire, including the *New York American* and *New York Journal*, Brisbane sat in the press section for the 1930 Max Schmeling-Jack Sharkey heavyweight championship fight to determine the successor to retired champion Gene Tunney. In the fourth round as Schmeling came up out of his crouch to throw a left hook, Sharkey countered with a wicked left hook that landed south of the border. Schmeling dropped to the canvas clutching his groin and referee Jim Crowley (one of college football's famous "Four Horsemen") began to count over the stricken fighter. But Schmeling's manager, Joe Jacobs, jumped into the ring hollering "Foul! Foul!" For three minutes, the ring officials argued over who had done what to whom and what to do about it, with only one of the judges claiming that he saw the low blow. But Brisbane shouted up at referee Crowley that if he didn't rule that Schmeling had been fouled and award him the fight then he would campaign to have boxing "banned" in New York. With Hearst's vast publishing empire behind him, Brisbane's "or else" was no idle threat. And the New York Athletic Commission got the hint, voting 2-1 to make Schmeling the champion—the only man ever to win the heavyweight championship on a foul.

5-4. Lou Nova and Max Baer. Although the first fight ever to be televised was the British light heavyweight championship bout between Len Harvey and Jack McAvoy on April 4, 1938, the first American bout to be televised in the United States was the Lou Nova-Max Baer fight from Yankee Stadium on June 1, 1939, won by Nova on a TKO in 11. Then, to cement their names in television history, the two again fought in the first fight televised from Madison Square Garden on April 4, 1941, a fight also won by Nova, this time on an eighth-round KO, Nova and Baer's two bouts serving as the beginning of televised boxing in America.

3. Dave Barry. A last-minute replacement as referee for the 1927 Jack Dempsey-Gene Tunney rematch, Dave Barry can be counted as one of the most famous referees in boxing history. Literally. Barry was at the center of "The Long Count" controversy that has resonated down boxing's long corridors ever since. The scene was Chicago's Soldier Field, where more than 100,000 fans assembled to watch Gene Tunney defend the heavyweight championship he had won from Dempsey the previous year. And for six rounds he defended it well indeed. But in the seventh, Dempsey caught Tunney with a sweeping left hook, driving the champion into the ropes. Dempsey then pounced on him, throwing a series of lefts and rights, every one of them landing on Tunney's unprotected chin. Slowly Tunney fell to the canvas while Dempsey moved to the corner just above him, hovering like an avenging angel of death to finish the kill if Tunney got up. But before the bout, both fighters had agreed to a rule stipulating that in the event of a knockdown, the standing fighter should go to a neutral corner, which was not the corner Dempsey was standing in. Barry directed Dempsey to a neutral corner, then began the count again. But instead of picking up the count, he started it all over again, intoning "One. . . . Two. . . . " Finally, at the count of "Nine," Tunney arose on legs that were strangers to him and proceeded to run away from Dempsey the rest of the round. One witness in the press section—former world lightweight champion Battling Nelson—had a split-second stopwatch that he hit when Tunney went down and stopped when he got up, recording 14.5 seconds as the time Tunney spent on the canvas. It became a matter of great controversy for a long time, with even contemporary wit Will Rogers weighing in, saying that when you open a parachute you "count to ten, then pull the rip cord. Ten will be an awful short count. They gave Gene Tunney a count of 14 against Dempsey."

2. WILLIAM MULDOON. The high priest of 19th-century physical fitness and a champion wrestler, Muldoon was prevailed upon by the manager of John L. Sullivan to take Sullivan, then living life to the fullest, in hand and train him for his 1889 heavyweight title defense against Jake Kilrain. Muldoon found Sullivan at his favorite watering hole doing battle with a stein of straight liquor. Himself an awesome presence, Muldoon lashed the stein to the floor with one blow and physically dragged Sullivan off to his health farm in western New York, where he subjected the champion to a rigorous regimen of training that turned Sullivan from 240 pounds of boozy

flab into a 209-pound bear of a man who would reduce Kilrain into plowshares over 75 hard-fought rounds. Muldoon thus became the father of American trainers, with his methods adopted by fight trainers everywhere in the years to come.

1. LOU HOUSEMAN. This sports editor of a Chicago newspaper was, not coincidentally, also the manager of Jack Root—a middleweight who was having trouble making his division's then-156-pound limit for an upcoming bout. With the next division north, the heavyweight division—ruled by Jim Jeffries, who weighed somewhere in the neighborhood of 220 pounds—representing a bridge too far for Root, Houseman felt that a halfway house between the two divisions was needed to keep Root in business. And so he came up with the idea of the light heavyweight division. The idea created controversy, but Houseman persevered, setting up a match between Root and Kid McCoy for the newly-minted "light heavyweight championship." The idea stuck, then multiplied over the years, leading to the creation of more new divisions between existing weight classes.

BOXING'S BEST CORNERMEN/TRAINERS

:: BY ANGELO DUNDEE

Note: Twice named Manager of the Year by the Boxing Writers Association, Angelo Dundee helped guide 15 boxers to world championships and was inducted into the International Boxing Hall of Fame in 1994. His Life Story, *My View from the Corner*, has been called a "classic" by *The Village Voice*. Over his long and illustrious career Dundee has come in contact with some of the other great trainers and cornermen, and here acknowledges those he considers "best."

12. CHARLEY GOLDMAN. Rocky Marciano's right-hand man. Little in stature, but huge in talent.

11. BILL GORE. Willie Pep's guy. Spoke very little.

10. CHRIS DUNDEE. Complete charge of corner.

9. GEORGE "CHICKIE" FERRERA. Great teacher. Showed me by doing.

8. LUIS SARRIA. My right-hand—and left-hand—man. Great Trainer. Misunderstood, didn't speak English. Luis Rodriguez's creator. (P.S. If Duran spoke English he would have equaled Ali in popularity.) Great talent and great sense of humor.

7. CUS D'AMATO. Did it by the numbers and it worked.

6. EDDIE FUTCH. Smooth in all aspects of getting the most out of his fighters. Produced Freddie Roach. 'Nuff said.

5. TEDDY ATLAS. Unique style of bringing the ultimate out of his fighters.

4. GIL CLANCY. Guided Emile Griffith from youngster to champion.

3. HARRY WILEY. Quiet, but effective. Ray Robinson's main man.

2. RAY ARCEL. Great knack for keeping fighters calm.

1. TEDDY BENTHAM. Trainer of Davey Moore and Jerry Quarry. Got the ultimate performances from them.

GREATEST PLAYBOYS OF THE BOXING WORLD

Nobody ever said that all boxers were altar boys in search of a service. For some, life added up to more than a little work + a little play, with their out-of-the-ring exploits as well-reported as their in-the-ring achievements. For others, it was lot more than a little play in that equation. These ten made hitting the bars and chasing women and fun as much a priority as chasing down and hitting their opponents during their inexplicably successful boxing careers.

10. JACK JOHNSON (1897-1932). The first African-American heavyweight champion became one of the first big celebrities of the 20th century, his every move fodder for the media, whether it involved him indulging his love of fast cars and equally fast women, drinking sloe gin or opening a nightclub in Chicago called *Café de Champion*, which served all comers. A spirit defiant, Johnson flaunted every excess to excess and lived life to its fullest, outraging the social mores of the day and the establishment.

9. WILLIE PASTRANO (1951-65). A slick performer inside the ring, light heavyweight champ Pastrano was just as slick outside the ring with women. And it didn't seem to matter with whom or when or where—as evidenced by his trainer Angelo Dundee once finding Pastrano the day before a fight in a hotel elevator in a compromising position with an airline stewardess.

8. CARLOS MONZON (1963-77). With matinee-idol looks—complete with delicately marked brows, an unmarked face and a body that could serve as a model for Hollywood beefcake pictures—Monzon was catnip to women. Even during his reign as middleweight champion, stories and pictures of him squiring models and actresses into nightclubs all over Europe and South America could be found regularly on the front pages of newspapers in his native Argentina. His pursuit of the high life, commingled with a taste for violence, ultimately resulted in the death of one of his companions and an 11-year prison sentence.

7. MAXIE ROSENBLOOM (1923-39). Rosenbloom never let success go to his training; remaining out all night before a fight or even the day of it, looking for excitement or just a female companion. Rosenbloom was a certifiable loony, twice as exciting outside the ring as he was inside. He lived the high life as a fighter before Hollywood beckoned him to a second career in acting where he became part of Tinseltown's social party scene.

6. TONY JANIRO (1943-52). A pretty boy playboy, Janiro was always on the look-out for female companionship, doing most of his training in the company of the fairer sex. His good looks played a key part in a sequence of scenes in the film *Raging Bull*; after Jake LaMotta's wife Vicki described her husband's next opponent Janiro as "good looking," Jake gave Janiro a brutal pounding, leading one mobster to say, "He ain't pretty no more."

5. JACK DELANEY (1919-32). Light heavyweight champ Delaney dedicated himself to the pastime known in the 1920s as "Making Whoopee." It was always midnight in the soul of this handsome French-Canadian version of Harry Greb. The Quebec native and Connecticut resident earned the nicknames "The Bridgeport Adonis" and "Bright Eyes" from the press for gathering a long string of well put-together chorines and hatcheck girls. His female fans earned the nickname "Delaney's Screaming Mamies" from the press for their enthusiastic vocal support for Delaney at his fights.

MAXIE ROSENBLOOM

4. HARRY GREB (1913-26). "The Pittsburgh Windmill" was as active outside the ring as he was in it—busy living life to the fullest and too busy trying to keep busy to stop. Somehow, Greb managed to squeeze more boxing and booze into his 32 years than any 32 men could have done, his only complaint being that each day contained only 24 hours. One of writer Damon Runyon's favorite fighters because of his colorful and flamboyant lifestyle, Greb took to wearing makeup and hair gel when he climbed into the ring. He became one of the 1920s' most legendary womanizers, boasting of his conquests in the dressing room before fights.

3. LEW JENKINS (1935-50). One of the most irrepressible, irresponsible whackos ever to come down the boxing pike, the "Sweetwater Swatter" was forever shoveling his purse monies into the pockets of friendly barkeeps. He stayed out all night, caroused with everyone he could find, sparred a few rounds with Canadian Club, and did his road work on something he called his "motorsickle," which he rode all over New York—and into anything in his way, like bridges, cars and store fronts. In spite of all his carousing, Jenkins' career had the sweet smell of success, as he knocked out Lou Ambers to win the lightweight title in 1940. However, that smell was usually 98 proof, the standing joke among sportswriters being that even Alcoholics Anonymous wouldn't let their members go to his fight. But even dead drunk, Jenkins could still knock out most everyone he fought.

2. MAX BAER (1929-41). Called "The Magnificent Screwball" and "Madcap Maxie," Baer viewed yesterday as a canceled check and today as money on the line. The heavyweight champ lit up Broadway more brightly than its faded neon signs as he pursued New York City's wine, women and song, not necessarily in that order.

1. MICKEY WALKER (1919-35). As Jim Murray wrote, "Mickey Walker will best be remembered as the middleweight who had the best left hook and the biggest thirst in the business. If it hadn't been for the one, the thirst, the other, the left hook, might have made him the only 155-pound heavyweight champion in modern history." A bouser and carouser of the first order, the welterweight and middleweight champion made the "Roaring Twenties" roar a little bit louder, going on his merry way, bottled and otherwise. With gin as his tonic, Walker and manager Don Kearns traveled the European continent for one month after Mickey had knocked out Tommy Milligan in London in defense of his middleweight crown in 1927, leaving no stone or bar unturned, returning to the States only when Walker had run out of money and Europe's bars out of alcohol.

POWDERPUFF PUNCHERS

While the knockout punchers are boxing's most popular fighters, their exploits the stuff of headlines, their KO's equivalent to the home runs of boxing, there are those who, in boxing parlance, "couldn't break an egg," their punches those of the powderpuff variety. Here are the most notable of the "powderpuff" brigade.

12. MAURICE BLOCKER (1982-95). An extremely tall welterweight at 6'2" but slim enough to work in an olive factory dragging the pimentos, through, Blocker relied on his ability to outbox rather than outpunch opponents. "The Thin Man" managed to record 20 knockouts, but almost all were knockouts owing to an accumulation of punches, not punching power.

11. SAMMY ANGOTT (1935-50). Lightweight champ Angott fit the profile of the talented and light puncher: fast, smart and elusive. His offensive arsenal included grabbing his opponents and hanging on, earning him the nickname "The Clutch." But his power was sorely lacking, as proven by his record of only 22 knockouts in a total of 125 fights.

10. WILLIE PASTRANO (1951-65). Known as "Willie the Wisp," Pastrano relied on quick defensive moves and fast hands that didn't have much power in them, scoring only 14 KOs in his 84 fights.

9. CORY SPINKS (1997-2005). You could use the words "pitter" and "patter" to describe the power behind Cory Spinks' punches. This southpaw "cutie" was good enough to use that "pitter-patter" style to win fight-after-fight, including one that gained him the welterweight title. But with only 11 KOs in his 43 fights, he earns inclusion in the "Powderpuff Punchers" club.

8. JOEY MAXIM (1941-58). Light heavyweight champ Joey Maxim threw his left jab like a machine gun. But rarely unsheathed his right from his holster, scoring only 21 KOs in 115 fights for a "slugging average" of only 18 percent.

7. BILLY GRAHAM (1941-55). Like many powderpuff punchers, Graham used a combination of hit-and-not-be-hit. With outstanding speed and movement Graham was never knocked off his pins. But then again, he rarely knocked any of his opponents off theirs, registering just 26 KOs in 126 bouts.

6. RALPH DUPAS (1950-66). Junior middleweight champion Ralph Dupas was known as a master boxer, slick and quick with great movement, good angles, and a fast counter. What he wasn't known for was his knockout power, his punches, while possessing snap and crackle, had no pop, his record showing only 19 knockouts in his 134 bouts.

5. JIMMY YOUNG (1969-88). In an era of great heavyweights, the 1970s, Jimmy Young was one of the best. Unfortunately, while he was a master of his craft, slick and able to deftly dodge punches and confuse opponents, he lacked a knockout punch, having only 11 KO's amongst his 34 wins, most of his opponents falling down from pure exhaustion trying to catch him than from any of his punches—as witnessed by George Foreman falling to the canvas in the last round of their 1977 fight, a result of exhaustion, not a punch.

4. JOHNNY DUNDEE (1910-32). With 322 bouts and only 19 KOs to his credit, featherweight and junior lightweight champ Dundee had a knockout rate of under six percent—one of the all-time lowest in the history of boxing. Standing just five-foot-four-and-one-half inches tall, Dundee was but a hint of a man. What he lacked in power, though, he more than made up for in ring generalship and movement.

3. MIGUEL CANTO (1969-80). Called "El Maestro" by his Mexican fans and the "Mexican Willie Pep" by observers, Miguel Canto was not your typical Mexican warrior, but instead was a busy, hit-and-not-be-hit fighter who had just 14 knockouts in his 68 total bouts—an average far below baseball's Mendoza line. As testimony to his lack of a punch, he successfully defended his flyweight championship 14 times, 13 of those going to a 15-round decision—a record never to be broken in this era of 12-round fights.

2. CORPORAL IZZY SCHWARTZ (1922-29; 1931). the flyweight champion from 1928 to 1929, Cpl. Izzy Schwartz was solely a boxer, a phantom in the ring who never stopped long enough to throw a hard punch, as attested to by his only having seven KO's in his 117 fights.

1. MAXIE ROSENBLOOM (1923-39). With 289 recorded fights and only 18 knockouts to his credit, this light heavyweight champion was boxing's equivalent of baseball's 1906 Chicago White Sox—the team called "The Hitless Wonder" for winning the World Series despite posting a team batting average of just .230. His best punches were his right—a slapping, open-handed blow which he called a "pouch" and earned him his nickname, "Slapsie Maxie"—and his left, which was roughly akin to an umbrella thrust by an old lady weighing all of 80 pounds.

HISTORY'S BUSIEST PUNCHERS

Before CompuBox and before we tried to quantify the number of punches thrown by a fighter, there was a perception of a "busy" fighter. And a boxing term: the fighter throwing "punches in bunches." Those listed below were famed for their workrate, sometimes their punches coming so fast they were almost impossible to see, let alone count.

10. JOE FRAZIER (1965-81). "Smokin' Joe" fought, as one observer had it, "like a wild beast caught in a thicket." His head bobbing up and down to the metronomic movement of his body, Frazier moved relentlessly and savagely, a runaway locomotive under full steam coming straight at his opponent, flailing away.

9. TOMMY "HURRICANE" JACKSON (1951-61). To describe Jackson's style as "style" would be to do a disservice to the very word itself. *Time Magazine* described this 1950s heavyweight as swatting away with a "wild assortment of slaps, jabs, backhanded cuffs and spectacular double uppercuts." Jackson less assaulted his opponents than surrounded them, his boundless energy and incredible stamina enabling him to beat many of the top heavies of the day and earning him a title shot against Floyd Patterson.

8. JACKIE "KID" BERG (1924-45). Described as a piston-shooting dynamo, this 1930s junior welterweight champ, nicknamed "The Whitechapel Whirlwind," made a career by throwing leather nonstop. There was little "science' to Berg's style, he just bored in, flailing away constantly until his opponent fell under the sheer volume of his punches.

7. PANCHO VILLA (1919-25). An earlier version of Manny Pacquiao, Filipino Pancho Villa was a vicious, rip-snorting boxer who could go 15 rounds at blinding speed and finish as fresh as when he started. Tagged by sportswriters as "Puncho Pancho," Villa was a non-stop puncher who won 71 fights and the 1920s flyweight championship with his all-out attack from the git-go.

6. FIGHTING HARADA (1960-70). The Japanese flyweight and bantamweight champion of the 60s fought like he was a typhoon, raining a cyclonic variety of punches to his opponents' heads, bodies and wherever else they left exposed. With little respect for his own safety, Harada threw punches from a bewildering variety of places in a never-ceasing, ever-relentless attack as he gradually eroded the will of his opponents.

5. BEAU JACK (1940-55). A non-stop punching machine, Beau Jack's style was almost no style at all as he flailed away from every conceivable angle, his hands ablur as he threw a smorgasbord of punches—bolos, hooks, crosses, and just about everything else imaginable—with either hand. Winner of 83 fights and two-time lightweight champion, Jack mainlined excitement and headlined Madison Square Garden cards 21 times, drawing 336,000 fans and $1,579,000 as New York's adoring fans flocked to see their Beau idol in action.

4. AARON PRYOR (1976-85). Aaron Pryor was a pinwheel out of control, fighting almost as if he were an endangered species in fear of losing his life. He practiced a fistic version of prefrontal lobotomy on his opponents as he gave the impression his gloves were caught in a revolving door.

3. TIGER FLOWERS (1918-27). The reigning middleweight champion for but one year, 1926, Flowers, better known to his fans as "The Georgia Deacon," was anything but in the ring, slashing and ripping at his opponents, throwing rights and lefts with blinding speed, most of his punches landing with the side of his fist almost as if he were incapable of landing a straight jab or swing. Still, Flowers parlayed his bunches of punches into 115 wins against only 13 losses and one world championship.

2. HARRY GREB (1913-26). Harry Greb was a ring marvel, a one-man destroyer who threw punches asfastasyoucanreadthis from any and all angles. Called "The Pittsburgh Windmill" for good reason, Greb was a whirling dervish in the ring who fought like an early-day terrorist, his style best described by boxing writer W.C. McGeehan as "The Manly Art of Modified Murder."

1. HENRY ARMSTRONG (1931-44). Armstrong suffocated his opponents with his swarming style, a perpetual-motion machine who imposed his will on his adversaries and earned him the monikers "Hurricane Hank" and "Hammerin' Hank."

COMPUBOX'S BUSIEST PUNCHERS :: BY BOB CANOBBIO

Note: Bob Canobbio owns and operates CompuBox, Inc., the company that in 1985 introduced a computer program to register the number—and types—of punches thrown and landed in a bout. The company's clients have included HBO, NBC and ESPN, as well as trainers Emanuel Steward and Eddie Futch, along with fighters such as Sugar Ray Leonard, Larry Holmes and Lennox Lewis. Here, Bob lists the 11 fighters who have kept him and his CompuBox employees busiest counting punches during fights.

11. TROY DORSEY. Although Dorsey outlanded his opponent, Jorge Paez, 620 to 340, throwing 1.365 total punches (or 114 per round), Paez got the decision in their featherweight bout. At least a draw would have been in order.

10. & 9. PHILLIP HOLLIDAY AND IVAN ROBINSON. Holliday won a 12-round decision over Robinson in a battle in which 990 punches were landed, with Holliday having the lion's share, 555. Robinson was also busy in his two wins over Arturo Gatti, landing 400-plus punches in each of the two.

8. DANIEL ZARAGOSA. The 39-year-old cigarette-smoking Zaragosa landed 504 punches in a decision win over the readily-available Wayne McCullough, an average of 42 combined punches landed per round.

7. & 6. SANTOS CARDONA AND KEVIN POMPEY. In just eight rounds the two combined to land 96 punches per round, nearly three times the CompuBox average for combined punches landed in a round.

5. & 4. ZACK PADILLA AND RAY OLIVERIA. The two combined to throw an astounding total of 3,020 punches in a 12-round fight. That's an average of 252 combined punches thrown per round, more than double the CompuBox average in one of the few fights CompuBox operators were happy to see the end of the bout due to finger fatigue.

3. JAMES TONEY. Toney landed 400-plus punches in a championship fight versus four different fighters–468 vs. Glenn Wolfe, 421 vs. Tony Thornton, 420 vs. Prince Charles Williams and 401 vs. Iran Barkley, an average of 45 punches landed per round.

2. ANTONIO MARGARITO. Margarito holds the record for most punches thrown in a fight, 1675 against Joshua Clottey in a 12-round decision with an average of 140 thrown per round, 82 more than the welterweight average per round.

1. VINCE PHILLIPS. Phillips threw the most punches in a round, 237 in the 12th round of his fight against Ray Oliveria, an average of 79 punches thrown a minute to break the record, ironically held by his opponent Oliveria (226).

THE MOST SIGNIFICANT FIGHTS IN HISTORY

'Tis said that all things are relevant, except maybe Eve telling Adam about all the men she could have married. The same thing can be said about boxing, where some fights pack more significance than others due to their impacts beyond the four corners of the ring on society, politics, and/or the rules of the sport. Here are the ten most significant of them.

10. MILTON McCRORY VS. COLIN JONES, MARCH 19, 1983, CONVENTION CENTER, RENO, NEVADA. Four months after the tragic death of Duk Koo Kim from injuries he sustained during his 14th-round KO by lightweight champion Ray Mancini, the WBC instituted a rule limiting title fights to 12 rounds. The first contest fought under the new restriction was this showdown for the vacant welterweight title between McCrory and Jones. Ironically, the fight ended in a draw, with a rematch five months later that McCrory won on a 12-round decision.

9. JAMES J. CORBETT VS. PETER COURTNEY, SEPTEMBER 7, 1894, LLEWELLYN, NEW JERSEY. Heavyweight champion Corbett's bout against the amateur Courtney was the first use of the motion picture camera to record a fight. The six-round exhibition was filmed at the Edison Laboratories' Kinetographic Theatre (known as "The Black Maria"), a studio painted black and set on a revolving base so it could be turned to follow the sunlight.

8. GENE TUNNEY VS. JACK DEMPSEY II, SEPTEMBER 22, 1927, SOLDIER FIELD, CHICAGO. Although known primarily for its infamous "Long Count" (see the "Boxing's Most Controversial Fights" list), the second Tunney-Dempsey fight set a new, higher standard for big fights, establishing attendance and gate records with an announced crowd of 104,943 packed into Chicago's Soldier Field paying $2,658,660 in Coolidge dollars (or over $30 million in Obama dollars).

7. LEN HARVEY VS. JOCK McAVOY, APRIL 7, 1938, HARRINGAY ARENA, LONDON, ENGLAND. Harvey won a 15-round decision over McAvoy for the British light heavyweight championship in the first boxing bout to be telecast, albeit not for the public. The first publicly screened bout came 10 months later when Eric Boon battled Arthur Danahar in Harringay Arena on February 23, 1939. The first major fight in the U.S. to be televised was the Lou Nova-Max Baer fight from Yankee Stadium on June 1, 1939.

6. JACK DEMPSEY VS. JESS WILLARD, JULY 4, 1919, BAY VIEW PARK ARENA, TOLEDO, OHIO. In the first major sporting event after World War I, Jack Dempsey stopped Willard on a third-round TKO to win the heavyweight title and usher in "The

Golden Age of Sports," an era when spectator sports like boxing and baseball began attracting much larger audiences and became a vital part of American life.

5. James J. Corbett vs. John L. Sullivan, September 7, 1892, Olympic Club, New Orleans.

In the first heavyweight championship bout contested under the Marquess of Queensberry rules, "Gentlemen Jim" Corbett used his scientific boxing techniques to knock out the reigning bareknuckle champion John L. Sullivan and usher in the beginning of boxing's modern era.

4. John C. Heenan vs. Tom Sayers, April 15, 1860, Farnborough, England.

The fight between the American heavyweight champion, "The Benicia Boy" John C. Heenan, and "The Napoleon of the Ring" and acknowledged British and European titleholder, Tom Sayers, is regarded as the first great international match. Heenan knocked down Sayers 25 times, while Sayers used his pinpoint punching accuracy to swell both of Heenan's eyes through 42 rounds. Finally, after two hours and twenty minutes with Sayers exhausted and Heenan virtually blind, the police intervened and stopped the fight, resulting in a draw. The referee awarded the championship belt to the defending champion Sayers, but Sayers offered half of it to Heenan in a gesture of international goodwill.

JACK JOHNSON (right) vs JIM JEFFRIES

3. Joe Frazier vs. Muhammad Ali I, March 8, 1971, Madison Square Garden, New York City. Called merely "The Fight," this was more than just a showdown at Boxing's Mecca between two undefeated heavyweight champions. Ali-Frazier set up as a war between two fighters with vastly different personalities, styles, faiths and—in the minds of their supporters—views on the ongoing Vietnam War still bitterly dividing America. In a fight that acquitted its build-up, Joe Frazier knocked Ali down in the 15th round to secure a unanimous decision.

2. Jack Johnson vs. Jim Jeffries, July 4, 1910, Reno, Nevada. The first bout to be called "The Fight of the Century" was more than just a fight, but an allegorical battle of black vs. white, invader vs. avenger. It pitted Johnson, who had become the first black heavyweight champion in 1908, against the undefeated former heavyweight champion Jeffries, who came out of retirement "to reclaim the heavyweight championship for the white race" after Johnson had turned back a string of "great white hopes." A predominantly white crowd of 15,760 jammed downtown Reno around a ring built for the occasion, chanting "Jeff, it's up to you." But Jeffries offered little competition as the once great symbol of white supremacy was reduced to a shambles and knocked out in the 15th round by a dominant Johnson.

1. Joe Louis vs. Max Schmeling II, June 22, 1938, Yankee Stadium, New York City. This was a rematch of a bout from two years before in which Germany's Schmeling knocked out the unbeaten American phenomenon Louis in 12 rounds. Louis managed to rebound from the loss, win the heavyweight title from Jim Braddock and line up a defense against Schmeling, still the only man to have defeated him. But with World War II looming, the bout became much more than just a chance for Louis to even the score; it was, in the words of Budd Schulberg, "a preview of the war to come". During the buildup, Louis had gone to the White House and had his arm felt by President Franklin Roosevelt, who said, "Joe, we need these muscles for democracy." Schmeling received a personal call in his dressing room before the fight from German leader Adolf Hitler, who saw a Schmeling victory as a way to further his case for Aryan supremacy. But Louis emphatically repudiated the Nazi notion of the so-called "master race" with a 124-second annihilation of the German that brought joy to millions of Americans, both black and white.

GREATEST IRISH-AMERICAN FIGHTERS

Ring archaeologists trace America's boxing roots to the mid-19th century, back when the sport was ruled by those from the Auld Sod with names like John C. Heenan and Tom Hyer. And for the next 60 years or so, up through the early 20th century, the "Sons of Erin"—with champions like John L. Sullivan, Jack McAuliffe, Nonpareil Jack Dempsey, James J. Corbett and others—continued to dominate the fight game. So powerful was the Irish hold on boxing that it became fashionable for fighters to adopt Irish names in the belief that it was the only way to make a "name," even if it wasn't their own name. Those appropriating Irish-sounding names included a Norman Selby who became Kid McCoy, a Joseph Youngs who became Tommy Ryan, a William J. Rothwell who became Young Corbett, a Vincent Morris Scheer who became Mushy Callahan, etc, etc., etc.—the et ceteras being enough to fill another five pages or more. It began to look like the old Irish saying made popular by Rudyard Kipling, "The Colonel's Lady and Judy O'Grady (were) sisters under the skin." Here are those greatest Irish-American fighters who achieved greatness without having to change their names.

10. MIKE GIBBONS (1907-22). Known as the "St. Paul Phantom" and "The Wizard," Mike Gibbons was the most damnably frustrating opponent one could ever face, driving grown men to tears and the great Harry Greb to scream at his manager during the course of one of their fights, "You sonuvabitch, from now on match me with one guy at a time!" One of boxing's greatest defensive artisans, Gibbons was grand opera in the ring, never out of position, his movements having a meaning all their own. Never a champion, Gibbons fought more than a dozen bouts with world champions, losing only three times in 127 fights.

9. BOB FITZSIMMONS (1885-1914). Called a "fighting machine on stilts" by John L. Sullivan, "Ruby Robert" took on anybody and everybody—despite weighing only 170 pounds tops—proudly proclaiming, "The bigger they are, the harder they fall." And fall they did, 67 of them, from elephantine heavyweights to lighter middleweights, as Fitzsimmons implanted his left almost up to the wrist in his opponent's midriff, as he did with his famous "Solar Plexus" punch to the midsection of heavyweight champion James J. Corbett in 1897 in what may have been the first pure left hook thrown in boxing history. With that left from hell Fitz won Corbett's title, 74 fights (67 by knockout) and became the first three-division champion in boxing.

8. TERRY McGOVERN (1897-1908). "Terrible Terry's" savage style was akin to mass mayhem. The little five-foot-four-inch McGovern waded into his opponents without any subtleties, throwing a frenzied orgy of punches with lightning speed, his objective to destroy them. "No bantamweight or featherweight," wrote Nat Fleischer, "ever packed a more dangerous punch than did 'Terrible Terry.'" No fighter of his weight piled up such a consistent record for tearing pell-mell into his adversaries and smothering them with wicked jolts, hooks, uppercuts, and vicious swings. In every sense of the phrase, he was a pugilistic marvel.

7. JOHN L. SULLIVAN (1879-92). An American tintype who was called everything from "The Boston Strongboy" to "His Fistic Highness" to "The Great John L." to "The Prizefighting Caesar," Sullivan was tailor-made for the lusty era in which he fought. He was an institution, a deity, a national treasure and obsession who often boasted, "I can beat any sonuvabitch in the house." The heavyweight bareknuckle champion for ten years, Sullivan possessed an awesome right hand, a blow which, according to one opponent, "felt like a telephone pole had been shoved against me endways." That right hand dispatched 33 of his opponents and, after it was extended to greet one of his many fans, inspired the catchphrase of his generation: "Shake the hand that shook the hand of the Great John L."

6. JAMES J. CORBETT (1886-1903). With every fight he fought, Corbett gave an exhibition of his "scientific boxing." Moving briskly but never urgently, Corbett would flash his opponents a come-hither look but never be at home when they called. Claiming the heavyweight title in 1892 by defeating the supposedly invincible John L. Sullivan in 21 rounds and challenging the rough-and-tumble standards that had dominated boxing for more than a century, Corbett served as the midwife to modern boxing, replacing strength with skill and immobility with finesse.

5. BILLY CONN (1934-48). A brash Irish leprechaun, Conn fought every fight with the bravado of someone going down aboard a ship humming, "Nearer My God to Thee." He took the measure of fighters from lightweight to heavyweight, from A-to-Z, from Fred Apostoli to Fritzie Zivic, and of no less than ten men who held titles at one time or another. Using his speed of foot, agile hands and the balls of a cat burglar, he beat opponents at any game they played. Unfortunately, his bravado got the better of him in 1941 in his classic first fight against Joe Louis, who came from behind to KO Conn in the 13th. But Conn won 63 other fights and the light heavyweight championship.

4. TOMMY LOUGHRAN (1919-37). James J. Corbett, the ring's first master boxer, once told Loughran, "You did things in the ring I wanted to do." And Max Baer, after losing a ten-round decision to Loughran jokingly implored his conqueror to "just show me how you do it with that left." Loughran was a master boxer on his own, one with lightning-fast hands and agile footwork that helped propel him to 96 victories in his 18-year career.

3. JIMMY McLARNIN (1923-36). McLarnin's right-hand wizardry and powerful left hook were so impressive that—long before the emergence of Sugar Ray Robinson—New York sportswriters called him "the greatest pound-for-pound fighter in the ring today." With the hands of an assassin and the face of a choirboy, the fighter known as "Baby Face" beat some of the best boxers of his era, including 10 former, present, and future champions.

2. GENE TUNNEY (1915-28). A boxer-puncher who mastered the art of boxing and possessed the power to dissect opponents, "The Fighting Marine" retired as heavyweight champion after an 83-bout career in which he lost only once—in a bout against Harry Greb, a defeat he avenged twice. Despite his greatness, Tunney was never fully appreciated in his day fighting as he did in the shadow of the man he defeated twice, Jack Dempsey.

1. MICKEY WALKER (1919-35). "The Toy Bulldog" always claimed he had been born with a black eye, and there was no reason to doubt him. A natural-born fighter who peaked at just 5'7", Walker was able to get inside the reaches of six-foot-plus heavyweights and bang their guts out. The welterweight and middleweight champ took on and beat heavies like Jim Maloney, King Levinsky, and Johnny Risko and drew with future heavy king Jack Sharkey during his 93-win career.

GREATEST JEWISH BOXERS :: BY MIKE SILVER

Note: Author of *The Arc of Boxing: The Rise and Decline of the Sweet Science*, Mike Silver is a boxing historian and expert on Jewish boxing history. The former promoter has served as a consultant for over a dozen boxing documentaries, including ones produced by ESPN, HBO, PBS and the History Channel. He has written on boxing for the *New York Times* and *The Ring* magazine. Silver served as curator for the 1994 exhibit *Sting Like a Macabee: The Golden Age of the American-Jewish Boxer* at the National Museum of American-Jewish History. Here, Mike offers his take on the top Jewish boxers in the history of the sport.

10. BATTLING LEVINSKY. Light heavyweight champion 1916–20. Pro record: 70 wins, 30 KOs, 20 losses, 15 draws, 179 no–decisions.

9. SID TERRIS. Top lightweight contender in the 1920s. Pro record: 105 wins, 15 KOs, 15 losses, five draws.

8. JACKIE "KID" BERG. Junior welterweight champion 1930-31. Pro record: 162 wins, 59 KOs, 26 losses, nine draws.

7. LEW TENDLER. Great lightweight of 1910s and 20s. Pro record: 135 wins, 39 KOs, 15 losses, nine draws, 13 no–contests.

6. JACKIE FIELDS. Welterweight champion 1929-30 and 1932-33. Pro record: 71 wins, 28 KOs, nine losses, two draws.

5. LOUIS "KID" KAPLAN. Featherweight champion 1925-27. Pro record: 102 wins, 17 KOs, 13 losses, 10 draws, seven no–decisions.

4. MAXIE ROSENBLOOM. Light heavyweight champion 1930-34. Pro record: 210 wins, 18 KOs, 35 losses, 23 draws, 19 no–decisions.

3. BARNEY ROSS. Lightweight champion 1933; junior welterweight champion 1933; welterweight champion 1934 and 1935-38. Pro record: 74 wins, 24 KOs, four losses, three draws.

ABE ATTELL

2. ABE ATTELL. Featherweight champion 1901-12. Pro record: 92 wins, 48 KOs, 10 losses, one draw, 50 no-decisions.

1. BENNY LEONARD. Lightweight champion 1917-24. Pro record: 89 wins, 71 KOs, five losses, one draw, 115 no-decisions.

GREATEST TRILOGIES

Some fights are so good they warrant a rematch. And some rematches are so good they deserve a third installment. With their drama and displays of courage and skill, the following three-part showdowns brought out the best in their fighters and from the sport of boxing itself making the word "trilogy" part of the boxing lexicon.

10. CARLOS ORTIZ vs. ISMAEL LAGUNA. A lightweight trilogy was one of the best of the 1960s between the lightning-fast Laguna and the ringwise Ortiz. Before their first fight in Laguna's hometown of Panama City, Ortiz's manager-advisor, "Honest" Bill Daly—called "Honest" because he wasn't, the type of man who go into a revolving door behind you and come out in front—thought he had the fight "in the bag" for his fighter, having one of the judges in his pocket. But even though Laguna outhustled and outsped the defending champion Ortiz for almost every second of every round, Daly's judge scored the fight a draw even though the other two scorecards had Laguna winning by 11 and 12 points. After the fight, the judge was chased by enraged Panamanian fans all the way back to his hotel. The second battle between the two, in San Juan in November of '65, was won by Ortiz handily as Ortiz out-thought and out-fought Laguna to regain his lightweight title. Their third fight, in 1967, was an outdoor affair at New York's Shea Stadium, and again Ortiz offset Laguna's speed afoot and ahand to win and retain his lightweight championship.

9. BATTLING NELSON vs. JOE GANS. Oscar Nielsen was born in Copenhagen in 1882, but raised in Chicago. He became known as "Battling Nelson" and established himself as one of the most celebrated fighters in the lightweight division, taking on the likes of Abe Attell and winning the world lightweight title from Jimmy Britt in 1905 with an 18th-round knockout. The new champ then faced "The Old Master", Joe Gans from Baltimore, the following year in Goldfield, Nevada. It was a bizarre fight, with Gans putting Nelson down a number of times before being declared the winner in the 42nd round when Nelson was disqualified for a low blow. Nelson got another chance at Gans on July 4, 1908, in Colma, California, and won back the crown by knocking out Gans in the 17th round. Two months later, Gans fought Nelson again in Colma and went down in the 21st round for a second Nelson victory in their three-act drama.

8. DICK TIGER vs. GENE FULLMER. Dick Tiger came over to America from Nigeria, through England, to establish himself as a top middleweight contender. He faced middleweight champion Gene Fullmer on October 23, 1962 in the first of what would prove to be three ring wars. Tiger won the opener with a 15-round decision over a bleeding and bruised Fullmer at Candlestick Park in San Francisco. They met in Las Vegas the following February for a rematch that ended in a draw, and then again for the historic finale in Ibadan, West Nigeria in the first world title bout held in Africa. Tiger battered Fullmer for seven rounds until the bout was stopped, with thousands of Tiger's countrymen cheering for their Nigerian champion.

7. EMILE GRIFFITH VS. BENNY "KID" PARET. A trilogy with tragic consequences, the Griffith-Paret fights were one part a normal fight and two parts a blood feud. Their first meeting at Miami Beach's Convention Center in April of 1961 was an even fight for the first 12 months between defending welterweight champion Paret and challenger Griffith. Between rounds, Griffith's trainer, Gil Clancy, told his charge, "it's now or never," and Griffith followed his exhortation, knocking down Paret with a left hook and a right hand in the 13th to win the welterweight title. Rematched five months later in Madison Square Garden, the bad blood between the two came to a boil at the weigh-in when Paret called Griffith a "maricón," gutter Spanish for homosexual, and the normally happy-go-lucky Griffith, smoldering like a volcano, vowed to fight Paret "right then and there." Paret would win a hard-fought split decision—which Griffith swore, "I know I beat him"—setting up their third fight. But not before Paret had slipped off to challenge middleweight champion Gene Fullmer for Fullmer's title. For 10 brutal rounds, Fullmer put Paret through a fearful beating, Fullmer later saying, "I never hit anybody with more punches harder then I hit Paret . . . I never beat anybody like that in my life." Despite his beating at the hands of Fullmer, four months later, Paret put his welterweight title on the line against Griffith. Still the fire that burned before their second fight burned in Griffith's heart, but was more than re-kindled by Paret again calling him a "maricón" at the weigh-in and putting his hand on Griffith. Griffith snarled at Paret, "Keep your hands off me, Paret!" and made as if to fight him then and there. The fight itself, held at Madison Square Garden, was a continuation of the weigh-in with Griffith winning the first five rounds before Paret floored Griffith in the sixth with a long left hook, Griffith shakily arising at the count of eight and steadying himself by holding onto the ropes, with referee Ruby Goldstein having to pry him loose. Coming back from the knockdown, Griffith caught Paret in the 10th with 30 unanswered punches, but Paret stood up under the fusillade. All of which served as a prelude to the 12th round when Griffith drove Paret into the corner with a right that sounded like waves striking shore, then surrounded the now helpless Paret, punching maniacally with uppercuts and lefts, holding up the by-now unconscious Paret by the force of his blows. Referee Ruby Goldstein, unable to get around Griffith and slow to react, finally made his way around Griffith to pull him away, and the unconscious Paret slid to the canvas, his arm still hooked on the ropes. Ten days later, Paret would succumb to the injuries suffered and die, with boxing on TV also suffering a similar fate, soon to disappear from national TV for almost a decade after the tragic ending.

6. FLOYD PATTERSON VS. INGEMAR JOHANSSON. Two boxers with distinctly different styles can make for intriguing and compelling fights. And that was the case with Floyd Patterson and Ingemar Johansson. A 1952 Olympic middleweight gold medal winner, the American Patterson rose to become heavyweight champion using his speed and his elusive "peek-a-boo" defense. Scandinavian heavyweight Johansson, who had been stripped of his Olympic silver medal for running away from Ed Sanders throughout their '52 gold medal bout, used his "Thunder and Lightning" power to pound his way to the top of the division. Johansson unleashed his powerful right hand to put Patterson on the canvas seven times in their June 26, 1959 bout before the fight was stopped in the third round. He became the new heavyweight champion and first European to defeat an American for the belt since 1933. But it was Patterson who delivered the thunder in their rematch the following June when he recaptured the heavyweight crown by landing a devastating left hook that left Johansson unconscious for more than five minutes. Their third bout the following year was another slugfest, with both fighters going down before Patterson stopped Johansson in the sixth round.

5. MUHAMMAD ALI VS. KEN NORTON. An ex-Marine, Ken Norton learned to box in the service, working as a sparring partner for Joe Frazier and eventually moving on to become a top heavyweight and the only fighter other than Smokin' Joe to face Frazier's nemesis, Muhammad Ali, three times in the ring. All the Norton-Ali bouts were close. The first one took place in Norton's hometown of San Diego on the last day of March in 1973, with the powerful Norton breaking Ali's jaw early in the fight and pounding his way to a split-decision victory. They fought again in September, with Ali prevailing, also on a split decision. They met a third time on September 28, 1976 at historic Yankee Stadium in a bizarre scene featuring a wild crowd unchecked by police, who were on strike at the time. Norton appeared to control the fight early, but Ali won some rounds with last-minute action and unleashed one final burst of energy in the 15th round to win a unanimous but controversial and disputed decision.

4. ARTURO GATTI VS. MICKY WARD. This was a riveting trilogy that no one really saw coming. Ward was a junior welterweight who was a fan favorite in New England, but hardly a star. After six years as a pro, Ward actually retired for three years before coming back in 1994 and establishing himself with a devastating left hook. Gatti, the former International Boxing Federation super featherweight champion, was an established fan favorite and television draw for his exciting style. Their first battle on May 18, 2002, in Atlantic City, was one for the ages, with both fighters attacking each other until Ward put Gatti down in the ninth round with a vicious left hook to the body and win a majority decision. It was a fight that demanded a rematch, and six months later they fought another spirited battle, this time with Gatti winning, setting up a June 7, 2003 rubber match that didn't disappoint. Gatti broke his right hand in the fourth round, but still managed to score and keep Ward at bay until the sixth when Ward caught him with a right hand. Gatti recovered and went on to earn a valiant decision. The first and third fights of this trilogy were acknowledged as the Fights of the Year by the boxing media.

3. TONY ZALE VS. ROCKY GRAZIANO. Rocky Graziano was the New York street kid who grew up to be one of the most popular fighters in boxing. He seemed poised to take the middleweight title from Tony Zale when the two met at Yankee Stadium on September 27, 1946. But Zale, as tough a fighter as the division had ever seen, was not ready to give up the belt. Right from the opening bell, the two went at it in a Pier-Six brawl, with Zale putting Graziano down with a left hook in the first round. But Graziano came back by the end of the round to put Zale in trouble. Zale took a beating from the second through the fifth, but came out for the sixth with an attack that dropped Graziano with a finishing left hook to the stomach. The rematch took place the following July at Chicago Stadium, and proved to be another slugfest. Zale came right after Graziano and hit him with a shot above the left eye that opened up a severe cut and closed the eye. But good corner work brought the cut under control and Graziano pushed the action until a series of right hands in the sixth draped Zale over the ropes for the stoppage. The third historic match took place on June 10, 1948 at Roosevelt Stadium in Newark, New Jersey. Graziano was the favorite going in, but Zale dropped him in the opening round and then knocked him out with a left hook in the third round to become the first middleweight champion to regain his crown since Stanley Ketchel 40 years earlier.

2. BARNEY ROSS VS. JIMMY MCLARNIN. This ethnic turf war between the outstanding Jewish and Irish fighters of their day produced three epic battles within 365 days. McLarnin, the reigning welterweight champion, was generally recognized as the best fighter in the game. But over and above his general reputation, McLarnin was viewed by Jewish boxing fans as "The Hebrew Scourge" and "Jew Killer," having taken on and taken out the best of the Ghetto heroes—Joey Glick, Sid Terris, Al Singer, Joey Sangor, Kid Kaplan, Ruby Goldstein, and that hero of heroes, Benny Leonard. Now the latest Jewish hero, Barney Ross, the lightweight and junior welterweight champion and winner of 55 of his 57 fights—including two wins over the great Tony Canzoneri—would challenge McLarnin for his welterweight title. It would be Ross's speed versus McLarnin's punching power. But in a reversal of form, Ross discarded his usual careful style that had served him well in previous 57 fights and matched McLarnin punch-for-punch. With each throwing punches and caution to the wind, the two battled evenly for eight rounds. Then, in the ninth, McLarnin nailed Ross and, for the first time in his career, knocked him down. Ross jumped up and tore into McLarnin, 45 seconds later knocking McLarnin down with two vicious lefts. Now it was McLarnin who leapt to his feet and came back at Ross. After 15 rounds of brutal give and take, the decision went to Ross with scores all over the map—11-2-2 and 13-1-1 for Ross and 9-1-5 for McLarnin. Their second battle, four months later, again at the Long Island Bowl, where no reigning champion had ever successfully defended his crown, would be another bruising battle, this time McLarnin winning a split decision, although 22 of the 29 ringside reporters gave the nod to Ross. Their third fight, eight months later and exactly one year to the day of their first fight in 1934, was another bruising battle with Ross breaking his right thumb in the sixth round but fighting with agony through the remaining nine rounds to win a unanimous decision which many thought McLarnin had won. The final tally for this epic 30s trilogy: Two wins for Ross, one of McLarnin, and three for boxing.

1. MUHAMMAD ALI VS. JOE FRAZIER. The three fights between these two great heavyweight champions established perhaps the greatest rivalry in the history of sports and produced two of the three greatest heavyweight title fights of all time. Ali was stripped of his heavyweight championship in 1967 when he refused induction into the armed services. It took him over three years to get re-licensed and back into the ring. In the interim, Frazier won a version of the heavyweight championship sanctioned by the New York State Athletic Commission, and then defeated Jimmy Ellis for the World Boxing Association belt. That set the stage for the two undefeated heavyweights to meet at Madison Square Garden on March 8, 1971. Billed as "The Fight," it was an event that transcended boxing. Frazier fought at a furious pace throughout much of the bout. But Ali withstood the assault until the 11th round when he was wobbled. Then, in the 15th round, Ali went down from a left hook that sealed the win for Frazier. With neither fighter entering the ring wearing a title belt, their 1974 rematch was hardly as memorable, Ali winning by unanimous decision. But their third and final battle, known as "The Thrilla in Manila," on October 1, 1975, is considered by many as the greatest heavyweight fight in history—a brutal ring war that went back and forth until Frazier's right eye was closed shut and his trainer Eddie Futch threw in the towel after the 14th round as the champion Ali collapsed in his corner from exhaustion with questions remaining to this day as to whether he could have answered the bell for the 15th round.

BIGGEST BOXING STORIES OF THE LAST 50 YEARS
:: BY ED SCHUYLER, JR.

Note: Ed Schuyler Jr. served as the national boxing writer for the Associated Press for over three decades, covering more than 6,000 fights and 300 world championship bouts. Honored with the Nat Fleischer Award for Excellence in Boxing Journalism in 1979 by the Boxing Writer's Association of America, Schuyler was inducted into the International Boxing Hall of Fame in 2010. Schuyler covered thousands of boxing stories during his time in the business; here are the ten stories that he thinks had biggest impact on the sport, sports in general and our lives over the past half-century.

10. THE RAY MANCINI-DUK KOO KIM FIGHT IN 1982. The Mancini-Kim fight, seen on national TV, led to Kim's tragic death, then a call for the banning of the sport and the institution of the 12-round limit.

9. THE POST-FIGHT MELEE AT MADISON SQUARE GARDEN AFTER THE RIDDICK BOWE-ANDREW GOLOTA FIGHT IN 1996. It wasn't a riot, nobody fired any shots, but it was damaging to boxing nevertheless.

8. ALI WINS THE "RUMBLE IN THE JUNGLE" IN 1974. Ali was supposed to be washed-up and this was to be his swansong. But his upset of the supposedly "invincible" Foreman was one of the biggest stories of 1974, or any other year.

7. ROBERTO DURAN QUITS AGAINST SUGAR RAY LEONARD IN THE "NO MAS" FIGHT IN 1980. Who would ever have expected that the quintessential warrior, Roberto Duran, would quit?

6. TYSON BITES OFF HOLYFIELD'S EAR IN 1997. A shocker to those who didn't understand things like that can happen in boxing.

5. "THE FIGHT"—ALI-FRAZIER I IN 1971. An "event" that opened the door for multi-million dollar paydays for athletes.

4. BUSTER DOUGLAS KNOCKS OUT MIKE TYSON IN 1990. The biggest upset in boxing history.

3. FLOYD PATTERSON MAKES BOXING HISTORY BY KNOCKING OUT INGEMAR JOHANSSON IN 1960. Patterson becomes the first man to regain the heavyweight championship by defeating the man who had taken it from him the previous year.

2. MIKE TYSON'S CONVICTION FOR RAPE IN 1992. Tyson went from the sports pages to the front pages of the tabloids and the three-year incarceration turned him into a smaller, slower fighter.

1. MUHAMMAD ALI'S REFUSAL TO ENTER THE DRAFT AND SUBSEQUENT EXILE IN 1967. If Ali had continued his career, he might have been out of boxing by 1978.

THE MOST UNDERAPPRECIATED BOXERS IN HISTORY

The public is, at best, fickle. Not only do they tend to forget good fighters who have fought in the past, they also often overlook some good current ones, especially—their eyes fixed upon heavyweights and nothing but heavyweights—those plying their trade in the lower weight classes. Sometimes those overlooked are neglected or unappreciated because they toil in the shadow of more famous boxers, don't get seen on TV, or simply get lost somewhere in the blind spots of history. Here are some of those who are most overdue their just due.

10. LEN HARVEY (1920–42). One of the best middleweights of his era, Britain's Len Harvey won 111 bouts with 51 KOs in a career that spanned 23 years. Fighting almost exclusively on his home turf, Harvey won the Commonwealth and British Empire middleweight and heavyweight championships. Unfortunately, all that is remembered of Harvey on this side of the Pond is the only time he ventured to the States—in 1931 to take on future middleweight champions Vince Dundee and Ben Jeby, losing twice to Dundee and once to Jeby. But in his battles in Britain, Harvey was virtually unbeatable, losing only 10 of his 130 fights.

9. MAXIE ROSENBLOOM (1923–39). Unfortunately, the man known as "Slapsie Maxie"—due to his tendency to slap his punches—is more well-known today as a character actor in old vintage Hollywood movies, usually of the Damon Runyon variety. Maxie fought 299 bouts and held the light heavyweight title, but is still remembered, when remembered at all, as a clown in the ring and on the screen.

8. SAM LANGFORD (1902–26). All Langford did was win a recorded 167 fights and score 117 KOs while fighting in all classes from lightweight to heavyweight. But he never got a title shot with Jack Dempsey and even his fellow African-American Jack Johnson turned down his offers for championship bouts. And so Sam Langford remained an uncrowned champion—the greatest in boxing history.

7. JIMMY WILDE (1910–23). The name Jimmy Wilde is lost for the ages. But this little flyweight was one of the greatest fighters of his time. All of five feet, two inches tall and weighing no more than 108 pounds, dripping wet, Wilde fought almost 100 times before suffering his first loss and overall won 131 times with 99 knockouts in one of the most astounding career records in all of boxing.

6. LARRY HOLMES (1973–2002). Despite ruling the heavyweight division for over seven years and winning his first 48 fights, one shy of Rocky Marciano's unblemished record, Larry Holmes was never fully appreciated, always overshadowed by the man he once served as a sparring partner for: Muhammad Ali.

5. EZZARD CHARLES (1940-59). To many with an eye for fistic delicacies, Ezzard Charles rates as the greatest light heavyweight they ever saw. An all-around performer who could box and punch and moved up to fight against heavyweights, Charles would meet and beat the best—including Charlie Burley, Jersey Joe Walcott (twice) and Archie Moore (three times). Unfortunately, Charles has never gotten his just due, despite his 87 wins and 49 knockouts, in large part because of one of his biggest wins—his 15-round decision over Joe Louis in 1950. Charles' win over the beloved Louis caused many fans to resent him and relegate Charles to Louis' footnotes for the rest of his career and beyond.

4. MARCEL CERDAN (1934-49). Maybe it was because he wasn't an American or because he only held the middleweight crown for nine months—winning it from Tony Zale and losing it to Jake LaMotta in his final fight. Whatever the reason, Marcel Cerdan doesn't get the historical billing he deserves as an all-time great. An Algerian *pied-noir*, Cerdan racked up 106 wins in 110 bouts with 61 knockouts during his career. Many servicemen who watched him giving exhibitions for the troops in North Africa during World War II called him the "greatest fighter" they had ever seen.

LARRY HOLMES (LEFT) vs MUHAMMAD ALI, 1980.

3. HAROLD JOHNSON (1947-71). Although Johnson won 76 bouts during his 24-year career and even wore the light heavyweight crown for two years, he is remembered, when remembered at all, by the boxing fan as only half the answer to a trivia question: what father and son were both KO'd by Jersey Joe Walcott? (The answer being Harold and his father, Phil.) But to those hardcore fans who saw Johnson, he stood out as a great technical fighter who was ranked as a top light heavyweight every year except one from 1951 to 1964.

2. JIMMY BIVINS (1940-55). Bivins fought for 16 years in both the heavyweight and light heavyweight divisions, winning 86 fights against the best in both, including the likes of Anton Christoforidis, Teddy Yarosz, Gus Lesnevich, Joey Maxim, Billy Soose, Ezzard Charles, Melio Bettina and Archie Moore—former or future champions all. And yet, Bivins never got a shot at a title even though he was declared the "Interim Heavyweight" and "Interim Light Heavyweight Champion" during World War II and continued to distinguish himself as a great boxer for a decade after the war.

1. CHARLEY BURLEY (1936-50). Few boxing fans remember the name Charley Burley, but those who do—like the great trainer Eddie Futch, who called Burley, "the finest all-around fighter I ever saw"—remember. And what they remember is a great black fighter out of Pittsburgh who, unfortunately, fought during the era of Jim Crow and couldn't break through boxing's color curtain. The closest Burley ever got to stardom came in 1942 when, after having been a ranked welterweight for four years, he fought "Showboat" Phil McQuillan in New York City. In little over one minute, Burley knocked out McQuillan, effectively ending two careers—that of McQuillan and his own. A victor by victory undone, Burley showed he was so good that night that nobody wanted to touch the man Archie Moore called, ". . . the toughest of them all."

MY ALL-TIME FAVORITE FIGHTERS :: BY IRAN BARKLEY

Note: Iran Barkley developed his appreciation for great fighters the hard way—by fighting a lot of them. During his career, the Bronx native climbed into the ring to face the championship likes of Roberto Duran, Michael Nunn, James Toney, Nigel Benn, and Tommy Hearns (twice), who between them held about a dozen titles. Barkley didn't do too badly himself, winning two world middleweight crowns and a light heavyweight championship, along with *The Ring* magazine's "Comeback Fighter of the Year" honor for 1992. He also became the only fighter to better Hearns twice, no mean feat. Here, Barkley shows that he is a student of the history of the sport of boxing—as well as someone who wrote himself into its history books—by listing his favorite fighters, some of whom enjoyed their heydays well before Barkley was born.

10. CARMEN BASILIO.

9. MAX SCHMELING.

8. JAKE LaMOTTA.

7. RENALDO SNIPES.

6. JACK DEMPSEY.

5. LARRY HOLMES.

4. JACK JOHNSON.

3. MUHAMMAD ALI.

2. JOE FRAZIER.

1. JOE LOUIS.

BOXING'S BIGGEST DISAPPOINTMENTS

Every manager worth his cigar and every trainer worth his Q-Tip looks for, hopes for, prays for the next champion, as Charlie Goldman found in Rocky Marciano. Their care and feeding of every prospect that comes along that they can hopefully mold into a champion takes many forms, from tweaking their style, to nursing them along, to setting up bouts that provide on-the-job training to gauge what their prospect has, all essential to the success of their fighter. But more than sometimes that "can't miss" prospect, thought to be prodigiously talented turns out to be more skim milk than the cream of the crop. Throughout history, many's the fighter who never quite acquitted his promise fighters like Fighting Bob Martin, Roscoe Toles, Ted Golick, Vinny Shomo, Alex Ramos, Shawn O'Sullivan, Willie de Wit, Earl Hargrove and even Gerry Cooney. And then there were those who were BIG disappointments, like the ten listed below.

10. RUBY GOLDSTEIN. Acclaimed by his fans as the next Benny Leonard, Ruby Goldstein, nicknamed "The Jewel of the Ghetto," ran off 23 consecutive wins at the beginning of his career, 13 by knockout, and was featured on the cover of *Ring Magazine*. However, in his 24th fight he was KO'd by Ace Hudins and lost his next fight when he couldn't continue due to a sprained ankle. But he resuscitated his career with six more wins before meeting another hero of the ghetto, Sid Terris, called "The Ghetto Ghost," in a neighborhood fight big enough to be held at the Polo Grounds. Goldstein floored Terris with a right hand in the first round, but after Terris arose at the count of nine, Goldstein raced in to finish him off and Terris, with one well-timed right, caught the onrushing Goldstein to knock him out. His rollercoaster career continued with 10 more wins before he was matched with Jimmy McLarnin on December 13, 1929, who KO'd him in two rounds. And although Goldstein would go on to record 54 wins, 38 by KO, with only six losses—all by KO—he would forever remain in the eyes of his followers a disappointment.

9. RICARDO WILLIAMS, JR. A silver medalist at the 2000 Olympics in the light welterweight class, Williams was called the cream of the Olympic class, gaining the nickname, "Slicky Ricky." With power in both hands, he was thought to be the next great prospect and began to acquit his promise by winning his first nine bouts as a pro. But, in his tenth fight, he lost to a journeyman named Juan Valenzuela, who was just 15-6 going in, and later to Manning Galloway. Then, in 2005, Williams was sentenced to three years for conspiracy to distribute cocaine. Although he tried to put his personal train back on its tracks upon his release, to all intents and purposes his once promising career was over.

8. JAMES J. BEATTIE. A mammoth six-foot-nine, 240-pound heavyweight from Minnesota, Beattie was culled in 1962 from a large list of potential heavyweights as the next "White Hope" by a syndicate known as "Kid Galahad, Inc." Moved from St. Paul to New York, Beattie was quickly inserted into bouts, losing a couple to another heavyweight prospect, James J. Woody. But somewhere along the way he discovered, as it was rumored, that "Kid Galahad" was backed by mob boss Frankie Carbo and wanted no part of it. He was threatened, even—as the story goes—having his water poisoned in one bout. Finally, free of his contract, Beattie returned home and became the heavyweight champion of Minnesota and later, appropriately enough, appeared in the movie *The Great White Hope*, playing the part of the fictional Jess Willard.

7. JACK DOYLE. Called "The Gorgeous Gael," the six-foot-five, dashing and handsome Jack Doyle was the beau idol of Ireland in the 1930s, undefeated as an amateur and winner of 14 of his first 15 pro bouts, losing the other on a DQ. In 1933 he challenged Jack Peterson for the British heavyweight title. Unfortunately, Doyle did his training for the bout in pubs, rousing and carousing up to the day of the fight—some even saying up to the very fight itself. Discovering soon after the opening bell that he didn't have a chance, he took to fouling and was disqualified. He would go on to win a few more bouts and be brought over to America to take on Buddy Baer—the younger brother of then-heavyweight champion Max Baer. And for the two minutes and 38 seconds that the bout lasted, the 11,547 at Madison Square Garden were treated to a slugfest as Doyle hurt the heavier Baer, but in return was dropped three times to end the fight. Doyle would reconsider his choice of careers, becoming a singer and actor instead of a boxer and marrying the Mexican movie star Movita, who later became the wife of Marlon Brando.

6. LEM FRANKLIN. In 1941 Lem Franklin was the second-ranking heavyweight in the world, behind only Billy Conn by virtue of his having beaten such heavyweight contenders as Curtis "Hatchetman" Sheppard, Jimmy Bivins, Abe Simon, and Lee Savold. But then in February of 1942, he was KO'd by the light-punching Bob Pastor and went on to lose six of his last nine fights, becoming, by the end of his career, an "opponent."

5. BILLY ARNOLD. A welterweight out of Philadelphia, Billy Arnold had won the Inter-City Golden Gloves and was thought, in boxing parlance, to be a "comer." After going undefeated in 25 fights, his brain trust brought him to New York, where, in his debut, he lost a decision to former welterweight champion Fritzie Zivic. But still, when he entered the ring at Madison Square Garden the night of March 9, 1945, to face Rocky Graziano, who had just lost two fights to Harold Green, Arnold was a 6-to-1 favorite. Graziano soon showed him that he was no longer in "The City of Brotherly Love," but instead in "The City of Brotherly Shove," as he shoved Arnold around the ring with his punches and drove him to the canvas three times in three rounds, KO'ing Arnold and his career.

4. VINCE FOSTER. A welterweight out of Omaha managed by the cagy Jack Hurley, Foster ran up a record of 20-1 fighting in the Midwest. Brought to New York, Foster knocked out Tony Pellone in seven rounds to set up a bout with Charley Fusari at Madison Square Garden on May 13, 1949. Knocked down three times in the first round, Foster turned away from Hurley who was hollering instructions—Hurley later saying, "I think he lost to spite me."—and was KO'd at 1:10 of the first round. Heartbroken, Foster turned to drink and two months later, while driving drunk, was killed in an auto accident.

3. JORGÉ LUIS GONZALEZ. The Cuban heavyweight won gold medals at the 1983 and '87 Pan Am Games, defeating Riddick Bowe and Lennox Lewis in the process. Gonzalez defected and turned pro in the U.S., running up a record of 23-0, with 22 knockouts. A fearsome-looking six-foot-seven fighter with a Mohawk haircut, Gonzalez never let success go to his training, telling his American trainers he had been trained by his Cuban trainers and refusing to listen to them. Climbing into the MGM Grand ring to face the same Riddick Bowe he had defeated in the Pan Am Games, Gonzalez showed his lack of training as Bowe took him out in six rounds. And Tim Witherspoon went Bowe one up, knocking out Gonzalez in five rounds the next year to effectively end his career with 31 wins and 27 KOs and eight losses.

2. MANUEL URTAIN. Dubbed "El Cid" by Spanish dictator Generalissimo Franco, Jose Manuel Ibar Urtain was a superman, pictured lifting cars and cattle, with no less an authority than Nat Fleischer of *The Ring* magazine saying, "No man who ever held the world heavyweight title could match Urtain's feats of strength." Urtain won his first fight in 17 seconds and ran up a record of 30-0, winning all by knockout, before being stopped in the ninth round by Henry Cooper in November, 1970 in a fight for the European heavyweight championship. Urtain's career ended seven years later after he was KO'd in the fourth round by the so-called "Lion of Flanders"—Jean-Pierre Coopman. After fighting Coopman the previous year, Muhammad Ali had said the Belgian "had nothing." Still, Coopman's "nothing" proved too much for Urtain.

1. DUANE BOBICK. The World Amateur Heavyweight champion in 1971 and the U.S. super heavyweight in the 1972 Olympic games, Duane Bobick turned pro in 1973, winning his first 15 fights by knockout. He added ten more wins in '74 and eight more in '75 and by 1976 was the third-ranked heavyweight in the world. On the night of May 11, 1977, he entered the ring at Madison Square Garden with a record of 38-0 and 32 knockouts to face Ken Norton, who had lost a close decision in a title fight with Muhammad Ali the previous year. And in just one minute and 48 seconds the bubble burst as Norton caught Bobick with a big looping right hand that staggered Bobick and followed with a barrage of punches that put Bobick down and out. Bobick would go on to suffer KO losses to Kallie Knoetze, John Tate, and George Chaplin, who ended Bobick's career in 1979 with a record of 48 wins, 42 KOs, and four losses (all by KO), along with the dubious title "King of the Disappointments."

GREATEST DEFENSIVE FIGHTERS

One of the most important skills for a great boxer, pure and simply, is the ability to avoid punishment. There have been great defensive fighters in the old-old days, fighters who, like Young Griffo, couldn't be hit by someone standing on the same handkerchief as them, and others, like Jem Welsh, who proudly wore cauliflower ears as testament to their ability to move just enough to avoid being hit anywhere but on the ears. In more recent times, some fighters — like Herol Graham and the more modern Floyd Mayweather, Jr. — have earned the label "slick" for their defensive abilities. But such skills are not appreciated by today's fans as much as they were in the days of yore. Here are the ten who remain most appreciated for their mastery of the fundamental skill of avoiding punishment in the ring.

12. Joey Maxim (1941-58). A survivor, Joey Maxim had a total of 115 fights against some of the hardest hitters of his day and was only knocked out once, that by Curtis "Hatchman" Sheppard—whom he came back to beat three weeks later—and then have 85 more fights without being stopped. Maxim, who fought off his back foot, which might explain his having only 21 KO's to his credit, could parry anything coming his way and still be in position to counter. In his memorable 1952 fight against Sugar Ray Robinson in defense of his light heavy crown with the temperature reaching 104 degrees under the hot Yankee Stadium lights, Maxim took everything Robinson could throw and stood up against the assault for 13 rounds in that sweltering hotbox before Robinson collapsed. Later, when a reporter told Maxim he had won only because of the temperature, he replied, "I was in that heat, too." And he was, surviving as he always did to win.

11. James J. Corbett (1886-1903). In his day—his day being the late 1800s and early 1900s—James J. Corbett's style was referred to as "The Sweet Science." But it was really the beginning of defensive boxing in an era when out-and-out slugging was the norm. Corbett used his footwork and hand speed in a manner unknown to boxingkind, anticipating blows and backing out of harm's way and fighting in balletic arcs, all the better to counter his opponents' wild swings. It was a style that frustrated and ultimately defeated the theretofore invincible John L. Sullivan—and ushered in a new era in boxing, with every defensive fighter since Corbett carrying part of his defensive DNA in their style.

10. Wilfred Benitez (1973-90). A disingenuous fighter, insincere in his moves, Benitez misled, deceived, tricked, and lied to his opponents as he offered them something to hit; but when they knocked, nobody was home. Sugar Ray Leonard admitted, after his fight with "El Radar," that Benitez had successfully "slipped" his best shots and "countered" him all night.

9. YOUNG GRIFFO (1886-1904). The original "Will o' the Wisp" was gifted with almost superhuman defensive skills and an ability to make any opponent look ridiculous with his dazzling feints, head fakes, sidestepping and impenetrable defense. Born in Australia as Albert Griffiths, this featherweight claimant was, in the opinion of *The Ring* magazine editor Nat Fleischer, "the cleverest boxer who ever performed under the Queensberry rules."

8. GENE TUNNEY (1915-28). Gene Tunney learned from the best—drawing on the styles of that prince of defense, Mike Gibbons, from his stablemate Benny Leonard, and the founder of modern-day scientific boxing, James J. Corbett—and put all their teachings into use, perfecting an almost impenetrable defense, one that carried him through 77 bouts against some of the 1920s greatest heavyweights and only being floored once—that once by a baker's dozen of murderous shots from Jack Dempsey in the most controversial knockdown in history, the one known as "The Long Count," from which he got up, whether at the referee's count of nine or the stop-watch's count of 14, to survive and win the fight.

7. JACK JOHNSON (1897-1932). In the words of Damon Runyon, "No greater defensive fighter than Jack Johnson ever lived." Although known primarily for his potent offensive skills, Johnson's ability to block and parry anything thrown at him also became legendary. Many of his fights took on the look of a game of patty cake, as he stood there nonchalantly catching everything his opponent threw, almost as if he were merely cruising on batteries, before coming back to batter his opponent into submission.

6. MAXIE ROSENBLOOM (1923-39). According to trainer Cus D'Amato, you could-n't hit Rosenbloom "in the backside with a handful of buckshot." This light heavyweight champion would give his opponents a "poosh and a tush," turning away, tying them up, and doing anything he could to evade their punches. Boxing scuttlebutt had it that the handlers of young undefeated prospect Joe Louis turned down a fight against "Slapsie Maxie," not because they doubted that Louis could beat him, but that he wouldn't look good doing so. Rosenbloom employed his eccentric and vexing defensive skills to stay basically unhit and unhittable during his 299-bout career.

5. MIKE GIBBONS (1907-22). "The St. Paul Phantom" dodged and befuddled opponents with a combination of reverse polarity and footwork worthy of his contemporary Vernon Castle, the king of ballroom dancing. After a fight against Eddie McGoorty, a ranking middleweight of the 1910s, Gibbons told newspaperman Hype Igoe, "I never let him hit me . . . not once. . . . He never laid a glove on me." Rarely did any of his other 126 opponents.

4. TOMMY LOUGHRAN (1919-37). Light heavyweight champ Loughran was an almost wraithlike presence in the ring, one who made such a fool of future heavyweight Max Baer that, after trying to locate the elusive Loughran round-after-futile round, he finally threw up his arms in exasperation with a "what-the-hell-can-you-do?" expression on his befuddled face. Known as "The Phantom of Philly," Loughran had such command of his ring performance that he would wind up in his corner at the bell ending the round, ensuring that he could just sit down and make his opponent walk across the ring to take his seat.

3. BENNY VALGAR (1916-29). Trainer Ray Arcel, who had been around since Cain & Abel, once said of Benny Valgar: "When it came to all-round ring generalship, Benny Valgar was on a par with Benny Leonard." But besides being a ring general with oak-leaf clusters, the boxer known as "The French Flash" was one of the greatest defensive fighters of his time—his time being the late 1910s and early 20s. With 184 recorded fights—and some historians listing as many as 239—this fancy jab-and-run fighter was never-ever knocked down or stopped.

2. PERNELL WHITAKER (1984-2001). Whitaker once said, "I don't care who I'm fighting. I don't care if it's God. If I don't want God to hit me, He's not going to hit me." And for 45 fights, no matter how much they tried, his opponents couldn't hit this gypsy phantom in front of them as he employed a Turkish bazaar of moves and motions, almost as if he had taken a four-way cold tablet and had to run three more ways to catch up with it.

1. WILLIE PEP (1940-66). Willie Pep was a Swiss movement to be watched, boxing's version of three-card-monte: now you see him, now you don't. Willie Pep fought with a "if-you-can't-convince-them-then-at-least-confuse-them" mentality. In his virtuoso performance, he won a round, literally, without throwing a punch. His opponent that night was Jackie Graves, a TNT-southpaw puncher. Before the fight, Pep had told a local Minneapolis writer he would not throw a punch in anger in the third round. And sure enough, he ducked, he feinted, he danced, he weaved and never threw a punch, winning the round on all three judges' scorecards. Pep proudly kept the write-up of the fight and his daring-do in his wallet till the day he died.

GREATEST FIGHTING FAMILIES :: BY MICHAEL ROSENTHAL

Note: Michael Rosenthal has been a sportswriter and editor in Southern California since 1987, first in newspapers in Los Angeles and San Diego for 20 years and then for *The Ring* magazine website, RingTV.com, since 2008. He started as a news reporter for a small suburban paper in 1982, but eventually found his niche in sports and reported on every major sport at one time or another. He covered his first fight in 1989 and was immediately hooked.

10. MAGRAMO (RIC, RONNIE, MELVIN AND RIC, JR.). Combined record: 142 wins, 0 losses, 12 draws.

9. CHAVEZ (JULIO CÉSAR, ROBERTO, OMAR AND JULIO CÉSAR, JR.). Combined record: 185 wins, 11 losses, four draws.

8. HILTON (DAVE, MATTHEW, ALEX AND STEWART AND DAVE, JR.). Combined record: 184 wins, 11 losses, four draws.

7. PENALOSA (CARL, DODIE BOY, GERRY, JONATHAN AND DODIE BOY, JR.). Combined record: 111 wins, 31 losses, 11 draws.

6. QUARRY (JERRY, MIKE AND BOBBY). Combined record: 124 wins, 34 losses, 12 draws.

5. FULLMER (GENE, DON AND JAY). Combined record: 129 wins, 31 losses, 10 draws.

4. ZIVIC (FRITZIE, JACK, PETE AND EDDIE). Combined record: 277 wins, 167 losses, 30 draws.

3. YAROSZ (TEDDY, TOMMY, JOEY AND EDDIE). Combined record: 202 wins, 31 losses, five draws.

2. MAYWEATHER (FLOYD, ROGER, JEFF, JUSTIN JONES AND FLOYD, JR.). Combined record: 166 wins, 29 losses, seven draws.

1. SPINKS (MICHAEL, LEON, CORY, DARRELL AND TOMMY). Combined record: 111 wins, 28 losses, four draws.

BOXING'S BIGGEST UPSETS

Ever since a horse named "Upset" defeated Man o' War in the great thoroughbred champion's only loss, the word has become part and parcel of the language of sport—particularly the sport of boxing, where upsets occur with more than some frequency. However, there are lowercased upsets and then there are BIG UPSETS—those so unexpected that they almost cause seismic shocks, like the ten below.

10. BATTLING SIKI VS. GEORGES CARPENTIER, SEPTEMBER 24, 1922, VELODROME BUFFALO ARENA, PARIS, FRANCE. Known as "The Orchid Man," Carpentier was the light heavyweight champion and overwhelming favorite of his Parisian fans and the oddsmakers, too, in his match against the Senegalese slugger Battling Siki. Before the bout, a rumor circulated that Siki had agreed to throw the fight. But after being knocked down by Carpentier in the first round and with Carpentier merely toying with him, Siki changed his mind and began fighting back. And hurting Carpentier. In the sixth round, Siki caught Carpentier with a left hook, flooring him. But referee Henri Bernstein ruled that instead of knocking down Carpentier, Siki had tripped him and declared the Frenchman the winner on a foul. However, the crowd disagreed and rioted, believing that an injustice had been done to Siki. Bernstein's decision was reversed and Siki was declared the winner and new light heavyweight champion.

9. FRITZIE ZIVIC VS. HENRY ARMSTRONG I, OCTOBER 4, 1940, MADISON SQUARE GARDEN, NEW YORK, NEW YORK. "Hammering Hank" simultaneously held the featherweight, lightweight and welterweight titles in 1938. He put his welterweight title on the line for the 20th time in 1940 to face brawler-boxer Fritzie Zivic, who came into the fight having, in his own words, "finished second" 23 times. And to listen to the pundits, the 4-1 underdog would soon add the 24th to that long list of "L's." However, Zivic—a somewhat-less-than-classic boxer who resorted to thumbs, elbows, or whatever else at his disposal—mauled, brawled and generally beat up Armstrong to win the welterweight crown and end Armstrong's long and glorious championship reign. The two would meet in a rematch three months later, with Armstrong again the betting favorite and Zivic again the winner, this time by a 12th-round knockout.

8. EVANDER HOLYFIELD VS. MIKE TYSON I, NOVEMBER 9, 1996, MGM GRAND, LAS VEGAS, NEVADA. Out of jail and champion again by way of "knocking out" Bruce Seldon, Mike Tyson finally, after several postponements, signed to fight Evander Holyfield. With fears about his health and a lackluster performance against Bobby Czyz in his last fight, Holyfield was thought to have so little chance that oddsmakers installed Tyson as the favorite by as much as 25-1. But Evander met Tyson toe-to-toe in the middle of the ring, thwarting his charges, backing him up and eventually beating him down, scoring a stoppage in the 11th round in what announcer Steve Albert called "A colossal upset."

7. SANDY SADDLER-WILLIE PEP I, OCTOBER 29, 1948, MADISON SQUARE GARDEN, NEW YORK. Two days before Halloween, 1948, featherweight champion Willie Pep stepped into the ring at Madison Square Garden to defend his title for the seventh time against an opponent he described as the "thin, weak-looking guy" named Sandy Saddler. Pep, who had only one loss in his previous 136 fights—that to former lightweight champion Sammy Angott, a human octopus who had tied Pep up in knots for 10 rounds—had held the title for five-plus years. Called "the Will o' the Wisp" for his ability to fake opponents out of their jocks with his many moves and feints, Pep was a prohibitive favorite over the challenger Saddler. But oddsmakers had only examined the bottle, not its contents in assessing Saddler. For Saddler had a snapping, twisting left and a powerful, sinewy right hand that had knocked out 56 opponents in his 85 wins and his 5' 8½" height and praying-mantis-like wingspan dwarfed the five-foot-five champion. Not allowing Pep to do that voodoo he did so well, Saddler attacked Pep from the beginning, finally getting to him in the third round and knocking him down twice, once from a solitary left hand. Then in the fourth, he drove Pep into the ground like a hammer to a nail with a dynamite right hand, ending the fight and setting up a four-fight rivalry that still remains one of the greatest in featherweight, if not boxing, history.

6. RANDY TURPIN VS. SUGAR RAY ROBINSON I, JULY 10, 1951, EARL'S COURT, LONDON, ENGLAND. After winning the middleweight title in 1951 from Jake LaMotta, Ray Robinson put on his own version of the European Grand Tour, complete with an entourage that resembled a troop movement. He fought Kid Marcel in Paris, Jean Wanes in Zurich, Jan de Bruin in Antwerp, Jean Walzack in Liege, Gerhard Hecht in Berlin, and Cyrille Delannoit in Turin. And then there was one last stop in England to face a fighter he had never seen, the European middleweight champion Randy Turpin for a then-impressive $100,000. But not merely wanting to be a party of the second part, the 2-1 underdog Turpin sliced open Robinson's eye in the seventh and outpunched him the rest of the way, to become the British Empire's first middleweight champion since Bob Fitzsimmons some half-a-century before—and hand Sugar Ray his first loss in eight years and only his second setback in over 125 fights.

5. MUHAMMAD ALI VS. GEORGE FOREMAN, OCTOBER 30, 1974, 20TH OF MAY STADIUM, KINSHASA, ZAIRE. Thought by many to be invincible and looking like the man Jack met at the top of the beanstalk, George Foreman put his title on the line against Muhammad Ali in what had been dubbed "The Rumble in the Jungle." With most of Ali's fans hoping for the best but fearing for the worst, if not his life, Ali put on a display far removed from his dancing days against another equally frightening opponent, Sonny Liston ten years before (see #4 on this list). This time he employed a defensive strategy he called "The Rope-a-Dope," leaning on the ropes and letting Big George pound away until be began to look like a hose after someone had turned off the water, going limp. Then, in the eighth, Ali caught George off balance and landed six straight shots, punctuated by a hard right that sent Foreman pirouetting to the canvas, there to be counted out.

4. CASSIUS CLAY VS. SONNY LISTON I, FEBRUARY 25, 1964, CONVENTION HALL, MIAMI, FLORIDA.

The young Cassius Clay literally baited the fighter he called "The Bear" into defending his heavyweight title against him, taunting Liston and haunting him in the ring and casinos in Vegas, issuing insulting challenge after insulting challenge until Liston decided to shut him up and fight him. Few gave Clay a snowball's chance in hell; others gave him less. The oddsmakers made Liston the 7-1 favorite, while comedian Joe E. Lewis, expressing the general consensus, said, "I'm betting on Clay . . . to live!" Clay's take on the odds: "If you'd like to lose your money, be a fool and bet on Sonny." And Liston's: "The odds should be ten-to-nothing that he doesn't last for the first round." At the opening bell, Liston lurched out of his corner, nearly running, determined to acquit his prediction. But Clay, moving away from Liston's potent jab, slid gracefully to his left. And for the next three rounds, Clay continued to move away, then pick openings with the care of a master craftsman, jolting the defending champion with pinpoint punches before moving back out of danger again. At the end of the fourth, Clay began to blink as if there was something in his eyes and for the fifth round, the half-blinded Clay got on his horse and stayed away from the heavy-handed champion. With his eyes cleared in the sixth, Clay put a beating on Liston who, after the round, spat out his mouthpiece, retiring in his corner as Clay leaned over the ropes, shouting, "Eat your words! Eat your words!" at the 46 members of the working press, 43 of whom had picked Liston.

3. JIM BRADDOCK VS. MAX BAER, JUNE 13, 1935, LONG ISLAND BOWL, LONG ISLAND CITY, NEW YORK.

Immortalized in the film, *Cinderella Man*, James J. Braddock, supposedly a washed-up former light heavyweight contender down on his luck and out of boxing for the better part of a year after breaking his hand in a September, 1933 fight against Abe Feldman, fought his way back into contention with wins over Corn Griffin, John Henry Lewis and Art Lasky to earn a shot at the heavyweight title held by Max Baer. Thought to have so little chance of dethroning Baer—who had won the title one year less a day earlier by flooring Primo Carnera 11 times—the oddsmakers installed Braddock as a 10-1 underdog. But Braddock outboxed Baer, who spent the entire 15 rounds posing and preening, to win the heavyweight crown in what was then called "a monumental upset."

2. MAX SCHMELING VS. JOE LOUIS I, JUNE 19, 1936, YANKEE STADIUM, NEW YORK, NEW YORK. Going into the fight with a record of 27 straight victories (23 by knockout), Louis was such a prohibitive favorite over the ex-heavyweight champion Schmeling—thought to be just one more ex-champion, like Carnera and Baer, who had been set up for Louis to knock down—that no New York boxing writer gave "Der Max" a chance of winning, let alone surviving. But Schmeling had, in his own words, "seed something"—Louis dropping his left hand after he jabbed. And, after absorbing Louis' jabs for three rounds, Schmeling caught Louis with an overhand right over Louis' low-held left, in the fourth, driving the invincible Louis to the floor for the first time in his career. From that point on, Louis had no memory of the fight, finally succumbing to Schmeling's right-hand smashes at 2:29 of the 12th round.

1. BUSTER DOUGLAS VS. MIKE TYSON, FEBRUARY 11, 1990, TOKYO DOME, TOKYO, JAPAN. The mother of all upsets, this UPSET is the standard by which all other upsets are measured, not just in boxing, but in all of sports. For here was Mike Tyson, the so-called "Baddest Man on the Planet," who was just two years removed from dispatching Michael Spinks in 91 seconds and who had taken all of 93 seconds to knock out Carl "The Truth" Williams in his last fight, taking on the underachieving Buster Douglas, described by HBO's Jim Lampley as "a plodding fighter who had difficulty looking spectacular." Douglas was thought to be just another body for Tyson, a "walk in the park," his chances so slim that the odds of his winning were an astronomical 42-to-1. But Douglas entered the ring that night with a determination, inspired by the recent death of his mother—to whom he dedicated the fight. Using his superior reach and powerful jab to beat Tyson to the punch time and again, Douglas dominated the fight. Tyson had his one brief moment, a knockdown of Douglas in the eighth round, but according to Tyson, ". . . when Douglas got up after I knocked him down and came back at me, I didn't have it in me." And come back he did, battering Tyson around the ring in the ninth round and knocking him out in the tenth to cap the greatest upset in boxing history.

BEST LINES ON INDIVIDUAL ASPECTS OF BOXING

Boxing entails so many different aspects—from training to the personalities of fighters to commentary from journalists to money, money and more money—that it generates a lot of good lines on the nature of its individual constituents, as well as on its general nature. Lines like these:

"I AM THE ASTRONAUT OF BOXING. JOE LOUIS AND DEMPSEY WERE JUST JET PILOTS. I'M IN A WORLD OF MY OWN." Heavyweight Champion Muhammad Ali, on his place in boxing history.

"NEW YORK'S LIKE A BOXING MATCH. IN HOLLYWOOD, IT'S LIKE A FELLINI MOVIE OR SOMETHING." Actor John Cusack, on the relationship between certain cities, boxing and Italian cinema.

"I HAVEN'T GOT 50 PERCENT OF HIM, HE'S GOT 50 PERCENT OF ME." Manager Jack Hurley, on his fighter Harry "Kid" Mathews.

"A MAN WITH A LICENSE TO MAKE A LIVING WHILE COMMITTING VAGRANCY." Sportswriter Jimmy Cannon, on boxing managers.

"WHERE LEGITIMATE BUSINESS IS A FIGURE OF SPEECH." Promoter Jimmy Johnston, on the commercial side of boxing.

"BOXING IS THE MOST INDIVIDUAL LIFESTYLE YOU CAN HAVE IN SOCIETY WITHOUT BEING AN ARTIST OR A CRIMINAL." Writer Peter Wood, on the boxer's way of life.

"IT AIN'T THE NUMBER OF SEATS YOU GOT, IT'S THE NUMBER OF ASSES THAT ARE IN THEM." Sugar Ray Robinson's manager, George Gainford, on how to assess a fight's potential.

"BOXING IS SORT OF LIKE JAZZ. THE BETTER IT IS, THE LESS PEOPLE CAN APPRECIATE IT." Heavyweight champion George Foreman on boxing, and a certain type of music.

"WHEN ARCHAEOLOGISTS DISCOVER THE MISSING ARMS OF VENUS DE MILO, THEY WILL FIND SHE WAS WEARING BOXING GLOVES." Film star John Barrymore, on the relationship between boxing and a certain piece of art.

"A HUSTLER WITH A PhD." Don King on the definition of a promoter.

GREATEST PUERTO RICAN FIGHTERS OF ALL TIME

:: BY MARIO RIVERA MARTINO

Note: "Many years ago, I wrote that 'possibly' no other country would produce as many boxing champions as this little speck of an island—close to invisible unless you squint at your Atlas," says longtime Puerto Rican boxing writer and World Boxing Organization (WBO) official Mario Rivera. "But it was within the realm of possibilities when, by 1983, we already had 15 titleholders, from the Sixto era to the Camacho era—and in between such greats as Carlos Ortiz, Chegui Torres, Alfredo Escalera, Wilfredo Gomez, Wilfred Benitez, and Chapo Rosario. It all started with bantam champion Sixto Escobar in 1934, with a little help from the island's unofficial boxing ambassador, *The Ring* magazine editor Nat Fleischer, when we counted on "The Bible of Boxing" to be the guiding force in recognizing *bonafide* champions. Not so today, when we have as many as four different champions recognized by four different boxing organizations in each and every division. But setting aside the four-tiered championship make-up of today, Puerto Rico still has more than enough Hall of Fame-quality champions to list them on a pound-for-pound basis. Here are my choices for the greatest all-time pound-for-pound Puerto Rican fighters."

10. EDWIN "CHAPO" ROSARIO. Lightweight champion, 1983-84, 1986-87 and 1989-91; junior welterweight champion 1991-92. Pro record: 47 wins, 41 KOs, six losses.

9. SIXTO ESCOBAR. Bantamweight champion 1934-35, 1936-37 and 1938-39. Pro record: 42 wins, 21 KOs, 18 losses, four draws.

8. PEDRO MONTAÑEZ. Lightweight and welterweight contender 1931-40. Pro record: 91 wins, 51 KOs, eight losses, four draws.

7. WILFREDO VÁZQUEZ. Super bantamweight champion 1992-95; featherweight champion 1996-98. Pro record: 56 wins, 41 KOs, nine losses, two draws.

6. MIGUEL COTTO. Junior welterweight champion 2004-06; welterweight champion 2006-08 and 2009; junior middleweight champion 2010. Pro record: 35 wins, 28 KOs, two losses.

5. JOSÉ "CHEGUI" TORRES. Light heavyweight champion 1965-66. Pro record: 41 wins, 29 KOs, three losses, one draw.

4. WILFRED BENITEZ. Junior welterweight champion 1976-77; welterweight champion 1978-79; junior middleweight champion 1981-82. Pro record: 53 wins, 31 KOs, eight losses, one draw.

3. CARLOS ORTIZ. Junior welterweight champion 1959-60; lightweight champion 1962-65 and 1965-68. Pro record: 61 wins, 30 KOs, seven losses, one draw.

2. FELIX "TITO" TRINIDAD. Welterweight champion 1993-99; junior middleweight champion 2000; middleweight champion 2001. Pro record: 42 wins, 35 KOs, three losses.

1. WILFREDO GOMEZ. Super bantamweight champion 1977-83; featherweight champion 1984; super featherweight champion 1985-86. Pro record: 44 wins, 42 KOs, three losses, one draw.

GREATEST *NEW YORK DAILY NEWS* GOLDEN GLOVES CHAMPIONS :: BY BILL FARRELL

Note: A *Daily News* reporter for more than 30 years, Bill Farrell covered the Golden Gloves for 20 of those years and is the author of *Cradle of Champions: 80 Years of New York Daily News Golden Gloves.*

10. DENNIS MILTON/ DAVEY MOORE. A toss-up. Both were unbeatable fan favorites and outstanding boxers, each undefeated in winning four Golden Gloves titles.

9. ZAB JUDAH. Had the speed, power, and instincts to impose his will on every opponent in winning 139-lb. championships in 1994 and 1995.

8. MITCH "BLOOD" GREEN. One of the most imposing heavyweights in the history of the Gloves, winner of four titles in five years.

7. MICHAEL BENTT. The heavyweight open champion from 1984-86, he skipped '87 to focus on the Olympic trials and returned to win a fourth championship in 1988.

6. HECTOR CAMACHO. Winner of three Golden Gloves championships, 1978-80, Camacho brought joy and enthusiasm to the ring.

5. HOWARD DAVIS, JR. A four-time Golden Gloves champion (1973-76), and Olympic gold medalist. One veteran official said Davis was the "perfect" Olympic-style boxer.

4. FLOYD PATTERSON. Unbeatable at 160 lbs. in 1951, he won the 175-lb. championship final with one punch in 1952 before going on to win an Olympic gold medal.

3. VINCENT SHOMO. In an era that featured Emile Griffith and Jose Torres, this knockout artist from Harlem was the headliner. He was the first four-time champion with a then-record 13 first-round knockouts.

2. SUGAR RAY ROBINSON. After losing his first sub-novice bout in 1939, Robinson returned as the premiere "must see," "can't miss," prospect, winning open championships in 1939 and 1940.

1. MARK BRELAND. The first five-time champion, Breland dominated the Gloves from 1980 through 1984, stopping 22 of his 23 opponents, 15 in the first round.

BOXING'S GREATEST METHUSELAHS

Boxing doesn't belong just to the young. Some of the all-time greats have fought so long that even their trunks were turning gray. But, as Archie Moore once said of his future opponents, "It's not this old gray head they're afraid of, it's these old gray fists." Here are ten fighters who washed away the improbability of the calendar, their "old gray fists" continuing to strike fear in the hearts of their opponents after their heads turned a touch of gray.

10. JEM MACE (BORN: 1831; CAREER: 1855-1896). The last London Prize Fight champion, Mace fought to the age of 59, winning as many times as he lost.

9. SUGAR RAY ROBINSON (BORN 1921; CAREER: 1940-52, 1954-65). The man whom many called "The Greatest Fighter of All Time" fought in 48 bouts after the age of 40, winning 31 of them with 16 KOs.

8. EVANDER HOLYFIELD (BORN: 1962; CAREER: 1984-). Like the little train that could, Evander willed himself to win after win, and kept right on chugging into middle age. As of this book's going to press, he'd fought eight times (once for the vacant IBF heavyweight title) and won five bouts since turning 40.

7. DANIEL MENDOZA (BORN: 1764; CAREER: 1787-1820). Mendoza was recognized by many as the father of what was later to be called "Scientific Boxing," revolutionizing the sport by incorporating defensive tactics into it. Despite standing only 5'7" and weighing just 160 pounds, Mendoza became the 16th heavyweight champion of the bareknuckle world. He fought and won a 53-round bout at the age of 42, fighting his last battle at the age of 56.

6. KID AZTECA (BORN: 1913; CAREER: 1930 OR 1932-1961). After turning 40, by his own calculations, the Mexican welterweight had 26 fights, winning all but one by KO. For his swan song at the age of 47, Azteca KO'd his opponent in the first round.

5. BERNARD HOPKINS (BORN: 1965; CAREER: 1988-). Hopkins promised his mother he would retire when he turned 40, but decided after his mother passed away the promise was no longer binding. So rather than pack his storied career in mothballs and lavender, he continued on, beating such top-ranked fighters as Winky Wright and Kelly Pavlik, who was, at the time, the undefeated middleweight champion and 17 years younger than Hopkins.

4. Saoul Mamby (born: 1947; career: 1971–2000, 2008). The former junior welterweight titleholder fought 25 times after his 40th birthday, including once at the age of 60, making him the oldest fighter ever to appear in an officially sanctioned bout.

3. Bob Fitzsimmons (born: 1863; career: 1883–1914). The former middleweight and heavyweight champion won the light heavyweight crown at the age of 40 and went on to fight for 11 more years.

2. George Foreman (born: 1949; career: 1969-77, 1987-97). Proclaiming that "forty is not a death sentence," Foreman fought 20 times after the age of 40, winning 17 of those with 12 KOs. He recaptured the heavyweight belt he'd lost 20 years before by knocking out undefeated 26-year-old champ Michael Moorer in 1994 at the advanced age of 45, becoming the oldest man ever to win the title.

1. Archie Moore (born: 1913 or 1916; career: 1936-63). Nobody knew exactly how old "the Ol' Mongoose" actually was, with his mother saying he was born in 1913, while Moore claimed it was 1916. (The quick-witted Moore had an answer for the discrepancy, saying, "I have given this a lot of thought and have decided that I must have been three when I was born.") But no matter who was keeping score, ol' Archie chalked up at least 30 fights after turning 40, including two challenges for the heavyweight belt and nine defenses of his light heavyweight title, which he still held at the advanced age of 48.

SADDEST FINALES

Unfortunately, boxers rarely know when to quit, staying on long after the footlights have dimmed and the curtains of their primes have come down. And as once-greats who are now once-wases, they become cannon fodder for young turks who have entered, stage left, to take their turn in the spotlight. For evidence of this unfortunate tendency, look to the fact that only six of the first 27 heavyweight champions exited their careers, stage right, with a "W." Here are ten of the saddest final fights of some of the all-time greats.

10. JERSEY JOE WALCOTT (1930–53). After losing his title to Rocky Marciano in 1952 in what had been one of the most exciting heavyweight title fights of all time, Jersey Joe met Marciano in a return bout on May 15, 1953 in an attempt to regain his crown. But the highly anticipated rematch turned out to be, in the words of the poet laureate of sportswriters, Red Smith, "one of the most sordid of all time." After Marciano threw the fight's first notable punch—a right "to the expression," according to Smith—Walcott took a seat on the floor and sat there while referee Frank Sikora tolled ten to end the fight. And Walcott's career.

9. JIMMY WILDE (1910–23). Acknowledged by all as the greatest flyweight of all time, "The Mighty Atom" Jimmy Wilde ended his career at New York's Polo Grounds on June 18, 1923 by losing his title to the hard-punching Pancho Villa. The Filipino battered and bloodied Wilde for seven rounds until the referee had seen enough—even if Wilde hadn't—and stepped in mercifully to stop the slaughter.

8. TONY CANZONERI (1925–39). A popular champion in three weight classes (featherweight, lightweight, and junior welterweight), Canzoneri ended his career on November 1, 1939 by serving as a punching bag for hard-hitting left-hook artist Al "Bummy" Davis, with the 19-year-old Davis handing the once-great Canzoneri his only KO loss in 176 career fights.

7. MIKE TYSON (1985–2005). Once, by his own declaration, "The Baddest Man on the Planet," Tyson was by 2004 anything but. After taking a beating from the unheralded Danny Williams in four rounds in July of 2004, Tyson came back in June 2005 to fight an even lesser opponent, Kevin McBride, who dominated a sluggish Tyson, making the former champion quit before the seventh round.

6. WILLIE PEP (1940-66). One of the greatest fighters of the 20th century, the man known as "The Will o' the Wisp" was still knocking out opponents into his 44th year. Pep thought his last fight—in Richmond, Virginia on March 16, 1966 against someone named Calvin Woodland—was supposed to be just an exhibition. Instead, it was ruled an official bout and a unanimous decision win for Woodland.

5. JIM JEFFRIES (1896-1910). After having retired as undefeated heavyweight champion in 1905, Jeffries was called back into the ring five years later by public outcry and the white establishment, which viewed African-American Jack Johnson's 1908 defeat of Tommy Burns for the heavyweight title an insult and worse— novelist Jack London exhorting him to "remove that golden smile from Jack Johnson's face . . . Jeff, the White Man must be saved!" Famous author Jack London wrote, "Jeffries must emerge from his alfalfa farm and remove that smile from Johnson's face. Jeff it's up to you!" Succumbing to the pleas, Jeffries entered the ring on July 4, 1910 to take back their title from Johnson. But in front of a hopeful crowd of 15,760 packed into the Reno outdoor arena, Johnson played with the sup- posedly invincible Jeffries for 14 rounds, then, in the 15th, as the crowd shouted, "Stop it! Don't let him get knocked out!" Johnson knocked down the exhausted and beaten-down Jeffries thrice to end the crusade and Jeffries' career.

4. BENNY LEONARD (1911-24; 1931-32). The all-time great lightweight champion retired in 1925 after ruling the lightweight roost for almost eight years, but was forced to make a comeback after being wiped out by the stock market crash of 1929. After 19 comeback fights without a defeat against, at best, mediocre compe- tition, Leonard was matched with the hard-hitting Jimmy McLarnin on October 7, 1932. The result was sadly predictable as McLarnin raked the balding, slow-moving Leonard, alternately hitting the once-great Leonard and pleading with the referee to stop the slaughter. Finally, with McLarnin pulling his punches to save Leonard from any more punishment, the referee took pity on Leonard in the sixth round and put an end to his ill-fated comeback.

3. SUGAR RAY LEONARD (1977-97). The most unretiring boxer in history, Leonard came out of a two-year retirement to face Terry Norris in 1991 and lost, going back into retirement for another six years until he decided he "missed the roar of the crowd." So much so that Leonard again came out of retirement again on March 1, 1997 to fight Hector Camacho. Unfortunately, there was to be no roaring from the crowd as the once ever-so-graceful Leonard was reduced to hobbling around the ring when his 40-year-old legs failed in their obligation to uphold him. The fight was called to a halt in the fifth round, marking the only time in his 40-fight career that Sugar Ray Leonard had been stopped.

2. MUHAMMAD ALI (1960-81). Coming back from a two-year retirement in 1980, Ali took what he called "a one-sided ass whuppin'" from his former sparing partner and then-heavyweight champion, Larry Holmes. But Ali came back again the following year on December 11, 1981 in the Bahamas against Trevor Berbick. With a cowbell serving as the ring bell, Ali's lost a 10-round decision, his storied career ending not with a bang, but with a cowbell's tinkle.

1. JOE LOUIS (1934-51). As glorious as his 13-year reign as heavyweight champion had been, his after-the-ring life and return to boxing bordered on the tragic. Retiring as undefeated champion in 1949 after 25 successful title defenses, Louis soon found himself hounded by the IRS for unpaid taxes and was forced to return to the ring the following year to face his successor, Ezzard Charles. Rusty and looking every bit his 36 years of age, Louis lost a unanimous decision. He continued his comeback in 1951, winning eight fights, three by knockout. But in his next fight, he entered the ring at Madison Square Garden on October 26, 1951 to face the young, up-and-coming Rocky Marciano. A shell of his former self, that old fire that had flamed at his every command in his younger days now but a flicker, Louis was knocked out in the eighth round by a devastating right hand that sent the former champ through the ropes, his head cradled by those in the press area in one of the saddest sights and nights the old Garden had ever witnessed.

MY FAVORITE SINGERS AND MUSICAL GROUPS

:: BY ERNIE TERRELL

Note: Heavyweight Ernie Terrell won 45 fights, including two defenses of his World Boxing Association title which he held from 1965-67. A tall, intelligent fighter, Terrell also enjoyed a successful musical career after retiring from the ring. He toured for over a decade as lead singer of his band "Ernie Terrell & the Knockouts," which also featured his younger sister Jean Terrell—who went on to become lead singer of The Supremes in the early 1970s. A longtime mainstay of the music scene in his adopted hometown of Chicago, Ernie has produced numerous records for other artists over the years and remains a musical connoisseur of everything from R&B to folk to funk to soul to country to Ol' Blue Eyes. Here, Ernie lists his favorite singers and musical groups, in no particular order.

THE DRIFTERS.

RAY CHARLES.

BOB DYLAN.

BO DIDDLEY.

JAMES BROWN.

TENNESSEE ERNIE FORD.

NAT KING COLE.

FRANK SINATRA.

THE TEMPTATIONS.

THE SUPREMES.

BEST BOXING SONGS

Boxing doesn't exactly rank up there with lost love and newfound lust as a common source of inspiration for songwriters. But plenty of songs reference boxers, from "That's Why the Lady Is A Tramp" to too many New York rap songs to count that use Zab Judah's name as a convenient way to fill out a couplet. Many other songs have become associated with boxers as musical accompaniments for their ring entrances or to inspire their workouts, like Sonny Liston's favorite, "Night Train." But the *bonafide* boxing song—one that focuses on, or at least includes a significant amount of lyrical content about a boxer or boxing or a particular bout, remains a relatively rare entity. Still, seek and ye shall find some good ones. Here are the dozen we put at the top of boxing song charts.

12. "EL CORRIDO DE JULIO CÉSAR CHAVEZ," PERFORMED BY BANDO EL RECORDO. Played in a traditional Mexican song style designed to celebrate heroic figures, this tribute to boxing legend Julio César Chavez gives you some idea of just how much joy and pride Chavez brought to his native Mexico and Mexicans everywhere—especially when he showed rival Hector "Macho" Camacho *quien es mas macho*. Plenty of bands have recorded this song, Bando El Recordo gets the nod here because their version has the best video, which includes lots of footage of Chavez.

11. "BODY OF AN AMERICAN," PERFORMED BY THE POGUES. The Irish heavyweight champion band of the post-Clancy Brothers/Tommy Makem era, the Pogues spit out this fierce, moving and funny as hell telling of the life of fictional Irish-American boxing champ Big Jim Dwyer—as told by a mourner drinking over Dwyer's body at a wake so raucous and loaded with mythos, you half-expect Tim Finnegan to enter and reanimate the corpse for a few rounds of sparring.

10. "I THINK I CAN BEAT MIKE TYSON," PERFORMED BY D.J. JAZZY JEFF AND THE FRESH PRINCE. This 1989 pranksta' rap tune came with a hit video about a brash punk who takes on then-heavyweight Godzilla Mike Tyson in a bout so one-sided the narrator punches out his own cornerman so he can flee the ring after the first round. Teen rapper Fresh Prince grew up to become movie star Will Smith, who played Muhammad Ali in the 2001 film *Ali*. Tyson vs. Ali in their primes. Imagine that fight. Or even a song about it.

9. "READY FOR THE FIGHT," PERFORMED BY THE YOUNG PUNX. Actually, you can get some help imagining what Tyson vs. Ali in their primes would have looked like from *EA Sports Fight Night 4* video game, whose demo mode features the two heavyweights going at it, plus a soundtrack with this Young Punx song that uses boxing as a metaphor for an all-too-typical day in the life.

8. "KING JOE," PERFORMED BY THE COUNT BASIE BAND WITH PAUL ROBESON. An accomplished athlete who gained First-Team All-American football honors at Rutgers and praise as "the greatest to ever trot the gridiron" from legendary football coach Walter Camp, Paul Robeson adds athletic authority and his deep-voiced talents to the Count Basie band's playful instrumental backup in this 1941 tribute to then-reigning heavyweight champ Joe Louis. The third verse offers a lullaby to Joe's opponents, most destined to catch at least ten winks soon after climbing into the ring with him.

7. "PANCHO VILLA," PERFORMED BY SUN KIL MOON. It's not about the early 20th-century Mexican revolutionary, but the great and exceedingly polite Filipino flyweight champion Pancho Villa, and Mexican featherweight champ Salvador Sanchez, and Cuban welterweight Benny "Kid" Paret. It's also about being great and brave and adored, then dying young, and all the uneasy thoughts and unfulfilled dreams and grief it leaves behind.

6. "SONG FOR SONNY LISTON," PERFORMED BY MARK KNOPFLER. A troubled and terrifying fellow best remembered for helping make the name—make that two names—of his nemesis Cassius Clay/Muhammad Ali, Sonny Liston isn't the kind of figure people usually write songs for. But he gets one from Dire Straits founder Mark Knopfler. And a nice one at that.

5. AND 4. "WHO KILLED DAVEY MOORE?" AND "THE HURRICANE," PERFORMED BY BOB DYLAN. The first song tells the story of doomed featherweight champion Davey Moore, who died as a result of injuries he suffered losing his belt to Sugar Ramos in 1963. The other testifies on behalf of controversial middleweight contender Ruben "Hurricane" Carter, who was arrested in 1966, then convicted and jailed for murder, with the conviction finally thrown out over 20 years later. Both tales are semi-fictionalized, mythologized and, best of all, Dylanized during two of the great singer-songwriter's half-dozen primes.

3. "THE BOXER," PERFORMED BY SIMON AND GARFUNKEL. Paul Simon's bittersweet (lyrics: bitter; melody: sweet) song about an unemployed loner wandering around a New York City with no use for him reveals its title when the narrator likens himself to a battered veteran fighter. The final chorus of "Lie-de-lie, lie-de-lie-lie-lie-de-lie . . . " might suggest that songwriter Paul Simon was also describing the business side of boxing. But Simon confessed that he just stuck all those "lie's" in there at the recording session because he couldn't think of anything else to sing.

2. "EYE OF THE TIGER," PERFORMED BY SURVIVOR. The first time you heard the song's opening killer guitar riff blaring out of a radio speaker in 1982, you probably swore you had heard it before. And you were destined to hear it again and again almost every time you walked into a fitness club or sporting arena or happened upon MTV, all of which had the song on heavy rotation for the simple reason that people loved it. Over a quarter century and no hits later, the band Survivor remains well-known because of this song and its association with the hit boxing film *Rocky III*.

1. "GONNA FLY NOW" (THEME FROM *ROCKY*), PERFORMED BY DEETTA LITTLE AND NELSON PIGFORD. The song provided the inspiring soundtrack in the Oscar-winning film's pivotal scene when Rocky Balboa triumphantly sprints to the top of the steps of the Philadelphia Art Museum (still a Mecca for boxing and Rocky Balboa fans decades later). The horn-driven tune also went on to soundtrack thousands of high school football halftime shows and late-game drives as marching bands sought to inject some Rocky spirit into their players.

GREATEST ROLES IN BOXING MOVIES

With their dangerous and dramatic lives always heading toward another violent showdown, boxers make for compelling film characters, as do ex-boxers and those trying to navigate the transition between those two stages in life. These roles and the actors who played them set the standard for boxing characters and performances in film, and also make for some fine and entertaining viewing that could help you gain greater understanding of fighters and the extraordinary challenges they face both inside and outside the ring.

10. MARLON BRANDO IN *ON THE WATERFRONT* (1954). Brando changed film acting forever with his early screen work, and this role as Terry Malloy, a former fighter turned stevedore, played a big part in that revolution. In the decades that followed, actors used Brando's work as a source of awe and inspiration, including the #9 actor on this list, who ended his performance in *Raging Bull* repeating Brando's famous "coulda been a contender" monologue from this film.

9. ROBERT DENIRO IN *RAGING BULL* (1980). In the role that still defines his great career, Robert DeNiro whipped himself into fighting shape to play destructive middleweight champion Jake LaMotta, then packed on 60 pounds of cellulite for the film's later scenes when the older LaMotta has to come to terms with the effects of his self-destructiveness. DeNiro won an Academy Award for his efforts, and probably deserved another for his remarkable physical and psychological transformation within the role.

8. JAMES CAGNEY IN *CITY FOR CONQUEST* (1940). An actor who seemed perpetually on the verge of slugging someone in many of his film dramas, Cagney was a natural to star in a boxing movie. He breaks a few jaws on his way toward the top to support the blind ambitions of his brother and sweetheart. And he will break your heart in the end when he's left blinded by an unscrupulous rival, displaying a side of his acting ability that is often forgotten but which helped make Cagney so unforgettable playing doomed, vulnerable tough guys like boxer Danny Kenny in *City for Conquest*.

7. PAUL NEWMAN IN *SOMEBODY UP THERE LIKES ME* (1956). Not many actors are good enough to play a public personality as willful, accomplished, charismatic and loaded with back-story as Rocky Graziano. But the role in this biopic, based on Graziano's autobiography of the same name, fit the wilder, younger Newman like a laced-up pair of gloves.

6. KIRK DOUGLAS IN *CHAMPION* (1949). The poor kid who punches his way to the right side of the tracks and then climbs up a high rise to fame and fortune while leaving his friends and ideals behind became a stock leading character in boxing films. But few brought as much energy and believability to it as Douglas in his portrayal of Midge Kelly. You love him, you hate him, but mostly, you understand him, thanks to Douglas.

5. AND 4. JACK PALANCE IN THE TV VERSION OF *REQUIEM FOR A HEAVYWEIGHT* (1956) AND ANTHONY QUINN IN THE CINEMA VERSION OF *REQUIEM FOR A HEAVYWEIGHT* (1962). Each fine actor brings his own special set of talents and emotions—Palance, his stark and almost superhuman intensity, Quinn his profound sense of the irony and agony of being human—to the role of a washed-up fighter who finds life outside the ring after retirement more daunting than an in-ring encounter with Cassius Clay, who kayos Anthony Quinn's boxing career in the cinematic remake.

3. BURT LANCASTER IN *THE KILLERS* (1946). Lancaster plays against type, not his usual energetic huckster or hero driving the story, but as Ole "Swede" Andersen, an ex-boxer and the main dupe of an elaborate plot you can't blame him for failing to figure out in time. By his end, which takes place in the movie's brilliant opening scene—with what led up to it told in subsequent flashbacks—Burt's former prizefighter is too depressed and disgusted to even bother dodging the hitmen he has been warned are coming to kill him. Yet Lancaster makes that unbelievable surrender seem all too believable.

2. ERROL FLYNN IN *GENTLEMAN JIM* (1942). A skilled amateur boxer in his younger days, Flynn brought physical authenticity and his usual charming roguery to his semi-fictionalized take on scientific boxing pioneer Gentleman Jim Corbett. Financed by rich men looking to make boxing respectable and legal in late-19th century San Francisco, the Irish upstart Corbett gets too big for his britches and becomes a target of his former benefactors, but just ends up buying bigger britches for himself and changing boxing forever.

1. ROBERT RYAN IN *THE SET UP* (1949). Robert Ryan is so convincing in this film's fight scenes, you may wonder why he didn't go into boxing—until you see how good he is as an actor in all the film's other scenes. Ryan plays a down-but-not-quite-counted-out fighter urged by everyone around him to quit, but determined to redeem his career and life by beating his rival. An overlooked classic with a great performance by a too-often overlooked actor, *The Set Up* may take a little digging to find, but Ryan makes it well worth the dig.

CHAMPIONSHIP FIGHTS THAT WOULD HAVE HAD A DIFFERENT RESULT UNDER THE CURRENT 12-ROUND LIMIT

As a result of the tragic aftermath of the Ray Mancini-Duk Koo Kim lightweight championship fight on November 13, 1982, the WBC instituted a new rule mandating that all championship fights be limited to 12 rounds, with other Alphabet Soup groups eventually following suit. Through the previous 100-plus years of boxing,many championship fights were scheduled for as many as 45 rounds, with the 15-round limit not becoming the norm until the early 1920s. It is interesting to look back on classic fights and consider which ones would have had a different result had they been 12 rounders, with the fight and the result changing. Here are ten of those bouts.

10. STEVIE CRUZ VS. BARRY MCGUIGAN, JUNE 23, 1986, LAS VEGAS NEVADA. McGuigan, who had won the featherweight title the previous year from the supposedly unbeatable Eusebio Pedrosa, made his second title defense under a hot afternoon summer sun against the lightly regarded Stevie Cruz. And for the early part of the 12-round fight the champion got the better of the action. However, for reasons that were never made clear, McGuigan was given the sun side of the ring and began to wilt in the later rounds, suffering three knockdowns in the 15th that changed the course of the fight and led to a close unanimous decision win for Cruz.

9. MATTHEW SAAD MUHAMMAD VS. YAQUI LOPEZ, JULY 13, 1980, MCAFEE, NEW JERSEY. For the first seven rounds, the two engaged in a toe-to-toe rock-'em-sock-'em fight. Then it got even better as Lopez knocked down Saad early in the eighth round, only to get knocked down himself in the round's closing seconds. Going into the 14th, Lopez, who had been ahead after 12, began to visibly slow down and Saad started to land more frequently. Then, in the 14th, Saad dropped Lopez with an uppercut. Up at the count of eight, Lopez was quickly floored again, this time by another right. Up again, Lopez ran into another right and went down for the third time, this time for a count of three. With the three-knockdown rule waived, the action, albeit now one-sided, continued, and when Saad knocked down Lopez a fourth time, the fight was stopped, 2:03 into the fateful 14th.

8. JIM JEFFRIES VS. JIM CORBETT, MAY 11, 1900, CONEY ISLAND, NEW YORK. In a bout scheduled for 25 rounds, former heavyweight champion Jim Corbett literally danced circles around defending champion Jim Jeffries for 22 rounds, befuddling him with jabs and moving in and out to evade the devastating punches of the champion considered by most boxing experts as one of the heaviest punchers in the history of the heavyweight division. However, in the 23rd, Corbett made the fateful mistake of bouncing off the ropes right into a Jeffries' right and was knocked down and counted out, ending the fight and his hopes of recapturing the title, which would have been his again 11 rounds earlier under today's 12-round limit for title fights.

7. SUGAR RAY LEONARD VS. TOMMY HEARNS, SEPTEMBER 16, 1981, LAS VEGAS, NEVADA.

In a bout labeled "The Showdown," WBC welterweight champion Sugar Ray Leonard and WBA welterweight champ Tommy Hearns engaged in a bout with enough ebbs and flows and drama to fill the pages of a Russian novel. Leonard rocked Hearns with a left hook in the sixth and "The Hit Man" reverted to the style that had him winning over 100 amateur fights, sticking his rapier-like left jab in Ray's face, puffing up Leonard's right eye and piling up points. Going into the 13th, with Tommy ahead on all scorecards, Leonard's trainer Angelo Dundee exhorted, "You're blowing it, son." And Leonard, responding to Dundee's urgings, went to work, staggering Hearns in the 13th and stopping him in the 14th to end one of the greatest comebacks in recent boxing history.

6. MIKE WEAVER VS. JOHN TATE, MARCH 31, 1980, KNOXVILLE TENNESSEE.

For 14 rounds WBA Heavyweight champ John Tate had had his way with challenger Mike Weaver, who had done little, with one minor exception—a wicked left hook that had shaken Tate in the 12th. But with less than a minute to the final bell in the 15th round, that left hook came into evidence again as Weaver shot it out and landed it, flush, on Tate's jaw, felling Tate like a tree, face first to the canvas, where he was counted out with just 45 seconds left in the 15th and final round.

5. JAKE LAMOTTA VS. LAURENT DAUTHUILLE, SEPTEMBER 13, 1950, DETROIT, MICHIGAN.

Challenger Laurent Dauthuille had taken the fight to the defending middleweight champion LaMotta, the Frenchman piling up points on the slower-moving LaMotta as he moved in and out with ease. As the bell rang for the 15th and final round, the bruised and battered champion came off his stool squinting through the narrow slit that once was his left eye, mindful of his corner's instructions that he'd have to "knock the Frog out." Though far ahead on the scorecards, Dauthuille had inexplicably been told to "go in and fight." During an exchange near the end of the final round, Dauthuille stepped back to survey his handiwork. It was the last look he got. For, with fewer than 45 seconds remaining in the fight, LaMotta caught Dauthuille with one deep-dish beauty of a left. Dauthuille staggered backward with Jake in pursuit, throwing a varied assortment of lefts and rights, all of which connected. Finally, LaMotta felled the challenger with one long, looping left, draping Dauthuille over the bottom rope where he was counted out with only 13 seconds to go in the fight.

4. JOEY MAXIM VS. SUGAR RAY ROBINSON, JUNE 25, 1952, NEW YORK, NEW YORK.

With the thermometer registering a record temperature of 104 degrees Fahrenheit—and the Yankee Stadium Klieg lights making in even hotter—middleweight champion Sugar Ray Robinson took on Joey Maxim for Maxim's light heavyweight title. The heat that night was so grueling that referee Ruby Goldstein had to be carried from the ring in the 11th round after succumbing to heat prostration. But for the first 11 rounds, Robinson had put on a boxing clinic, moving and dancing around the almost statue-like Maxim, landing and moving back out of the way before Maxim could respond. However, with an unbeatable lead and a third world championship in his grasp, Robinson collapsed on his stool at the end of the 13th, unable to continue and the title and the fight belonged to Maxim, who responded to those who claimed he had won only because of the heat by saying, "I fought 13 rounds under the same heat."

3. JOE LOUIS VS. BILLY CONN, JUNE 18, 1941, NEW YORK, NEW YORK.

Making the 18th defense of his heavyweight title and the seventh in seven months, Joe Louis took on former light heavyweight champion Billy Conn. But Conn was no "Bum of the Month," a phrase sportswriter Jack Miley had used to describe Louis' monthly opponents. For 11 rounds Conn went into Louis' vaunted wheelhouse and exchanged with the champ, beating him to the punch and then moving away before Louis could react. In the 12th he staggered the champion, who had to hold on to survive. With the title in sight and ahead on all three scorecards, Conn chose to ignore his corner's directives to stay away and instead went for the knockout. But the knockouter became the knockoutee as Louis connected with several right-hand uppercuts, snapping Conn's head back. And Conn, defying his prefight statement that he would run away to fight another day, stayed in close, fighting back. Louis landed a volley of lefts and rights to Conn's head, and another right spun Conn around and he fell, almost as if in slow motion, there to be counted out for the first time in his career with just two seconds to go in the 13th round.

2. JOE LOUIS VS. JERSEY JOE WALCOTT, DECEMBER 5, 1947, NEW YORK, NEW YORK.

Jersey Joe Walcott gave heavyweight champion Joe Louis a boxing lesson for 12 rounds. Practicing a form of fistic breakdancing, slip-slip-sliding to his right before planting his right foot and crossing over with his right, Walcott had twice floored Louis and out-maneuvered the plodding champion for 12 rounds. But his corner, mindful of the mistake Billy Conn had made six years earlier of trying to slug it out with Louis and losing his gamble, implored the challenger not to make the same mistake and Walcott, heeding their advice, got on his bicycle, shuffling one way, then the other through the closing rounds, staying out of range of Louis' firepower. It was a strategy that cost him, dearly, the final tally on the scorecards showing that Louis had captured the final three "Championship rounds" to win a close split decision. After the fight Louis walked over to Walcott and said quietly, "I'm sorry." Walcott was even sorrier.

1. ROCKY MARCIANO VS. JERSEY JOE WALCOTT, SEPTEMBER 23, 1952, PHILADELPHIA, PENNSYLVANIA. Right from the opening bell Walcott made liars out of those naysayers who said he was too old and that Marciano, the favorite, was "too strong" for him, flooring Marciano for the first time in The Rock's career midway through the opening round. For the next four rounds it was more of the same, Walcott pitching and Marciano catching as Jersey Joe piled on the punches and the points. In the sixth Rocky had taken the battle to Walcott, backing the champion to the ropes and blazing away with lefts and rights. But during one of their heated exchanges, their heads collided and Marciano suffered a deep gash to the head and Walcott a cut eye. Both fighters were administered solution to stem the flow of blood, but somehow, someway that solution got into Rocky's eyes and by the end of the next round he had trouble seeing. He continued half-blind for the next three rounds with Walcott doing that voodoo he did so well, moving in and catching Marciano and then moving out. And all the while piling up points. Ahead on all three scorecards with just three more rounds—"the championship rounds"—to go, the two came out for the 13th. Thirty seconds into the round Walcott unexplainably backed into the ropes, bouncing off to throw a right hand. It was a right hand that never landed as Marciano beat him to the punch with his own short right hand that caught Walcott flush. As a grazing left passed by Walcott's head, Walcott fell slowly, almost oozed, to the canvas where referee Charley Daggert counted 10 over the fallen form of the now ex-champion. He could have counted to 100 and it would have made no difference, Walcott being OUT, as in O-U-T.

GREATEST CUBAN FIGHTERS

Given its relatively small size, Cuba has produced a remarkable quantity and quality of pugilistic talent. Even after a Communist revolution limited emigration for Cubans, the country continued to export great fighters and develop Olympic champions, enough to make Bert and Teddy both want to do a list of Cuba's ten finest.

BERT'S LIST

10. JOEL CASAMAYOR. Super featherweight champion 2000-02. Pro record: 37 wins, 22 KOs, five losses, one draw.

9. TEÓFILO STEVENSON. Olympic super heavyweight champion 1972, 1976 and 1980.

8. FLORENTINO FERNANDEZ. No championships. Pro record: 50 wins, 43 KOs, 16 losses, two draws.

7. LUIS RODRIGUEZ. Welterweight champion 1963-64. Pro record: 107 wins, 49 KOs, 13 losses.

6. JOSÉ LEGRA. Featherweight champion 1968-69 and 1972-73. Pro record: 137 wins, 50 KOs, 12 losses, four draws.

5. BENNY "KID" PARET. Welterweight champion 1960-61 and 1961-62. Pro record: 35 wins, 10 KOs, 12 losses, three draws.

4. ULTIMINIO "SUGAR" RAMOS. Featherweight champion 1963-64. Pro record: 54 wins, 39 KOs, seven losses, four draws.

3. JOSÉ NAPOLES. Welterweight champion 1969-70 and 1971-75. Pro record: 76 wins, 54 KOs, eight losses.

2. KID GAVILAN (GERARDO GONZALEZ). Welterweight champion 1951-55. Pro record: 106 wins, 27 KOs, 30 losses, six draws.

1. KID CHOCOLATE (ELIGIO SARDINAS MONTALVO). Featherweight champion 1932; junior lightweight champion 1931-33. Pro record: 145 wins, 64 KOs, 10 losses, six draws.

10. TEÓFILO STEVENSON. Olympic Super Heavyweight champion 1972, 1976 and 1980.

9. JOSE LEGRA. Featherweight champion 1968-69 and 1972-73. Pro record: 137 wins, 50 KOs, 12 losses, four draws.

8. FLORENTINO FERNANDEZ. No championships. Pro record: 50 wins, 43 KOs, 16 losses, two draws.

7. ULTIMINIO "SUGAR" RAMOS. Featherweight champion 1963-64. Pro record: 54 wins, 39 KOs, seven losses, four draws.

6. BENNY "KID" PARET. Welterweight champion 1960-61 and 1961-62. Pro record: 35 wins, 10 KOs, 12 losses, three draws.

5. KID GAVILAN (GERARDO GONZALEZ). Welterweight champion 1951-55. Pro record: 106 wins, 27 KOs, 30 losses, six draws.

4. "KID TURNERO" (EVELIO CELESTINO MUSTELIER). Heavyweight contender 1937-48. Pro Record: 97 wins, 37 KOs, 32 losses, 16 draws.

3. LUIS RODRIGUEZ. Welterweight champion 1963-64. Pro record: 107 wins, 49 KOs, 13 losses.

2. JOSÉ NAPOLES. Welterweight champion 1969-70 and 1971-75. Pro record: 76 wins, 54 KOs, eight losses.

1. KID CHOCOLATE (ELIGIO SARDINAS MONTALVO). Featherweight champion 1932; junior lightweight champion 1931-33. Pro record: 145 wins, 64 KOs, 10 losses, six draws.

MOST DISAPPOINTING HEAVYWEIGHT TITLE FIGHTS

For every great heavyweight championship fight—Marciano vs. Walcott I, Louis-Conn I, Jeffries-Sharkey—there have been at least twice as many that have been anything but. Some have been so uninspiring and dreary they might well have been the ones Stanley Ketchel's manager Wilson Mizner was commenting on when he said, "After the fight, the fighters were arrested on suspicion of fighting, but the case was dropped for lack of evidence." Other fights were so one-sided they could have passed for fungo practice, or so lacking in excitement they could have qualified for the bore-snore award of the year. Here are a few that were, for whatever reason, the most disappointing heavyweight championship fights in history.

12. LARRY HOLMES VS. RANDY "TEX" COBB, NOVEMBER 26, 1982. Larry Holmes' opponent for his 13th title defense was Randy "Tex" Cobb, whose stock-in-trade seemed to be catching punches with his face, a trait that was very much in evidence that night in the Houston Astrodome in a fight that might best be called, in Muhammad Ali's words, "a one-sided ass whuppin'." Howard Cosell, announcing the fight for ABC-TV, excoriated referee Steve Crosson in the fifth round for allowing the fight to continue, saying, "Doesn't he know that he is constructing an advertisement for the abolition of boxing?" And , in the ninth, Cosell called the fight "an assault on the sense of any civilized human being...twenty-six unanswered punches..." all by Holmes. The only thing Cobb could do besides absorbing punches was turn to referee Crosson and holler, "You're white...Help me!!!" But nobody could help Cobb who just stood there, a human sponge, absorbing everything Holmes threw until his face, in the words of Cosell, "looked like hamburger meat." After the fight Cosell signed off with, "I will not dignify this fight with any interviews. I think what you have seen tonight speaks for itself," then put down the mike and walked away from professional boxing—which for many fans, was the least disappointing part of the fight.

11. MUHAMMAD ALI VS. JEAN PIERRE COOPMAN, FEBRUARY 20, 1976. After his life-and-death struggle with Joe Frazier in Manila just four months before, Muhammad Ali was looking for an "easy" title defense. And now, with his going-price for appearances one million dollars per, no matter whom he fought, the Ali brain trust scrapped the bottom of the heavyweight barrel to come up with one of those "no matter who's," a Belgian named Jean Pierre Coopman. Nicknamed "The Lion of Flanders" for no apparent reason, Coopman proved to have limited abilities, more a pussycat than a lion. After the first round, Ali went over to the ropes to communicate his opinion of Coopman to CBS-TV announcers Pat Summerall and Tommy Brookshier, shouting down, "You guys in trouble... This cat's got nothin'...Ain't no way you gonna get all your commercials in..." Four rounds later, after toying with Coopman and slapping him to death, Ali finally took him out in as embarrassing a heavyweight title fight as ever seen.

10. LARRY HOLMES VS. MARVIS FRAZIER, NOVEMBER 25, 1983. Unfortunately for him and for boxing, Larry Holmes was just too good—too good for the heavyweight division he ruled for seven years and too good to really be appreciated by fans and journalists who craved the kind of dramatic heavyweight title fights they regularly got from Muhammad Ali in the previous decade. Coming along at a time when the heavyweight division—unlike its heyday a decade earlier—was devoid of top talent except for Holmes himself, Holmes starred in a boxing version of *Snow White and the Seven Dwarfs* (pun unintended), with Larry forced to defend his title against many fighters who weren't even household names in their own households. For his 17th title defense, he finally got to share the marquee with a recognizable name: Frazier—not "Smokin' Joe," but his son Marvis. An amateur champion, Marvis was making his first appearance on the national stage. And for about one minute of the first round he acted like he belonged, dancing around, dropping his hands and taunting Holmes. But at about the two-minute mark, Holmes dropped Marvis on his backside. And then, after Frazier had arisen on legs that were strangers to each other, Holmes proceeded to belabor him with punches, all the while looking to referee Mills Lane to call a halt to the one-sided ass whupin'. Finally, Lane had seen enough, even if Papa Joe, screaming from his son's corner, hadn't, and called an end to the fight, such as it was.

9. JESS WILLARD VS. FRANK MORAN, MARCH 25, 1916. A leviathan of a man at 6'6" and 250-plus pounds, Jess Willard became heavyweight champion in 1915 by dethroning Jack Johnson in 26 rounds and ending the "Great White Hope" era. Less than a year later, Willard looked to put his belt on the line, but the list of legitimate contenders numbered just four: Fred Fulton, Jack Dillon, Sam Langford, and Frank Moran. Willard immediately dismissed Fulton and Dillon, invoked the "color line" against Langford and opted for Moran, whom he had already beaten two years earlier. The fight, at Madison Square Garden under the auspices of promoter Tex Rickard was notable only for the fact that William Randolph Hearst's New York paper *The American* had prepared an editorial demanding the abolition of boxing for being "too brutal." Unfortunately for Hearst, whose paper came out after the fight, and for fans packed into the second Garden, the fight itself was a bore-snore, going ten rounds to a no-decision.

8. JOE LOUIS VS. BILLY CONN II, JUNE 19, 1946. Five years earlier, Louis and Conn engaged in a classic battle, one in which Conn came close to becoming the 16th heavyweight champion of the world, but instead became Louis' 16th knockout victim in defense of his crown when Conn attempted to trade punches with the heavy-hitting Louis. During the intervening five years, while both were in the service, they had a chance to meet during their boxing tours for the troops. Conn, ever the brash leprechaun, needled Louis, saying, "Joe why didn't you lend me the title for 12 months. We could have made a lot of money in a rematch." Louis, with his remarkable economy of words, replied, "Billy, I lent it to you for 12 rounds and you didn't know what to do with it." With the war over, their long anticipated rematch was scheduled for Yankee Stadium. And the sports-starved public, deprived of major sporting events during the Duration, flocked to see the two again, buying $100 ringside seats, 10,574 of them, enough to add up to the first million dollar gate in almost 30 years. Unfortunately, Conn had nothing left in his tank, succumbing to rust and Louis in eight listless rounds.

7. LENNOX LEWIS VS. OLIVER McCALL II, FEBRUARY 7, 1997. While Tom Hanks told his players, "There's no crying in baseball," there was crying—oceans of it—in the second Lewis-McCall match. Their first time around McCall won the WBC title by somehow landing a shot with his eyes closed that closed Lennox's. Now, three years later with Lewis again the WBC champ, the two met for the second time. But this time, it was less a fight than a sob story . . . literally, as Oliver McCall experienced a mental breakdown and began walking around the ring crying—an episode he later tried to explain in a rambling and bizarre alibi as a "Rope-a-dope" designed to lure Lewis into something or other that was never explained. Amid pleas from his cornerman Georgie Benton of "Don't do this to yourself," McCall continued to cry and refused to fight until referee Mills Lane stopped the fight in the fifth round, ruling it a TKO, although Lewis had never hit him.

6. WLADIMIR KLITSCHKO VS. SULTAN IBRAGIMOV, FEBRUARY 23, 2008. Wladimir Klitschko added the WBO belt to his IBF hardware in a lopsided fight so devoid of action that there wasn't enough caffeine in the house at Madison Square Garden that night to stop the crowd from dozing off and someone in the press section turning around to another journalist and telling him, "Quit snoring...you're keeping me awake." It was a fight where one of the so-called combatants couldn't and the other wouldn't. Writer Ron Borges called Ibragimov "a guy whose battle plan apparently was not to engage in a battle if one could be avoided." And Klitschko's trainer, Manny Steward said of his non-warrior, "Wladimir could have thrown more punches." Whatever it was, it was the most booooooring fights in the long history of boring heavyweight title fights, not even so-bad-it-was-good. It was terrible.

5. MIKE TYSON VS. BRUCE SELDON, AUGUST 6, 2008. On the comeback trail after his incarceration for rape, Mike Tyson entered the ring to challenge WBA titleholder Bruce Seldon, with one of Tyson's entourage wearing a vest reading, "Loved by few, hated by many, but respected by all." But what many that Vegas evening didn't respect was the ending of the fight, which lasted all of one minute and forty-nine

seconds. A Tyson punch—which was probably his elbow posing as a punch—grazed Seldon's forehead and Seldon, who apparently had a China forehead, went down and out, with the crowd shouting "Fix. . . . Fix" as it ended.

4. MICHAEL DOKES VS. MIKE WEAVER I, DECEMBER 10, 1982. In his third defense of the WBA version of the heavyweight title, champion Mike Weaver took on leading contender Michael Dokes. At the bell, Dokes rushed at Weaver and stunned him with a left hook, then followed with a right and another hook, dropping him. Weaver was up quickly and took a mandatory eight from referee Joey Curtis. But as soon as Curtis had stepped away, Dokes was back at Weaver and pummeled him with an 18-punch volley, pinning him on the ropes. Referee Curtis stepped between the two as though to break them from a clinch, but instead held up Dokes' hand signifying a stoppage at 1:03 of the first round. Broadcasting the fight, Sugar Ray Leonard said that Curtis had "panicked" and former heavyweight champion Larry Holmes could only look on in amazement and add, "Curtis couldn't referee my kids in a baseball game." Even Dr. Donald Romeo, the ringside physician, contributed, "They shouldn't have stopped it. The referee was wrong. Weaver was fine." But referee Curtis was nowhere to be seen, having quickly escaped through the ropes.

3. SONNY LISTON VS. FLOYD PATTERSON II JULY 22, 1963. Floyd Patterson had been there before, having been knocked silly and then successfully regaining his heavyweight championship in a return bout—as he had against Ingemar Johansson three years before. This time around he was trying to reclaim his title from Sonny Liston who, just 10 months earlier, had destroyed Patterson with one bodacious right hand in just two minutes and six seconds of the first round. Bob Hope made fun of the outcome saying on his show the next week: "I almost invited Sonny Liston and Floyd Patterson on the show, but the last time they were together they almost got into a fight." And Patterson, so ashamed of his performance in the fight, had sneaked out of Chicago in a beard and mustache, vowing to take back his championship, something his fans hoped he would, as he had before. But their second fight was almost like the watering of last year's crops, the same result with Liston taking only four seconds longer to reduce Patterson into resin in a fight totally devoid of drama.

2. MAX SCHMELING VS. JACK SHARKEY I, JUNE 12, 1930. The elimination tournament following the retirement of heavyweight champion Gene Tunney culminated in a title fight between Max Schmeling and Jack Sharkey at Yankee Stadium. And what happened is still the subject of controversy. With Sharkey ahead on the scorecards going into the fourth round, the two met in mid-ring, exchanging blows. Schmeling came out of a crouch and started a left hook; at that moment, Sharkey started his own left hook. But Schmeling stood straight up into the path of the punch—which would have scored to the rib cage but instead landed palpably low.

Schmeling fell to the ground, writhing and grimacing in agony, his left hand holding his left thigh. With Schmeling's corner screaming, "Stay down," pandemonium broke out and referee Jim Crowley, confused as to what happened, went over to consult with the judges. Schmeling was dragged to his corner after the bell ending the fourth round. A minute later at the bell signaling the start of the fifth, Sharkey rushed across the ring, but Crowley restrained him and awarded the fight on a foul to the still grimacing Schmeling, seated on his stool, in the most unsatisfactory conclusion to a heavyweight championship fight since British policemen called a halt to the Sayers-Heenan contest some 70 years before.

1. ROCKY MARCIANO VS. JERSEY JOE WALCOTT II, MAY 15, 1953. In their first fight the previous September, Jersey Joe had given lie to the slander that he was too old and "The Rock" too much for him by flooring Marciano in the first round and giving him a boxing lesson for 11 more, until a deep-dish beauty of a right hand at 43 seconds of the 13th not only knocked the crown off Walcott's head, but damned near tore his head off as well. In a rematch eagerly awaited by the boxing public, the two met again, this time with Marciano defending his newly-won crown against the challenger Walcott. Just two minutes and thirty-five seconds into the first round, with many of the fans still filing into Chicago Stadium, Walcott went down and out again—more from remembrances of the punch from the first fight than from any punch Marciano threw in the rematch. In the words of sportswriter Red Smith: "Last autumn's wildly wonderful battle, one of the finest, closest and most exciting of all heavyweight title fights, was replayed as one of the most sordid of all time."

GREATEST HEAVYWEIGHT CHAMPIONSHIP FIGHTS

:: BY MUHAMMAD ALI

Note: Three-time heavyweight champion Muhammad Ali remains such a gigantic figure in sport and culture—even decades after his retirement—that he really requires no further introduction. "The Greatest" offers his take on the greatest heavyweight title fights of all time, listed chronologically.

JACK JOHNSON VS. JAMES J. JEFFRIES, JULY 4, 1910, RENO, NEVADA.

JACK DEMPSEY VS. LUIS FIRPO, SEPTEMBER 14, 1923, POLO GROUNDS, NEW YORK, NEW YORK.

GENE TUNNEY VS. JACK DEMPSEY II, SEPTEMBER 22, 1927, SOLDIER FIELD, CHICAGO, ILLINOIS.

JOE LOUIS VS. MAX SCHMELING II, JUNE 22, 1938, YANKEE STADIUM, NEW YORK, NEW YORK.

JOE LOUIS VS. BILLY CONN I, JUNE 18, 1941, POLO GROUNDS, NEW YORK, NEW YORK.

ROCKY MARCIANO VS. JERSEY JOE WALCOTT I, SEPTEMBER 23, 1952, MUNICIPAL STADIUM, PHILADELPHIA, PENNSYLVANIA.

JOE FRAZIER VS. MUHAMMAD ALI I, MARCH 8, 1971, MADISON SQUARE GARDEN, NEW YORK, NEW YORK.

MUHAMMAD ALI VS. GEORGE FOREMAN, OCTOBER 30. 1974, STADE DU 20 MAI, KINSHASA, ZAIRE.

MUHAMMAD ALI VS. JOE FRAZIER III, OCTOBER 1, 1975, ARANETA COLISEUM, QUEZON CITY, PHILIPPINES.

BUSTER DOUGLAS VS. MIKE TYSON, FEBRUARY 11, 1990, TOKYO DOME, TOKYO, JAPAN.

MOST CONTROVERSIAL DECISIONS

:: BY HAROLD LEDERMAN

Note: Harold Lederman worked as an official boxing judge on every continent but Antarctica from 1967-2001, scoring over 100 world title fights, including Ali-Norton III. The Bronx native became the official "unofficial" judge in 1986 for HBO, where he explains fight rules for viewers before bouts and breaks in every third round to review his scorecard for the fight. His daughter, Julie, is currently a respected judge who has scored a few title fights of her own, including Joe Calzaghe vs. Roy Jones, Jr. in 2008. Harold gained induction into the World Boxing Hall of Fame in 1997 and won the 2006 Good Guy Award from the Boxing Writers Association of America—a decision that no one disputed. Here, Harold offers a dozen decisions that a lot of people disputed.

12. ANGEL MANFREDY VS. JULIO DIAZ, OCTOBER 6, 2001, MEMORIAL COLISEUM, CORPUS CHRISTI, TEXAS. Manfredy was awarded a split decision win in a 12-round IBF lightweight eliminator fight, during which Diaz had outboxed the hard-charging Manfredy and used his legs and jab to clearly earn the decision.

11. LUPE PINTOR VS. CARLOS ZÁRATE, JUNE 3, 1979, CAESARS PALACE, LAS VEGAS, NEVADA. Lupe Pintor won the WBC bantamweight championship on a 15-round split decision that brought audible gasps from the Caesars Palace crowd when it was announced.

10. PERNELL WHITAKER VS. JULIO CÉSAR CHAVEZ, SEPTEMBER 10, 1993, THE ALAMODOME, SAN ANTONIO, TEXAS. In front of thousands of Chavez supporters who went silent during the bout when they realized Whitaker was giving Chavez a boxing lesson, the judges were blind to the action, calling it a "draw." Judge Jack Woodruff scored it 115-113 for Whitaker, but WBC judge Mickey Vann and Franz Marti had it 115-115 for a majority draw. Several members of the press expressed their disgust with the verdict, with *Boxing Illustrated* captioning a photo of the bout on its next cover with: "If you think this fight was a draw, don't buy this issue."

9. JOSÉ LUIS RAMIREZ VS. PERNELL WHITAKER, MARCH 12, 1988, STADE DE LEVALLOIS, LEVALLOIS-PERRET, FRANCE. The decision favoring Ramirez in this WBC lightweight title fight was generally considered a "robbery." British judge Harry Gibbs scored the fight 117-113 for Whitaker, while judges Newton Campos (118-113) and Louis Michel (116-115) gave it to Ramirez. The magazine *Boxing 88* scored it 118-111 for Whitaker and most ringsiders had Whitaker winning by at least that large a margin. The two fought again the following year in Norfolk, Virginia, with Whitaker pitching a 12-round shutout.

8. ROCKY MARCIANO VS. ROLAND LASTARZA, MARCH 24, 1950, MADISON SQUARE GARDEN, NEW YORK, NEW YORK. In a battle of heavyweight contenders, Rocky Marciano won a close fight, aided by a fourth-round flash knockdown of LaStarza. Referee Jack Watson and judge Artie Schwartz gave the fight to Marciano, while judge Artie Aidala scored it for LaStarza. The split decision for Marciano was condemned around ringside as a miscarriage of justice.

7. LENNOX LEWIS VS. EVANDER HOLYFIELD, MARCH 13, 1999, MADISON SQUARE GARDEN, NEW YORK, NEW YORK. The fight between WBC champion Lewis and Holyfield, the WBA and IBF titlist, was declared a "draw" by the judges—a decision that New York Mayor Rudy Giuliani declared a "travesty." In a post-fight CNN/SI poll, 91 percent of the participants said that Lennox Lewis was robbed. And British judge Larry O'Connell was quoted after the fight saying he had probably made a mistake in casting his vote for Holyfield.

6. BOB FOSTER VS. JORGE VICTOR AHUMADA, JUNE 17, 1974, UNIVERSITY ARENA, ALBUQUERQUE, NEW MEXICO. Making the 14th defense of his light heavyweight crown, Foster got a gift in the 15-round draw decision, with almost everyone—except the judges—rating the rugged Ahumada a clear winner.

5. JOEY GIARDELLO VS. BILLY GRAHAM, DECEMBER 19, 1952, MADISON SQUARE GARDEN, NEW YORK, NEW YORK. Giardello originally won a split decision when referee Ray Miller (5-4 in rounds and five points each) and judge Joe Agnello (6-4 in rounds and five points each) voted for Giardello, while Charley Shortell (7-3 in rounds and 10-4 in points) gave the fight to Graham. However, New York State Athletic commissioners Robert Christenberry and C.B. Powell seated at ringside altered Agnello's scorecard after the fight to reverse the decision and award it to Graham. Giardello sued and the New York State Supreme Court reversed the reversal the following February, giving the decision back to Giardello.

4. JAMES TONEY VS. DAVE TIBERI ON FEBRUARY 8, 1992, TRUMP TAJ MAHAL, ATLANTIC CITY, NEW JERSEY. Toney won a split decision over Tiberi in defense of his middleweight title when judges William Lerch and Frank Garza scored the fight 115-112 for the champion, overruling Frank Brunette, who had it 117-111 for Tiberi. The decision prompted U.S. Senator William Roth from Tiberi's home state of Delaware to call for a federal investigation of boxing. Tiberi retired after the fight and, in 2009, Toney admitted he had lost.

3. JOE LOUIS VS. JERSEY JOE WALCOTT, DECEMBER 5, 1947, MADISON SQUARE GARDEN, NEW YORK, NEW YORK. Despite being knocked down in rounds one and four and so sure he had lost that he tried to leave the ring before the decision was announced, defending heavyweight champion Louis was gifted a 15-round decision over challenger Walcott. Even Louis' old army buddy—scoring referee Ruby Goldstein—voted for Walcott, but was overruled by judges Frank Forbes and Marty Monroe. Louis would win the rematch six months later via an 11th-round knockout.

2. KID GAVILAN VS. BILLY GRAHAM, AUGUST 29, 1951, MADISON SQUARE GARDEN, NEW YORK, NEW YORK. Gavilan won a split decision when referee Mark Conn cast the decisive vote for the defending welterweight champion. Conn needed a police escort to get him out of the ring. A UP poll of writers at ringside had 12 declaring Graham the winner and only three favoring Gavilan.

1. ALFREDO ESCALERA VS. TYRONE EVERETT, NOVEMBER 30, 1976, THE SPECTRUM, PHILADELPHIA, PENNSYLVANIA. In what may be history's worst decision, Alfredo Escalera was awarded the WBA super featherweight belt when the scorecard of judge Lou Tress had Escalera up by two points in what should have been a landslide victory for the hometown favorite Everett. The decision was so bad that the scores were not announced at fight's end to prevent a riot and no one knew who had won until the next day. Tress never worked as a judge again.

GREATEST MEXICAN BOXERS

Few countries can stand toe-to-toe with Mexico when it comes to producing great fighters. We even needed to add a pair of extra slots to our list of the best of them. Even then, we couldn't agree on the same dozen and made it into two lists, one by Teddy and one by Bert. Both should give you an idea of—along with a healthy dose of awe over—just how many great fighters have come out of Mexico.

BERT'S LIST

12. ERIK MORALES. Super bantamweight champion 1997-2000; featherweight champion 2001-02 and 2002-03; super featherweight champion 2003-04 and 2005. Pro record: 48 wins, 34 KOs, six losses.

11. RAUL (RATON) MACIAS. Bantamweight champion 1955-57. Pro record: 36 wins, 22 KOs, two losses.

10. MARCO ANTONIO BARRERA. Super Bantamweight champion 1995-96 and 1998-2002; featherweight champion 2002; super featherweight champion 2004-07. Pro record: 66 wins, 43 KOs, seven losses.

9. MIGUEL CANTO. Flyweight champion 1975-79. Pro record: 59 wins, 14 KOs, five losses, four draws.

8. RAFAEL MARQUEZ. Bantamweight champion 2003-07; super bantamweight champion 2007. Pro record: 39 wins, 35 KOs, five losses.

7. VICENTE SALDIVAR. Featherweight champion 1964-67 and 1970. Pro record: 36 wins, 25 KOs, three losses.

6. JUAN MANUEL MARQUEZ. Featherweight champion 2004-07; Lightweight champion 2009-. Pro record: 51 wins, 37 KOs, five losses, one draw.

5. SALVADOR SANCHEZ. Featherweight champion 1980-82. Pro record: 44 wins, one loss, one draw.

4. RICARDO LOPEZ. Minimumweight champion 1990-99; flyweight champion 1999-2002. Pro record: 51 wins, 38 KOs, zero losses, one draw.

3. CARLOS ZÁRATE. Bantamweight champion 1976-79. Pro record: 54 wins, 53 KOs, two losses.

2. RUBEN OLIVARES. Bantamweight champion 1969-70 and 1971-72; featherweight champion 1974-75 and 1975. Pro record: 87 wins, 77 KOs, 11 losses, two draws

1. JULIO CÉSAR CHAVEZ. Super featherweight champion 1984-87; lightweight champion 1987-89; super lightweight champion 1989-94 and 1994-96. Pro record: 107 wins, 86 KOs, six losses, two draws.

TEDDY'S LIST

12. MARCO ANTONIO BARRERA. Super bantamweight champion 1995-96 and 1998-2002; featherweight champion 2002; super featherweight champion 2004-07. Pro record: 66 wins, 43 KOs, seven losses.

11. ERIK MORALES. Super bantamweight champion 1997-2000; featherweight champion 2001-02 and 2002-03; super featherweight champion 2003-04 and 2005. Pro record: 48 wins, 34 KOs, six losses.

10. MIGUEL CANTO. Flyweight champion 1975-79. Pro record: 59 wins, 14 KOs, five losses, four draws.

9. RODOLFO "BABY" CASANOVA. Bantamweight contender 1932-42. Pro record: 54 wins, 31 KOs, 17 losses, one draw.

8. RAUL (RATON) MACIAS. Bantamweight champion 1955-57. Pro record: 36 wins, 22 KOs, two losses.

7. RICARDO LOPEZ. Minimumweight champion 1990-99; flyweight champion 1999-2002. Pro record: 51 wins, 38 KOs, zero losses, one draw.

6 VICENTE SALDIVAR. Featherweight champion 1964-67 and 1970. Pro record: 36 wins, 25 KOs, three losses.

5. CARLOS ZÁRATE. Bantamweight champion 1976- 79. Pro record: 54 wins, 53 KOs, two losses.

4. BABY ARIZMENDI. Featherweight champion 1934-35. Pro record: 60 wins, 26 KOs, 13 losses.

3. SALVADOR SANCHEZ. Featherweight champion 1980-82. Pro record: 44 wins, one loss, one draw.

2. RUBEN OLIVARES. Bantamweight champion 1969-70 and 1971-72; featherweight champion 1974-75 and 1975. Pro record: 87 wins, 77 KOs, 11 losses, two draws.

1. JULIO CÉSAR CHAVEZ. Super featherweight champion 1984-87; lightweight champion 1987-89; super lightweight champion 1989-94 and 1994-96. Pro record: 107 wins, 86 KOs, six losses, two draws.

JULIO CÉSAR CHAVEZ

GREATEST "KILLER INSTINCT"

Many of the all-time great knockout "artists" had that so-called "killer Instinct," the ability to finish off opponents when they had them in trouble. Here are some of the best at not letting their opponents off the proverbial hook once they smelled blood.

10. RUBEN OLIVARES (1965-88). With a big left hook that could knock down a building, this little bantamweight and featherweight personally retired entire divisions. He reduced his first 23 opponents into smaller, neater pieces and then stepped over the prone bodies of 55 more over the course of his long career. Olivares would throw whole timbre and pallet into his left hook, his bread-and-butter punch, nearly breaking his opponents in two as he won titles in both the bantamweight and featherweight divisions, earning the nickname "Rockabye Ruben" from his adoring fans.

9. "TERRIBLE" TERRY McGOVERN (1897-1908). No more savage warrior than Terry McGovern ever climbed through the ring ropes. McGovern was "terrible" in name and deed alike, his style, one of mass mayhem. Nat Fleischer of *The Ring* magazine wrote, "no bantamweight or featherweight ever packed a more dangerous punch than did 'Terrible Terry.'" His wicked hooks, uppercuts and vicious swings—all thrown in a pell-mell manner—took out 42 of his opponents, 23 of those KOs coming in the first three rounds.

8. SAM LANGFORD (1902-26). So sure was this welterweight-*cum*-heavyweight of his prowess as a knockout puncher that he frequently called his shots—long before Muhammad Ali took up the practice. One time, while awaiting the call to action, he saw the seconds of his opponent slicing up oranges. "What ya' doin' with all them oranges?" Langford called over. "I'm slicing them up for my man to suck on between rounds," came the answer. "Man, you ain't gonna need them oranges," promised Sam, who went out and dispatched his opponent in one short round. Another time, one of his opponent's seconds was screaming for his man to do something or other and he would tell him what to do when he came back that way again. Langford looked at the corner and said, "Man, he ain't comin' back this way again," and coldcocked his foe one punch later.

7. ROBERTO DURAN (1968-2001). You don't acquire the nickname "*Manos de Piedra*" ("Hands of Stone") without finishing off a few opponents. In Duran's case, it was more than a few; it was 70 of them to be exact, including 11 of 12 contenders in defense of his lightweight title. He fought with a will to destroy all those who had the gall to stand up to him, and once Duran hit an opponent, it was *adios*—as it was for challenger Ray Lampkin, who was being carried off on a stretcher while Duran was being interviewed. Duran, taking a glance over his shoulder at the semi-limp body, said in a deadly Derringer tone, "Next time, I send him to the morgue."

6. STANLEY KETCHEL (1903-10). A man-made tornado who rushed into his opponent head-down with hate in his heart and murder in his eyes—eyes which *The Ring* magazine editor Nat Fleischer wrote, "were the eyes of a killer"—the fighter known as "The Michigan Assassin" fought with a feral joy, employing both a murderous left and an equally lethal right hand to destroy 49 of his opponents, many times vaulting over the ropes when his opponent's bottom had hit the canvas, then running down the aisle before the referee had counted to ten without bothering to look over his shoulder, so sure was he of the outcome.

5. MIKE TYSON (1985-2005). "Iron Mike" became the very embodiment of boxing's "killer" instinct. Delivering a one-round KO of Hector Mercades in his pro debut, he went on to win his first 19 bouts by knockout. Tyson's prowess as a "killer" was never more in evidence than in his 1996 fight against Bruce Seldon, with Seldon fairly swooning after one of Tyson's punches barely brushed his forehead. Tyson's philosophy: "I always try to catch my opponents right on the tip of the nose because I try to push the bone right into the brain."

4. ROCKY MARCIANO (1947-55). The undefeated heavyweight champion had the fierceness that defines a finisher. Marciano's powerful overhand rights finished off most of his 43 knockout victims in his 49 wins. And when they landed, they left a lasting impression, as in his 13th-round KO of Jersey Joe Walcott with a right-handed howitzer that Walcott remembered into their second fight, when he fell down the first time it landed, a vestigial reminder of that first-fight right.

3. JACK DEMPSEY (1914-27). "The Manassa Mauler" was at his best when he smelled blood, finishing off his opponents when he trapped them. And the one time he didn't— against Gene Tunney in the seventh round of their second fight— became one of the most memorable knockdowns in history, a knockdown that might have lasted as long as 14 seconds and will forever be known as "The Long Count." In 48 other fights, his opponents weren't so lucky, unable as they were to beat the 10-count.

ROCKY GRAZIANO

2. ROCKY GRAZIANO (1942-52). With a right hand from hell, "Da Rock" was the ultimate finisher, even when woefully behind on points—as witnessed by his knock-outs of Freddie "Red" Cochrane and Charley Fusari in the tenth and final rounds.

1. JOE LOUIS (1934-51). When the great heavyweight champion caught up with his challengers, he usually finished them off—as he did with 22 of his 25 opponents in title defenses. Sometimes in dramatic fashion, as witnessed by his finally getting to Billy Conn in the 13th round of their first fight after chasing Conn for 12 rounds.

BEST POST-FIGHT LINES

The ring announcer doesn't always get the last word about a fight. Plenty of fighters have had important, wise or at least humorous things to say after the end of a bout, especially these ten guys.

"WELL, OUTSIDE OF A BUSTED JAW, A CRACKED RIB AND MY HANDS ALL BUSTED UP, I FEEL ALRIGHT." Kid Broad, when asked how he felt after a tough fight.

"WHAT'S THE SENSE OF BEING IRISH IF YOU CAN'T BE STUPID?" Billy Conn, after his first Joe Louis fight, in response to sportswriter Jesse Abramson asking him, "You were ahead after 12 rounds and had the fight won...What happened in there?"

"MAMMY, YOUR BOY IS BRINGING HOME THE BACON WITH LOTS OF GRAVY ON IT." Joe Gans, in a telegram to his mother, after winning a lightweight title bout against Battling Nelson.

"NO, BUT HIS MANAGER WAS." Sonny Liston, responding to a reporter who asked whether Chuck Wepner was "the bravest man you've ever fought" after Liston had beaten Wepner in nine one-sided rounds.

"I GOT TOO GODDAMNED CARELESS." Tami Mauriello, after being knocked out in the first round by Joe Louis.

"I DON'T KNOW, BUT BRADDOCK CAN USE THE TITLE. HE HAS THREE KIDS. I DON'T KNOW HOW MANY I HAVE." Max Baer, responding to the question, "What happened in there?" after he'd lost his heavyweight belt to underdog Jimmy Braddock.

"I DIDN'T KNOCK HIM OUT 'CAUSE THEY PAID TO SEE ME FIGHT 15 ROUNDS." Willie Pep, when asked why it took him 15 rounds to win a decision over an opponent who looked like he should have been knocked out earlier.

"I ZIGGED WHEN I SHOULD HAVE ZAGGED." Jack Roper, after being KO'd in one round by Joe Louis.

"WELL, HE FELL AWKWARDLY." Jerry Quarry, when asked if his opponent, Jack Bodell, whom he had knocked out in just over a minute, was awkward.

"HE TRAINED FOR SIX MONTHS AND DIDN'T EVEN GET A CHANCE TO USE HIS STOOL." Curtis Cokes, former welterweight champion, on heavyweight contender Duane Bobick, after Bobick was knocked out 58 seconds into the first round by Ken Norton.

MOST FAMOUS DISQUALIFICATIONS

The word "foul" can be found in Webster's tome sandwiched between the words "fought" and "four-flusher." "Foul" can also be found in the lexicon of boxing, probably between the same two words. By the late 1920s and early 1930s, what had once been the exception had become the rule, and fouls became an epidemic as fighter after fighter fell gloves-over-teakettle to the canvas, hollering "foul" and holding his groin while the public held their collective noses. One of the more imaginative suggestions for curbing this ill came from sportswriter Wilbur Wood, who proposed, "When a low blow is landed, the recipient should be given a free shot, as is the case in soccer. This fellow would have the offender backed into a corner and held there by the fouled man's second while the boxer hit low repays in kind." Nonetheless, foul blows resulting in disqualifications—or, as they're entered in the record books, "DQs"—continued and played a part in the sport. Here are the most famous "DQs" in boxing history.

10. INGEMAR JOHANSSON VS. ED SANDERS, AUGUST 2, 1952. In the super heavyweight final of the 1952 Helsinki Summer Olympics, the American Ed Sanders faced Sweden's Ingemar Johansson. Wary of Sanders' power, Johansson spent the first round-and-a-half backpedaling without throwing a punch. After receiving several warnings from the referee, he was finally DQ'd for not "giving his best" and denied his silver medal. Years later, after Johansson had won the world heavyweight championship from Floyd Patterson, the Olympics relented and awarded him his silver medal.

9. ROY JONES, JR. VS. MONTELL GRIFFIN, MARCH 21, 1997. In a fight he appeared to be winning handily, having knocked down Griffin in the seventh round, Jones floored Griffin again in the ninth and then, for good measure, swatted him when he was down, resulting in a DQ and his first loss, not to mention the loss of his light heavyweight title. In the rematch five months later, Jones avenged his "loss" by knocking Griffin out in the first.

8. TOM SHARKEY VS. BOB FITZSIMMONS, DECEMBER 2, 1896. In one of the more controversial "won-by-foul" fights in history, middleweight champion "Ruby Bob" Fitzsimmons was disqualified for a low blow in the eighth round by referee Bat Masterson (yes—*that* Bat Masterson!) after delivering what appeared to most observers a legal knockout blow to "Sailor" Tom Sharkey's midriff. It was rumored that Masterson, who wore a gun into the ring, had bet money on Sharkey.

7. JOE GANS VS. BATTLING NELSON, SEPTEMBER 3, 1906. In the first bout ever promoted by legendary promoter Tex Rickard, Gans successfully defended his lightweight title against "The Durable Dane," Battling Nelson, when Nelson, thoroughly beaten and exhausted, deliberately fouled Gans in the 42nd round to save his backers their money—as bets were not paid off when a bout ended on a foul back in the old days.

6. AL "BUMMY" DAVIS VS. FRITZIE ZIVIC, NOVEMBER 15, 1940. In a battle of fouls—Zivic employing his patented thumb-to-the-eye punches and Davis delivering low blows—the two "boxers" befouled the sport with their efforts, with Davis disqualified in the second round for his transgressions.

5. TERRY NORRIS VS. LUIS SANTANA, APRIL 8, 1995. In a foul rematch, former junior middleweight champion "Terrible" Terry Norris, who had lost his title to Santana the previous autumn on a fifth-round foul after hitting him in the back of the head, repeated his foul tactics, this time hitting Santana after the bell ending the third round and being DQ'd again. In their third match in August of '95, Norris played it by the rules and knocked out Santana in two rounds to regain his belt.

4. RIDDICK BOWE VS. ANDREW GOLOTA I, JULY 11, 1996. WBO heavyweight champion Bowe took on the undefeated Golota at Madison Square Garden in what promised to be a punchfest between two of boxing's heaviest hitters. What it didn't promise to be was a fight decided by south-of-the-border punches. Golota, nicknamed "The Foul Pole" for his efforts in this fight, was ahead on all three scorecards—despite having three points deducted already for low blows. Ignoring several warnings, Golota continued to hit Bowe in the *cajones*—as many as 25 times, according to some ringside observers—and finally was DQ'd in the seventh round after delivering one particularly lethal punch to Bowe's nether region. The blow and disqualification precipitated a riot during which one of Bowe's entourage raced into the ring and hit Golota's manager, 74-year-old Lou Duva, over the head with a cell phone. Rematched four months later, Golota repeated his foulfest, being disqualified again, this time in the ninth round.

3. JACK BRITTON VS. BENNY LEONARD, JUNE 26, 1922. King of all he surveyed in the lightweight division, Leonard moved up in class to challenge Britton for his welterweight crown. In a match between two boxing masters, Leonard had the best of it for 12 rounds. Then, in the 13th, Leonard knocked Britton down and, for good measure, raced over to swat Britton while he was on the canvas. As Leonard's brother—who, it was rumored, had placed a sizable bet on Britton—dashed into the ring, referee Patsy Haley stopped the fight. Haley ruled that Leonard had fouled Britton intentionally and disqualified him, handing Leonard only his fourth loss in 181 fights.

2. MIKE TYSON VS. EVANDER HOLYFIELD II, JUNE 28, 1997. Despite being as much as a 25-1 underdog, Holyfield had dominated Tyson in their first fight, stopping him in the 11th round. Rematched seven months later in a bout labeled, "Sound and Fury," with Tyson again the favorite, "Iron Mike" spent the first two rounds complaining to referee Mills Lane that Holyfield was head butting him. Receiving no satisfaction from Lane, Tyson took matters into his own hands, or mouth, biting Holyfield's ears—not once, but twice. Adding insult to injury, Tyson pushed the wounded Holyfield, who was jumping up and down like Rumpelstiltskin, in the back and into the ropes. After the bell ending the third, Lane went over to Tyson's corner and disqualified him, leading to a near riot in the ring as Tyson tried to get at Holyfield to avenge what he later called "attacks on my children."

1. MAX SCHMELING VS. JACK SHARKEY, JUNE 12, 1930. In the final elimination bout to decide the successor to retired heavyweight champion Gene Tunney, Schmeling took on Jack Sharkey at Yankee Stadium in front of 80,000 fans. For three rounds Sharkey outjabbed the onrushing Schmeling, punctuating his attack with powerful right hands. In the fourth, the two stood mid-ring exchanging left hooks when a Sharkey left wandered low, dropping Schmeling to the ground, writhing and groaning in agony, his left hand holding his groin. As his corner shouted for him to "stay down," referee Jim Crowley hesitated and tried to figure out what to do. Schmeling's cornermen jumped into the ring, demanding their fallen warrior be awarded the bout on a foul. Finally, after much confusion in the ring, Crowley concluded that the heavyweight championship had been decided on a foul and proclaimed Schmeling, seated on his stool, the winner and new champion.

MY MOST MEMORABLE LAS VEGAS FIGHTS

:: BY ROYCE FEOUR

Note: Royce Feour has been honored as Writer of the Year by the North American Boxing Federation and gained boxing journalism's equivalent of the heavyweight belt in 1996 when he was given the Nat Fleischer Award for Excellence in Boxing Journalism by the Boxing Writer's Association of America. A member of the Southern Nevada Sports Hall of Fame, Feour served for 37 years as boxing writer for the *Las Vegas Review Journal*, covering pretty much every big bout that's happened in Las Vegas. Here are his top dozen matchups.

12. LARRY HOLMES VS. KEN NORTON, JUNE 9, 1978, CAESARS PALACE. Holmes captured the WBC heavyweight championship with a 15-round split decision over Ken Norton in a bout highlighted by the final round, still considered one of the best rounds in boxing history.

11. RIDDICK BOWE VS. EVANDER HOLYFIELD I, NOVEMBER 13, 1992, THOMAS & MACK CENTER. Bowe took a unanimous decision over Holyfield in a battle highlighted by the 10th round, one of the best rounds in Las Vegas history.

10. JULIO CÉSAR CHAVEZ VS. MELDRICK TAYLOR I, MARCH 17, 1990, LAS VEGAS HILTON. Chavez won when referee Richard Steele stopped the fight with just two seconds remaining in the 12th and final round. It was controversial because Taylor was leading the fight on two of the judges' scorecards.

9. LARRY HOLMES VS. GERRY COONEY, JUNE 11, 1982, CAESARS PALACE. Larry Holmes won over Gerry Cooney in the 13th round when referee Mills Lane disqualified Cooney because his trainer, Victor Valle, came into the ring as Holmes was on the verge of stopping Cooney anyway. Cooney was hailed as "The Great White Hope" and the much-hyped fight drew 29,214 paid fans to a Caesars Palace parking lot.

8. MARCO ANTONIO BARRERA VS. ERIK MORALES TRILOGY: FEBRUARY 19, 2000, MANDALAY BAY; JUNE 22, 2002, MGM GRAND; NOVEMBER 27, 2004, MGM GRAND. Barrera won narrow decisions twice, but all three fights were close. Some thought all three fights could have gone either way.

7. RIDDICK BOWE VS. EVANDER HOLYFIELD II, NOVEMBER 6, 1993, CAESARS PALACE. Holyfield won a majority 12-round decision over Bowe. But the fight will be most remembered for the "Fan Man" who parachuted out of the Las Vegas sky in the seventh round. The intrusion by the "Fan Man" delayed the fight for 20 minutes and he was beaten by Bowe's entourage.

6. MIKE TYSON VS. EVANDER HOLYFIELD I, NOVEMBER 9, 1996, MGM GRAND GARDEN. Evander Holyfield beat the heavily favored Mike Tyson when referee Mitch Halpern stopped the fight in the 11th round with Holyfield dominating.

5. MIKE TYSON VS. EVANDER HOLYFIELD II, JUNE 28, 1997, MGM GRAND GARDEN. Evander Holyfield's third round victory over Mike Tyson in the infamous "Bite Fight" came when Tyson actually bit Holyfield twice and referee Mills Lane disqualified Tyson.

4. DIEGO CORRALES VS. LUIS CASTILLO I, MAY 7, 2005, MANDALAY BAY. Diego Corrales stopped Jose Luis Castillo in the 10th round. Somehow, Corrales came back from two 10th-round knockdowns to achieve the victory. For sheer action and drama, this was an unbelievable fight.

3. SUGAR RAY LEONARD VS. TOMMY HEARNS I, SEPTEMBER 16, 1981, CAESARS PALACE. Hearns was leading by two, three and four points on the judges' scorecards when Sugar Ray Leonard rallied and stopped Hearns in the 14th round of their classic fight.

2. SUGAR RAY LEONARD VS. MARVIN HAGLER, APRIL 6, 1987, CAESARS PALACE. Leonard edged Marvin Hagler on a 12-round split decision with a brilliant box-and-move strategy. Leonard was coming off a three-year layoff and was given little chance by the experts. It was close and many fans thought Hagler won. A bitterly disappointed Hagler never fought again.

1. MARVIN HAGLER VS. TOMMY HEARNS, APRIL 15, 1985, CAESARS PALACE. Hagler knocked out Hearns in the third round. Tremendous action between two great Hall of Fame fighters, even though it only lasted three rounds.

FIGHTERS MORE REMEMBERED FOR THEIR LOSSES THAN THEIR WINS

It's a funny thing, but as our minds look back they tend to remember some successful people more for their big losses than for all their wins. Thus, Napoleon and Custer are recalled more for their respective defeats at Waterloo and Little Big Horn than for their dozens of triumphs in other important battles. This curious tendency carries over to boxing, where many highly accomplished fighters live on in our memories as the losers of big fights and not as the winners of so many others—a tendency that these ten fighters understood all too well.

10. TOM HEENEY (1920-33). Dubbed "The Hard Rock from Down Under" by writer Damon Runyon, this New Zealander came to America in 1927 to compete in the wide-open heavyweight division. He beat Johnny Risko, Jack Delaney and Jim Mahoney, and drew with Jack Sharkey. All of which earned him a #4 ranking and a 1928 fight for the title then held by Gene Tunney—the fight for which Heeney is best remembered, if he is remembered at all. Tunney stopped the overmatched Heeney in 11 rounds, but praised him afterwards, saying, "He had the most courage of anyone I fought."

9. FRANK BRUNO (1982-1996). The London native had 40 career wins, 38 by KOs and was, for a short time, the WBC heavyweight champion. But it was his five losses, all KOs at the hands and gloves of heavyweight champions—Tim Witherspoon, Bonecrusher Smith, Lennox Lewis and Mike Tyson (twice)—for which Bruno is best remembered. Especially his second loss to Tyson in 1996, when the petrified Bruno entered the arena on his way into the ring crossing himself a double-digit number of times.

8. LEW TENDLER (1913-28). Called "the greatest southpaw in ring history" by Nat Fleischer and winner of 135 fights, Tendler had the misfortune to fight in the same era and division as the legendary lightweight champion Benny Leonard. He fought Leonard twice, the first time knocking Leonard down in the eighth round. But when Leonard started talking to him, telling him his punches "were low," Tendler became convinced that Leonard wasn't hurt and hesitated to follow up, the bout going to a "no-decision" conclusion, Leonard keeping his title. In their rematch on July 24, 1923 at Yankee Stadium, Leonard gave Tendler nothing to hit, moving in angles away from the left-hander, and winning the decision, leaving Tendler with two fights to remember and boxing fans two fights to remember Tendler by.

7. ALFONSO ZAMORA (1973-80). Zamora won 29 consecutive fights by KO and the WBA bantamweight championship. Then he faced undefeated WBC bantamweight champion Carlos Zárate, (who had 45 consecutive wins, 44 by KO) in a non-championship fight called "The Battle of the Z's" on April 23, 1977. It was a sure bet that the bout wouldn't be going to the scorecards. And it didn't, with Zamora controlling the action until a crazed fan jumped into the ring, interrupting the action, after which Zárate took over and scored a fourth-round knockout.

6. TOMMY GIBBONS (1911-25). One of the greatest ring generals in boxingdom, the winner of 57 fights and a member of the Boxing Hall of Fame, Gibbons is remembered only as the party of the second part in his losing effort against Jack Dempsey in Shelby, Montana, a fight that bankrupted the town.

5. BARRY McGUIGAN (1981-89). McGuigan, who had beaten Eusebio Pedroza for the WBA featherweight belt the year before, put his title on the line against challenger Stevie Cruz on the afternoon of June 23, 1986 in Las Vegas. It was a hot, sweltering day—even by Las Vegas standards—and for reasons still unexplained McGuigan took the corner on the sunny side of the ring and was drying up like a raisin in the sun by the 14th round. Cruz scored two knockdowns in the 15th and final round, winning the bout by one point on two of the judge's scorecards in a decision directly attributed to McGuigan having, in the words of Noel Coward's famous song, "gone out in the noonday sun."

4. MELDRICK TAYLOR (1984-2002). Taylor was one of boxing's bright prospects of the 1980s, the winner of the featherweight gold medal at the 1984 Los Angeles Olympics and the IBF junior welterweight championship four years later. With an undefeated record in his first 25 fights, Taylor met Julio César Chavez, also an undefeated junior welterweight champion, in a bout called "Thunder and Lightning" to unify the title on March 3, 1990. And for 11 rounds and two minutes and 58 seconds, Taylor was on his way to becoming the unquestioned king of the junior welterweight division. Then, behind on two of the three judges' scorecards, Chavez knocked Taylor down and when Taylor didn't respond to referee Richard Steele Steele had no option but to stop the fight with two seconds to go. It was a moment that still lives in the memory of all who saw it, particularly in the memory of Taylor, who titled his autobiography, *Two Seconds from Glory*.

3. CHUCK DAVEY (1949-55). Back in the early 1950s, when television was a veritable boxing gymnasium with fights broadcast almost every night of the week, a handsome, college-educated white southpaw out of Detroit with what the *Los Angeles Times* called a "squeaky clean image" named Chuck Davey became TV boxing's glamour boy. He appeared on the popular *Pabst Blue Ribbon Wednesday Night Fights* show seven times in 1952 alone, becoming as familiar to viewers as "Bill the

Bartender," who poured glasses of Pabst between rounds. Undefeated in 39 fights, Davey gained a title fight against welterweight champion Kid Gavilan on February 11, 1953. But the bout proved to be less a match than a mismatch as Gavilan exposed Davey, knocking him down in the third round, then mimicking Davey's southpaw stance in the fifth and sixth "just for the fun of it." Thoroughly beaten, Davey was retired by his corner before the start of the 10th round to end a fight that had been, according to the Associated Press, "a cruel awakening to the legions of TV fans mesmerized by Davey's cute southpaw style."

2. TOMMY BURNS (1902-20). Heavyweight champion from 1906-08, Burns successfully defended his title 11 times, scoring a record eight consecutive knockouts in title defenses. However, Burns is remembered only for his 12th title defense, staged in Sydney, Australia on the day after Christmas in 1908, when he lost on a 14th-round stoppage to Jack Johnson, with Johnson becoming the first black heavyweight champion and Burns getting a close look at one of the most important moments in boxing history.

1. BILLY CONN (1934-48). Although he won the light heavyweight championship and 63 fights, Billy Conn is mostly remembered for losing his two heavyweight championship bouts against Joe Louis in 1941 and 1946, the only two times in his career he was knocked out.

GREATEST CAREER COMEBACKS

There have been career comebacks and then there have been career comebacks. Some comebacks consist of just one or two fights, like that of Danny "Little Red" Lopez, while others constitute a whole second career, like that of George Foreman. And whether the comeback follows a layoff—voluntary (see the Sugar Rays) or involuntary (see Muhammad Ali)—or an injury (see Vinny Pazienza), its success is judged here not merely by the quantity of fights the fighter fought, but the quality of his achievements after he came back. That said, here are boxing's greatest career comebacks.

10. Benny Leonard (1911-24; 1931-32). Master of all he surveyed in the lightweight division and out of challenges, Leonard retired in 1924. But after being financially wiped out by the stock market crash, he made a comeback seven years later, going unbeaten through his first 20 fights and giving hope to his legions of followers that the fighter known as "The Great Leonard" was back on top. Unfortunately, his 21st fight came against Jimmy McLarnin, who beat the bejabbers out of Leonard for six rounds before the referee ended the fight, along with Leonard's comeback and career and his followers' dreams.

9. Georges Carpentier (1908-14; 1919-26). Having already won the European heavyweight championship and the "white" heavyweight championship, Georges Carpentier left the fistic wars to join a bigger one, enlisting in the French *armee* during World War I and winning the *Croix de Guerre* and *Medaille Militaire* for his military exploits. After marching home again with all the Johnnies and Jacques and other returning veterans, Carpentier picked up where he had left off. He defended his European heavyweight title four times, won the world light heavyweight crown in 1919, and earned a shot at Jack Dempsey's world heavyweight belt in 1921.

8. Eugene Criqui (1910-14; 1917-1928). Criqui also took time off to serve in the French military during World War I and suffered severe injuries from a sniper's bullet that shattered his jaw, necessitating reconstructive surgery. Returning to the ring after the war, he won the French and European featherweight titles, then beat Johnny Kilbane in 1923 to end Kilbane's 11½-year reign as world featherweight champ.

7. Sugar Ray Robinson (1940-52; 1955-65). After piling up over 130 wins and ruling the middleweight division for years, Robinson lost his bid to also become light heavyweight champ when he couldn't go on after 13 rounds in the 104-degree summer heat at Yankee Stadium against Joey Maxim, despite being well ahead on all three judges' cards. Then the man called "The Greatest Boxer of All Time" by almost everyone who saw him in action decided to walk away from the ring and try his hand (and foot) at showbiz. However, 17 months after retiring, he made a comeback, one that would take him to the middleweight title again . . . and again . . . and again. Robinson reclaimed his middleweight belt from Bobo Olson in 1955 with a second-round KO, almost as if he had just "lent" Bobo the title during his showbiz sabbatical. He also had title-reclaiming wins against Gene Fullmer and Carmen Basilio among his over three-dozen victories during his decade-long comeback.

6. EDER JOFRE (1957-66; 1969-76). After going undefeated for over 50 fights (with 37 KOs) and claiming the world bantamweight title, Jofre lost twice to Fighting Harada in Japan and retired. But, after a hiatus of 26 months, Jofre came back to win 25 consecutive bouts, along with the world featherweight championship from fellow Brazilian José Legra in 1973.

5. SUGAR RAY LEONARD (1977-82; 1984; 1987-89; 1989; 1997). Sugar Ray Leonard's comeback must be discussed in plural terms, as he returned from retirement no less than four times—the first time for just one fight (a disappointing win over Kevin Howard in 1984) and twice, briefly, at the end of his career because he "missed the roar of the crowd." But it's his glorious second comeback that gains him entry onto this list. Incredibly, three years after the Howard fight, Leonard came back again to defeat Marvelous Marvin Hagler for the middleweight championship in 1987.

4. WILLIE PEP (1940-47; 1959; 1965-66). The winner of 109 of 111 fights, featherweight champion Willie Pep suffered near-fatal injuries in an airline crash on January 6, 1947. His career, if not his ability to walk, was thought to be over. Or so it seemed. But miraculously, "The Will o' the Wisp" willed himself back into the ring only six months later, even before he could collect the insurance. He fought until 1959, took six years off, then returned again to the ring for a successful year-long stint in the mid-1960s when he was well into his 40s.

3. MUHAMMAD ALI (1960-67; 1970-78; 1980-81). Stripped of his heavyweight title and barred from boxing for three-and-a-half years during the Vietnam "conflict" because of his refusal to step forward for the draft, Ali came back to reclaim his heavyweight title, win 27 times and serve as the main attraction in some of the biggest fights in boxing history. He retired again in 1979 after regaining his title and avenging his surprise loss to Leon Spinks, then staged another brief comeback.

2. VINNY PAZIENZA (1983-91; 1992-2004). After defeating Gilbert Dele for the WBA light middleweight title in 1991, "Vinny Paz" was seriously injured in an automobile accident that hospitalized him for three months. Told he would never fight again, he defied his doctors' orders and returned to the gym wearing a halo protector. Less than a year after his car accident, Pazienza beat future world middleweight champ Luis Santana and continued fighting for another dozen years. He won 19 of 24 fights following his comeback (including his first nine) and claimed two super middleweight titles.

1. GEORGE FOREMAN (1969–77; 1987-97). After his defeat in 1977 to Jimmy Young, George turned his massive back on boxing to serve as a pastor of the Church of the Lord Jesus Christ. Ten years later he embarked on an improbable comeback, winning his first 24 fights, 23 by knockout, and earning a shot at the heavyweight crown against Evander Holyfield. Although he lost that challenge, he kept Everlasting at it until he got a second chance, this time against heavyweight titlist Michael Moorer. Two months shy of his 46th birthday, Foreman knocked out the 26-year-old Moorer to become—two decades after losing his title to Muhammad Ali in Zaire—the oldest world heavyweight champ ever.

BOXING'S GREATEST: DIVISION-BY-DIVISION

When the editor asked us to compile our lists of the greatest all-time boxers in each weight division, we were faced with several dilemmas, not the least of which was how to resolve one of boxing's favorite bar arguments: Who could beat Whom?—a dispute in which there can never be a winner, no matter which fighter you select.

But over and above that, we were confronted with another problem: that of coming up with ten all-time greats in some of boxing's "super" or "junior" classes. For the traditional eight divisions—heavyweight, light heavyweight, middleweight, welterweight, lightweight, featherweight, bantamweight and fly-weight—there was enough history and more than enough great fighters to make our selections. However, some of those "super" or "junior" divisions go only as far back as the 1980s (the cruiserweight and strawweight divisions). And the names of many of their champions are not even household names in their own households. Not only that, but those halfway houses between the traditional divisions were only brief stopovers for some fighters on their way up to the next traditional division. Take Sugar Ray Leonard, who, on the way to his classic 1981 welterweight title matchup with Tommy Hearns, stopped off long enough to fight Ayub Kalule for his junior middleweight title and pick up a belt he never defended. Then there was Carlos Ortiz, who, on the cusp of a light-weight title bout in 1959, was given a title shot not for the title he coveted but instead for the junior welterweight title, a newly re-minted title that had been put in mothballs and lavender for 13 years, then resurrected just for Ortiz.

Another problem arose in rating the "greatest" in these divisions when Teddy pointed out that "some of the better guys in these junior classes did not have the best parts of their careers or stay long enough in those weight classes to be rated."

What to do with these halfway houses created out of whole cloth? There was even some opposition to even rating the "greatest" in these divisions. Nonetheless, we decided to rate them one-to-five instead of one-to-ten to acknowledge them, giving their existence partial acknowledgement.

And so we give you our "Top Ten"—and, in some divisions, "Top Five"—all-time rankings for all 17 of boxing's weight classes for your consideration and argumentation.

10. JOE FRAZIER (TITLE REIGN: 1970-73).

9. SAM LANGFORD (TITLE REIGN: NONE).

8. LARRY HOLMES (TITLE REIGN: 1978-85).

7. GEORGE FOREMAN (TITLE REIGNS: 1973-74; 1994-96).

6. ROCKY MARCIANO (TITLE REIGN: 1952-55).

5. GENE TUNNEY (TITLE REIGN: 1926-28).

4. JACK DEMPSEY (TITLE REIGN: 1919-26).

3. JACK JOHNSON (TITLE REIGN: 1908-15).

JACK JOHNSON

2. MUHAMMAD ALI (TITLE REIGNS: 1964-67; 1974-76; 1978-79).

1. JOE LOUIS (TITLE REIGN: 1937-49).

TEDDY'S TOP TEN ALL-TIME HEAVYWEIGHTS

10. SONNY LISTON (TITLE REIGN: 1962-64).

9. LARRY HOLMES (TITLE REIGN: 1978-85).

8. JOHN L. SULLIVAN (TITLE REIGN: 1882-92).

7. SAM LANGFORD (TITLE REIGN: NONE).

6. JACK DEMPSEY (TITLE REIGN: 1919-26).

5. GENE TUNNEY (TITLE REIGN: 1926-28).

4. ROCKY MARCIANO (TITLE REIGN: 1952-55).

3. JACK JOHNSON (TITLE REIGN: 1908-15).

2. MUHAMMAD ALI (TITLE REIGNS: 1964-67; 1974-76; 1978-79).

1. JOE LOUIS (TITLE REIGN: 1937-49).

BERT'S TOP FIVE ALL-TIME CRUISERWEIGHTS

5. TOMASZ ADAMEK (TITLE REIGN: 2008-09).

4. MARVIN CAMEL (TITLE REIGNS: 1980-81; 1983-84).

3. DWIGHT MUHAMMAD QAWI/BRAXTON (TITLE REIGN: 1985-86).

2. CARLOS DELEON (TITLE REIGNS: 1980-82; 1983-84).

1. EVANDER HOLYFIELD (TITLE REIGN 1986-88).

TEDDY'S TOP FIVE ALL-TIME CRUISERWEIGHTS

5. MARVIN CAMEL (TITLE REIGNS: 1980-81; 1983-84).

4. JUAN CARLOS (TITLE REIGN: 1998-2001).

3. ORLIN NORRIS (TITLE REIGN: 1993-95).

2. CARLOS DeLEON (TITLE REIGNS: 1980-82; 1983-84).

1. EVANDER HOLYFIELD (TITLE REIGN: 1986-88).

BERT'S TOP TEN ALL-TIME LIGHT HEAVYWEIGHTS

10. MICHAEL SPINKS (TITLE REIGN: 1981-86).

9. PHILADELPHIA JACK O'BRIEN (TITLE REIGN: 1905-12).

8. ROY JONES, JR. (TITLE REIGNS: 1996-97; 1997-2003).

7. HAROLD JOHNSON (TITLE REIGN: 1961-63).

6. BOB FOSTER (TITLE REIGN: 1968-74).

5. BILLY CONN (TITLE REIGN: 1939-40).

4. MAXIE ROSENBLOOM (TITLE REIGN: 1930-34).

3. TOMMY LOUGHRAN (TITLE REIGN: 1927-29).

2. EZZARD CHARLES (TITLE REIGN: NONE).

1. ARCHIE MOORE (TITLE REIGN: 1952-62).

TEDDY'S TOP TEN ALL-TIME LIGHT HEAVYWEIGHTS

10. JACK DELANEY (TITLE REIGN: 1926-27).

9. MAXIE ROSENBLOOM (TITLE REIGN: 1930-34).

8. JOHN HENRY LEWIS (TITLE REIGN: 1935-39).

7. BOB FOSTER (TITLE REIGN: 1968-74).

6. MICHAEL SPINKS (TITLE REIGN: 1981-86).

5. HAROLD JOHNSON (TITLE REIGN: 1961-63).

4. TOMMY LOUGHRAN (TITLE REIGN: 1927-29).

3. BILLY CONN (TITLE REIGN: 1939-40).

2. ARCHIE MOORE (TITLE REIGN: 1952-62).

1. EZZARD CHARLES (TITLE REIGN: NONE).

BERT'S TOP FIVE ALL-TIME SUPER MIDDLEWEIGHTS

5. NIGEL BENN (TITLE REIGN: 1992-96).

4. ROY JONES, JR. (TITLE REIGN: 1994-96).

3. SVEN OTTKE (TITLE REIGN: 1998-2008).

2. GRACIANO ROCCHIGIANI (TITLE REIGN: 1988-90).

1. JOE CALZAGHE (TITLE REIGN: 2006-08).

TEDDY'S TOP FIVE ALL-TIME SUPER MIDDLEWEIGHTS

5. ROY JONES, JR. (TITLE REIGN: 1994-96).

4. CHONG-PAL PARK (TITLE REIGN 1987-88).

3. NIGEL BENN (TITLE REIGN: 1992-96).

2. JOE CALZAGHE (TITLE REIGN: 2006-08).

1. SVEN OTTKE (TITLE REIGN: 1998-2008).

BERT'S TOP TEN ALL-TIME MIDDLEWEIGHTS

10. BERNARD HOPKINS (TITLE REIGN: 1995-2005).

9. JAKE LAMOTTA (TITLE REIGN: 1949-51).

8. TONY ZALE (TITLE REIGN: 1940-47; 1948).

7. MARVELOUS MARVIN HAGLER (TITLE REIGN: 1980-87).

6. SUGAR RAY ROBINSON (TITLE REIGNS: 1951; 1951-52; 1955-57; 1957-58; 1958-60).

5. MARCEL CERDAN (TITLE REIGN: 1948-49).

4. CARLOS MONZON (TITLE REIGN: 1970-77).

3. MICKEY WALKER (TITLE REIGN: 1926-31).

2. STANLEY KETCHEL (TITLE REIGNS: 1907-08; 1908-10).

1. HARRY GREB (TITLE REIGN: 1923-26).

TEDDY'S TOP TEN ALL-TIME MIDDLEWEIGHTS

10. JAKE LAMOTTA (TITLE REIGN: 1949-51).

9. JACK "NONPAREIL" DEMPSEY (TITLE REIGN: 1884-91).

8. TONY ZALE (TITLE REIGN: 1940-47; 1948).

7. TIGER FLOWERS (TITLE REIGN: 1926).

6. SUGAR RAY ROBINSON (TITLE REIGNS: 1951; 1951- 52; 1955-57; 1957-58; 1958-60).

5. MICKEY WALKER (TITLE REIGN: 1926-31).

4. MARVELOUS MARVIN HAGLER (TITLE REIGN: 1980-87).

3. CARLOS MONZON (TITLE REIGN: 1970-77).

2. STANLEY KETCHEL (TITLE REIGN: 1907-08; 1908-10).

1. HARRY GREB (TITLE REIGN: 1923-26).

BERT'S TOP FIVE ALL-TIME JUNIOR MIDDLEWEIGHTS (SUPER WELTERWEIGHTS)

5. TERRY NORRIS (TITLE REIGNS: 1990-93; 1994; 1995-97).

4. SANDRO MAZZINGHI (TITLE REIGNS: 1963-65; 1968).

3. OSCAR DE LA HOYA (TITLE REIGNS: 2001-03; 2006-07).

2. MIKE MCCALLUM (TITLE REIGN: 1984-87).

1. TOMMY HEARNS (TITLE REIGN: 1982-86).

TEDDY'S TOP FIVE ALL-TIME JUNIOR MIDDLEWEIGHTS

5. AYUB KALULE (TITLE REIGN: 1979-81).

4. WILFRED BENITEZ (TITLE REIGN: 1981-82).

3. TERRY NORRIS (TITLE REIGNS: 1990-93; 1994; 1995-97).

2. MIKE MCCALLUM (TITLE REIGN: 1984-87).

1. TOMMY HEARNS (TITLE REIGN: 1982-86).

10. KID GAVILAN (TITLE REIGN: 1951–55).

9. JACK BRITTON (TITLE REIGNS: 1915; 1916–17; 1919–22).

8. JIMMY McLARNIN (TITLE REIGNS: 1933–34; 1934–35).

7. TED "KID" LEWIS (TITLE REIGNS: 1915–16; 1917–19).

6. JOSÉ NAPOLES (TITLE REIGNS: 1969–70; 1971–75).

5. SUGAR RAY LEONARD (TITLE REIGNS: 1979–80; 1980–82).

4. EMILE GRIFFITH (TITLE REIGNS: 1961; 1962–63; 1963–66).

3. BARNEY ROSS (TITLE REIGNS: 1934; 1935–38).

2. HENRY ARMSTRONG (TITLE REIGN: 1938–40).

1. SUGAR RAY ROBINSON (TITLE REIGN: 1938–40).

TEDDY'S TOP TEN ALL-TIME WELTERWEIGHTS

10. CHARLEY BURLEY (TITLE REIGN: NONE).

9. EMILE GRIFFITH (TITLE REIGNS: 1961; 1962-63; 1963-66).

8. TED "KID" LEWIS (TITLE REIGNS: 1915-16; 1917-19).

7. SUGAR RAY LEONARD (TITLE REIGNS: 1979-80; 1980-82).

6. KID GAVILAN (TITLE REIGN: 1951-55).

5. BARNEY ROSS (TITLE REIGNS: 1934; 1935-38).

4. JOSÉ NAPOLES (TITLE REIGNS: 1969-70; 1971-75).

3. MICKEY WALKER (TITLE REIGN: 1922-26).

2. HENRY ARMSTRONG (TITLE REIGN: 1938-40).

1. SUGAR RAY ROBINSON (TITLE REIGN: 1938-40).

BERT'S TOP FIVE ALL-TIME JUNIOR WELTERWEIGHTS (SUPER LIGHTWEIGHTS)

5. KOSTYA TSZYU (TITLE REIGN: 1999-2003).

4. TONY CANZONERI (TITLE REIGNS: 1931-32; 1933).

3. NICOLINO LOCHE (TITLE REIGN: 1968-72).

2. JULIO CÉSAR CHAVEZ (TITLE REIGN: 1994-96).

1. AARON PRYOR (TITLE REIGN: 1980-83).

TEDDY'S TOP FIVE ALL-TIME JUNIOR WELTERWEIGHTS (SUPER LIGHTWEIGHTS)

5. EDDIE PERKINS (TITLE REIGN: 1963-65).

4. DUILIO LOI (TITLE REIGNS: 1960-62; 1962).

3. JULIO CÉSAR CHAVEZ (TITLE REIGN: 1994-96).

2. NICOLINO LOCHE (TITLE REIGN: 1968-72).

1. AARON PRYOR (TITLE REIGN: 1980-83).

BERT'S TOP TEN ALL-TIME LIGHTWEIGHTS

10. TONY CANZONERI (TITLE REIGNS: 1930-33; 1935-36).

9. JOE BROWN (TITLE REIGN: 1956-62).

8. CARLOS ORTIZ (TITLE REIGNS: 1962-65; 1965-68).

7. ALEXIS ARGUELLO (TITLE REIGN: 1981-83).

6. JULIO CÉSAR CHAVEZ (TITLE REIGN: 1987-89).

5. PERNELL WHITAKER (TITLE REIGN: 1988-92).

4. IKE WILLIAMS (TITLE REIGN: 1945-51).

3. JOE GANS (TITLE REIGN: 1902-08).

2. ROBERTO DURAN (TITLE REIGN: 1971-79).

1. BENNY LEONARD (TITLE REIGN: 1917-24).

TEDDY'S TOP TEN ALL-TIME LIGHTWEIGHTS

10. LOU AMBERS (TITLE REIGNS: 1938-38; 1939-40).

9. JOE GANS (TITLE REIGN: 1902-08).

8. JULIO CÉSAR CHAVEZ (TITLE REIGN: 1987-89).

7. IKE WILLIAMS (TITLE REIGN: 1945-51).

6. BARNEY ROSS (TITLE REIGN: 1933).

5. HENRY ARMSTRONG (TITLE REIGN: 1938-39).

4. PERNELL WHITAKER (TITLE REIGN: 1988-92).

3. TONY CANZONERI (TITLE REIGNS: 1930-33; 1935-36).

2. ROBERTO DURAN (TITLE REIGN: 1971-79).

1. BENNY LEONARD (TITLE REIGN: 1917-24).

BERT'S TOP FIVE ALL-TIME JUNIOR LIGHTWEIGHTS (SUPER FEATHERWEIGHTS)

5. KID CHOCOLATE (TITLE REIGN: 1931-33).

4. JULIO CÉSAR CHAVEZ (TITLE REIGN: 1984-87).

3. JOHNNY DUNDEE (TITLE REIGNS: 1921-23; 1923-24).

2. FLASH ELORDE (TITLE REIGN: 1960-67).

1. ALEXIS ARGUELLO (TITLE REIGN: 1978-80).

TEDDY'S TOP FIVE ALL-TIME JUNIOR LIGHTWEIGHTS (SUPER FEATHERWEIGHTS)

5. FLOYD MAYWEATHER, JR. (TITLE REIGN: 1998-2001).

4. AZUMAH NELSON (TITLE REIGN: 1988-94).

3. FLASH ELORDE (TITLE REIGN: 1960-67).

2. JULIO CÉSAR CHAVEZ (TITLE REIGN: 1984-87).

1. ALEXIS ARGUELLO (TITLE REIGN: 1978-80).

BERT'S TOP TEN ALL-TIME FEATHERWEIGHTS

10. JOHNNY KILBANE (TITLE REIGN: 1912-23).

9. HARRY JEFFRA (TITLE REIGNS: 1937-38; 1940-41).

8. PERNELL WHITAKER (TITLE REIGN: 1989-92).

7. ALEXIS ARGUELLO (TITLE REIGN: 1974-77).

6. DANNY "LITTLE RED" LOPEZ (TITLE REIGN: 1976-80).

5. SALVADOR SANCHEZ (TITLE REIGN: 1980-82).

4. GEORGE DIXON (TITLE REIGNS: 1891-97; 1898-1900).

3. SANDY SADDLER (TITLE REIGNS: 1948-49; 1950-57).

2. ABE ATTELL (TITLE REIGN: 1901-12).

1. WILLIE PEP (TITLE REIGNS: 1942-48; 1949-50).

TEDDY'S TOP TEN ALL-TIME FEATHERWEIGHTS

10. JOHNNY DUNDEE (TITLE REIGN: 1923-24).

9. AZUMAH NELSON (TITLE REIGN: 1984-88).

8. VICENTE SALDIVAR (TITLE REIGNS: 1964-67; 1970).

7. WILFREDO GOMEZ (TITLE REIGN: 1984).

6. GEORGE DIXON (TITLE REIGNS: 1891-97; 1898-1900).

5. SALVADOR SANCHEZ (TITLE REIGN: 1980-82).

4. KID CHOCOLATE (TITLE REIGN: 1932).

3. ABE ATTELL (TITLE REIGN: 1901–12).

2. WILLIE PEP (TITLE REIGNS: 1942–48; 1949–50).

1. SANDY SADDLER (TITLE REIGNS: 1948–49; 1950–57).

BERT'S TOP FIVE ALL-TIME JUNIOR FEATHERWEIGHTS (SUPER BANTAMWEIGHTS)

5. MANNY PACQUIAO (TITLE REIGN: 2001–04).

4. ISRAEL VAZQUEZ (TITLE REIGNS: 2004–07; 2007–10).

3. ERIK MORALES (TITLE REIGN: 1997–2000).

2. DANIEL ZARAGOZA (TITLE REIGNS: 1988–90; 1991–92; 1995–97).

1. WILFREDO GOMEZ (TITLE REIGN: 1977–83).

TEDDY'S TOP FIVE ALL-TIME JUNIOR FEATHERWEIGHTS (SUPER BANTAMWEIGHTS)

5. ERIK MORALES (TITLE REIGN: 1997–2000).

4. JEFF FENECH (TITLE REIGN: 1987).

3. DANIEL ZARAGOZA (TITLE REIGNS: 1988–90; 1991–92; 1995–97).

2. ISMAEL VAZQUEZ (TITLE REIGNS: 2004–07; 2007–10).

1. WILFREDO GOMEZ (TITLE REIGN: 1977–83).

BERT'S TOP TEN ALL-TIME BANTAMWEIGHTS

10. JIMMY BARRY (TITLE REIGN: 1894–99).

9. RAUL MACIAS (TITLE REIGN: 1955–57).

8. Fighting Harada (TITLE REIGN: 1965-68).

7. Orlando Canizales (TITLE REIGN: 1988-95).

6. Manuel Ortiz (TITLE REIGNS: 1942-47; 1947-50).

5. Pete Herman (TITLE REIGNS: 1917-20; 1921).

4. Carlos Zárate (TITLE REIGN: 1976-79).

3. Ruben Olivares (TITLE REIGNS: 1969-70; 1971-72).

2. Panama Al Brown (TITLE REIGN: 1929-35).

1. Eder Jofre (TITLE REIGN: 1960-65).

TEDDY'S TOP TEN ALL-TIME BANTAMWEIGHTS

10. Pete Herman (TITLE REIGNS: 1917-20; 1921).

9. Raul Macias (TITLE REIGN: 1955-57).

8. Jeff Chandler (TITLE REIGN: 1980-84).

7. Orlando Canizales (TITLE REIGN: 1988-95).

6. Manuel Ortiz (TITLE REIGNS: 1942-47; 1947-50).

5. Fighting Harada (TITLE REIGN: 1965-68).

4. Carlos Zárate (TITLE REIGN: 1976-79).

3. Ruben Olivares (TITLE REIGNS: 1969-70; 1971-72).

2. Eder Jofre (TITLE REIGN: 1960-65).

1. Panama Al Brown (TITLE REIGN: 1929-35).

BERT'S TOP FIVE ALL-TIME JUNIOR BANTAMWEIGHTS (SUPER FLYWEIGHTS)

5. VIC DARCHINYAN (TITLE REIGN: 2008-10).

4. GILBERTO ROMAN (TITLE REIGNS: 1986-87; 1988-89).

3. DANNY ROMERO (TITLE REIGNS: 1996-97).

2. JOHNNY TAPIA (TITLE REIGN: 1994-98).

1. KHAOSAI GALAXY (TITLE REIGN: 1984-91).

TEDDY'S TOP FIVE ALL-TIME JUNIOR BANTAMWEIGHTS (SUPER FLYWEIGHTS)

5. DANNY ROMERO (TITLE REIGN: 1996-97)

4. VIC DARCHINYAN (TITLE REIGN: 2008-10).

3. MARK JOHNSON (TITLE REIGN: 2003-04).

2. JOHNNY TAPIA (TITLE REIGN: 1994-98).

1. KHAOSAI GALAXY (TITLE REIGN: 1984-91).

BERT'S TOP TEN ALL-TIME FLYWEIGHTS

10. SMALL MONTANA (TITLE REIGN: 1935-37).

9. FRANKIE GENERO (TITLE REIGNS: 1928-29; 1929-31).

8. PONE KINGPETCH (TITLE REIGNS: 1960-62; 1963; 1964-65).

7. MIGUEL CANTO (TITLE REIGN: 1975-79).

6. PETER KANE (TITLE REIGN: 1938-43).

5. BENNY LYNCH (TITLE REIGN: 1937-38).

4. **Pancho Villa** (TITLE REIGN: 1923–25).

3. **Ricardo Lopez** (TITLE REIGNS: 1990–97; 2002).

2. **Pascual Perez** (TITLE REIGN: 1954–60).

1. **Jimmy Wilde** (TITLE REIGN: 1916–23).

TEDDY'S TOP TEN ALL-TIME FLYWEIGHTS

10. **Fidel LaBarba** (TITLE REIGN: 1927).

9. **Peter Kane** (TITLE REIGN: 1938–43).

8. **Midget Wolgast** (TITLE REIGN: 1930–35).

7. **Frankie Genaro** (TITLE REIGNS: 1928–29; 1929–31).

6. **Masao Ohba** (TITLE REIGN: 1970–73).

5. **Miguel Canto** (TITLE REIGN: 1975–79).

4. **Pascual Perez** (TITLE REIGN: 1954–60).

3. **Ricardo Lopez** (TITLE REIGNS: 1990–97; 2002).

2. **Pancho Villa** (TITLE REIGN: 1923–25).

1. **Jimmy Wilde** (TITLE REIGN: 1916–23).

BERT'S TOP FIVE ALL-TIME JUNIOR FLYWEIGHTS

5. **Ivan Calderon** (TITLE REIGN: 2007–10).

4. **Humberto "Chiquita" Gonzalez** (TITLE REIGNS: 1989–90; 1991–93; 1994–95).

3. **Yoko Gushiken** (TITLE REIGN: 1976–81).

2. **Michael Carbajal** (TITLE REIGNS: 1990–94; 1996–97; 1999).

1. RICARDO LOPEZ (TITLE REIGN: 1999-2002).

TEDDY'S TOP FIVE ALL-TIME JUNIOR FLYWEIGHTS

5. RICARDO LOPEZ (TITLE REIGN: 1999-2002).

4. MICHAEL CARBAJAL (TITLE REIGNS: 1990-94; 1996-97; 1999).

3. IVAN CALDERON (TITLE REIGN: 2007-10).

2. YOKO GUSHIKEN (TITLE REIGN: 1976-81).

1. HUMBERTO "CHIQUITA" GONZALEZ (TITLE REIGNS: 1989-90; 1991-93; 1994-95).

BERT'S TOP FIVE ALL-TIME STRAWWEIGHTS (MINIMUMWEIGHTS)

5. JOSE ANTONIO AGUIRRE (TITLE REIGN: 2000-04).

4. RATANAPOL SOR VORAPIN (TITLE REIGN: 1992-97).

3. IVAN CALDERON (TITLE REIGN: 2003-07).

2. DONNIE NIETES (TITLE REIGN: 2007-10).

1. RICARDO LOPEZ (TITLE REIGN: 1990-98).

TEDDY'S TOP FIVE ALL-TIME STRAWWEIGHTS (MINIMUMWEIGHTS)

5. DONNIE NIETES (TITLE REIGN: 2007-10).

4. RATANAPOL SOR VORAPIN (TITLE REIGN: 1992-97).

3. ROMAN GONZALEZ (TITLE REIGN: 2008-10).

2. IVAN CALDERON (TITLE REIGN: 2003-07).

1. RICARDO LOPEZ (TITLE REIGN: 1990-98).

BOXING'S GREATEST ALL-TIME POUND-FOR-POUND FIGHTERS

What else can you say about the men on this list? Well, plenty—because they were, in our opinion, the best pound-for-pound fighters in the history of boxing. If you're interested in gaining additional information about them, you will find plenty of it in numerous other lists in this book. For the purposes of this final dual list—one part by Bert, the other by Teddy—we will only give you what Sergeant Joe Friday used to ask for: just the facts, and the most basic ones at that. They speak for themselves. And do so loudly.

BERT'S LIST

13. GENE TUNNEY (1915-28). Heavyweight champion from 1926-28. Pro record: 61 wins, 45 KOs, one loss, one draw, one no contest.

12. TONY CANZONERI (1925-39). Featherweight champion 1928; lightweight champion 1930-33 and 1935-36; junior welterweight champion 1931-32 and 1933. Pro record: 137 wins, 44 KOs, 24 losses, 10 draws, four no-decisions.

11. MICKEY WALKER (1919-35). Welterweight champion 1922-26; middleweight champion 1926-31. Record: 93 wins, 60 KOs, 19 losses, four draws, 46 no-decisions.

10. JACK JOHNSON (1897-1932). Heavyweight champion 1908-15. Pro record: 77 wins, 48 KOs, 13 losses, 14 draws, 19 no-decisions.

9. JACK DEMPSEY (1914-27). Heavyweight champion 1919-26. Pro record: 61 wins, 50 KOs, six losses, eight draws.

8. ROBERTO DURAN (1968-2001). Lightweight champion 1972-79; welterweight champion 1980; junior middleweight champion 1983-84; middleweight champion 1989. Pro record: 103 wins, 70 KOs, 16 losses.

7. MUHAMMAD ALI (1960-81). Heavyweight champion 1964-67, 1974-78 and 1978-79. Pro record: 56 wins, 37 KOs, five losses.

6. BENNY LEONARD (1911-24; 1931-32). Lightweight champion 1917-24. Pro record: 85 wins, 69 KOs, five losses, one draw, 115 no-decisions.

5. HARRY GREB (1913-26). Middleweight champion 1923-26. Pro record: 105 wins, 48 KOs, eight losses, three draws, 170 no-decisions.

4. JOE LOUIS (1934-51). Heavyweight champion 1937-49. Pro record: 68 wins, 54 KOs, three losses.

3. WILLIE PEP (1940-66). Featherweight champion 1942-48 and 1949-50. Pro record: 230 wins, 65 KOs, 11 losses, one draw.

2. HENRY ARMSTRONG (1931-45). Featherweight champion 1937-38; lightweight champion 1938-39; welterweight champion 1938-40. Pro record: 151 wins, 101 KOs, 21 losses, nine draws.

1. SUGAR RAY ROBINSON (1940-65). Welterweight champion 1946-51; middleweight champion 1951-52, 1957-58 and 1958-60. Pro record: 175 wins, 109 KOs, 19 losses, six draws.

TEDDY'S LIST

13. CARLOS MONZON (1963-77). Middleweight champion 1970-77. Pro record: 87 wins, 59 KOs, three losses, nine draws.

12. JACK JOHNSON (1897-1932). Heavyweight champion 1908-15. Pro record: 77 wins, 48 KOs, 13 losses, 14 draws, 19 no-decisions.

11. JOE LOUIS (1934-51). Heavyweight champion 1937-49. Pro record: 68 wins, 54 KOs, three losses.

10. GENE TUNNEY (1915-28). Heavyweight champion 1926-28. Pro record: 61 wins, 45 KOs, one loss, one draw, one no contest.

9. ROBERTO DURAN (1968-2001). Lightweight champion 1972-79; welterweight champion 1980; junior middleweight champion 1983-84; middleweight champion 1989. Pro record: 103 wins, 70 KOs, 16 losses.

8. MUHAMMAD ALI (1960-81). Heavyweight champion 1964-67, 1974-78 and 1978-79. Pro record: 56 wins, 37 KOs, five losses.

7. MICKEY WALKER (1919-35). Welterweight champion 1922-26; middleweight champion 1926-31. Pro Record: 93 wins, 60 KOs, 19 losses, four draws, 46 no-decisions.

6. HARRY GREB (1913-26). Middleweight champion 1923-26. Pro record: 105 wins, 48 KOs, eight losses, three draws, 170 no-decisions.

5. SAM LANGFORD (1902-26). No championships. Pro record: 167 wins, 117 KOs, 38 losses, 37 draws.

4. BENNY LEONARD (1911-24; 1931-32). Lightweight champion 1917-24. Pro record: 85 wins, 69 KOs, five losses, one draw, 115 no-decisions.

WILLIE PEP (LEFT) VS ALBERT "CHALKY" WRIGHT, NEW YORK CITY, NOV. 20, 1942

3. WILLIE PEP (1940-66). Featherweight champion 1942-48 and 1949-50. Pro record: 230 wins, 65 KOs, 11 losses, one draw.

2. HENRY ARMSTRONG (1931-45). Featherweight champion 1937-38; lightweight champion 1938-39; welterweight champion 1938-40. Pro record: 151 wins, 101 KOs, 21 losses, nine draws.

1. SUGAR RAY ROBINSON (1940-65). Welterweight champion 1946-51; middleweight champion 1951-52, 1957-58 and 1958-60. Pro record: 175 wins, 109 KOs, 19 losses, six draws.

Made in the USA
Middletown, DE
19 January 2022

59159575R00142